Widows in India

About the Authors

Bindeshwar Pathak, a Ph.D. and D.Litt. in Sociology, is the Founder of Sulabh Sanitation and Social Reform Movement. A leading social reformer and humanist of contemporary India, he is renowned the world over for his liberating work for scavenging untouchables (who manually clean human excreta), widows and other weaker sections of society. His invention of Sulabh toilet technology has been internationally recognized as one of the best global practices for safe disposal of human waste. Besides his other achievements, he transformed the sanitation scenario in India by developing a self-sustaining model of public sanitation. He has written extensively on social issues, and has developed the concept of Action Sociology. Dr. Pathak is the winner of several national and international awards – Padma Bhushan (1991); the Saint Francis Prize for Environment (1992); the Scroll of Honour by UN-Habitat at Rio-de-Janeiro (Brazil) (2003); the Global 500 Roll of Honour Award by UNEP at Beirut (Lebanon) (2003); Stockholm Water Prize (2009), the LEGENDE DE LA PLANETE Congress Fondateur Jeux Ecologiques at UNESCO, Paris; (2013), to name just a few.

Satyendra Tripathi is trained as a social scientist in India, The Netherlands, United Kingdom and the USA. He helped establish the departments of Sociology at Utkal University, Kumaon University and Banaras Hindu University (BHU). Formerly Professor on SBI Chair and Director of the Centre of Integrated Rural Development Programme as well as Head of the Department of Sociology, BHU, he has worked in United Nations as UN Fellow in Asia-Pacific countries. While working with Sulabh International, he organized training programmes in Africa for the senior officials on Water and Sanitation in collaboration with Human Habitat Centre, Nairobi. His specialization is social change and development in developing countries, and he has travelled widely and delivered lectures in centers of higher learning in Europe, USA and South Asia.

Widows in India

Study of Varanasi and Vrindavan

Bindeshwar Pathak
Satyendra Tripathi

Sulabh International Social Service Organisation
Sulabh Gram, Mahavir Enclave, Palam Dabari Marg, New Delhi

RAWAT PUBLICATIONS
Jaipur • New Delhi • Bangalore • Guwahati • Kolkata

ISBN 978-81-316-0772-5

Published by
Prem Rawat for **Rawat Publications**
Satyam Apts, Sector 3, Jawahar Nagar, Jaipur 302 004 (India)
Phone: 0141 265 1748 / 7006 Fax: 0141 265 1748
E-mail: info@rawatbooks.com
Website: www.rawatbooks.com

New Delhi Office
4858/24, Ansari Road, Daryaganj, New Delhi 110 002
Phone: 011 2326 3290

Also at *Bangalore, Guwahati* and *Kolkata*

Typeset by Rawat Computers, Jaipur
Printed at Chaman Enterprises, New Delhi

Dedicated to
Hon'ble Shri Narendra Modi
Prime Minister of India
(A Man of Mission, Vision and Social Transformation)

A widow tying Rakhi, a colourful thread that symbolizes the bond of love between sister and brother, on the wrist of Hon'ble Prime Minister Shri Narendra Modi, while others wait for their turn.

Contents

Preface

In a patriarchal society, women have always been considered inferior to men, both in biological and mental spheres. It is only in the recent time that they have started competing with men, especially in achievable spheres such as education, employment, political power and authority, etc. But their competition or competitive spirit, coupled with favourable socio-economic condition and patronage of their family, has not percolated down to the large majority of women living both in rural and urban areas. In fact, women as a separate gender category have not yet been accepted as a separate social category in the male-dominated society in India, where their segregation or subordination has been legitimized by the religious scriptures. This is more so in the case of Hindu social system in which a host of specific norms, rituals and even behaviour patterns have been both proscribed and prescribed for the women, and even more for the widows. These prescriptions and proscriptions, since centuries, have shaped the mindset of men and women in the society, which regulates their attitudes and behaviour patterns though some positive changes or relaxations are definitely visible, both in urban and rural areas.

The Constitution of India treats both men and women as equal civilizen, and does not discriminate the latter on the basis of sex or a separate gender category. Rather, it makes some specific provisions for their progress and development. A number of specific laws have also been enacted for the betterment even of widows of all ages and socio-economic backgrounds. But all these constitutional provisions and related laws have not yet fully succeeded in overcoming the age-old societal resistance against their betterment and treating them as equal human beings. Needless to say that the widows of the upper castes of all economic strata have been the worst sufferers of the resistance of their own family kins, and customs and practices, though the efforts had been, even in the past, to provide them social justice and treat them equally. In numerous cases, widows even from the upper castes have asserted, time and again, for the accord of social justice and equal human treatment to them. But all these have not yet brought any qualitative change in their wretched socio-economic condition and the fractured emotions or emotional bonds with their family members, kins, neighbours, and society as a whole of which they are integral part.

Since time immemorial, the socio-cultural codes of the patriarchal Hindu society have demanded widows to detach themselves from worldly affairs and lead a life of ascetism or '*sanyas*' soon after their husbands' death. The consequential deprivation, which they face, has multiple forms since they are deprived both materially and emotionally and are placed in the material and ideological structures legitimized by the given cultural codes (Chakravarti, 1995: 2248–56). The *Dharmashastras,* which is the sacred law-book of the Hindus that lays down all the rules which historically all Hindus had to follow according to their place in society, depending on their caste and sex, prescribed that 'widows should give up adorning their hair, chewing betel-nut, wearing perfumes, flowers, ornaments and dyed clothes, taking food from a vessel of bronze, taking two meals a day and applying kajal to their eyes. She should wear a white garment, should curb her senses and anger, she should not resort to deceit and tricks, should be free from laziness and sleep, should be pure and of good conduct, should always worship God, should sleep on the floor at night on a mat of *kusa* grass, she should be intent on concentration of mind, and in the company of the good'.

These dictates of the *Dharmashastras* have been followed over centuries by Hindu widows, especially those belonging to the upper castes, irrespective of the age at which they became widows. Though they live in family and in society, but for all practical purposes they are outcasts. More precisely, widows practically remain 'outsider', though structurally and to some extent functionally, they are incorporated as 'insider' in both their affiant and natal homes (Chakravarti, 1995: 2248–56). They are deprived of their rights over both the parental and in-laws' or deceased husband's properties and are left to depend on others for their material survival (although the apex court of India has conferred a right of their share in the latter's property through its recent judgment, but its result is yet to be assessed). Thus, they virtually live a life of a destitute and an ostracized entity with little concern felt by anyone about their miserable existence.

Since renunciation of worldly life and leading the life of an ascetic is considered to be the sacred duty of widows, a common practice in Bengal was and still is to send widows to Varanasi (known as Kashi in the ancient time, Banares during the colonial period) and Vrindavan. Varanasi (in the present day people's usage) and Vrindavan are regarded as the supreme religious centres by the Hindus of India. Hindus of different castes and creeds from several parts of the country visit Varanasi and Vrindavan throughout the year, take a holy dip in the rivers Ganges and Yamuna, pay their reverence and obeisance to Lord Shiva, Lord Krishna and to numerous other deities at their shrines there, and offer oblation and ablution to their ancestors. These cities have also acted as a quasi-permanent abode for both male and female ascetics and renouncers by inspiring them to stay here and seek *moksha* or salvation on the banks of rivers Ganges and Yamuna. Thus, the widows who had to live in Varanasi after attaining widowhood are certain to attain *moksha* since the religious environment of the place will invariably induce feelings of ascetism within them. Varanasi or earlier Kashi has attracted Bengali widows since the past many centuries, and even today there is a large population of Bengali widows there. They easily outnumber widows of all other regions, although one can find widows from Rajasthan, Maharashtra and a few other regions also there. The huge number of widows in Varanasi is the reason why it is often described as the city of widows, bulls, stairs or steps at the Ganga *ghats,* and of the ascetics. The actual usage reads as *raand* (widows), *saand* (bulls), *sidi* (stairs or steps), *sanyasi* (ascetics), *inse bache to seve Kashi* (if one is saved from the widows, bulls, stairs and ascetics, only then one may live comfortably in Kashi or Varanasi). Although it is not known when this couplet was composed, this describes the preponderance of all the four in the city of Varanasi. According to 1991 Census, the total number of widows living in Varanasi city and in the tehsil towns in the Varanasi district was 22,870, of which a very large percentage comes from Bengal.

The present study is a step in this direction. It is an exploration of the various forms of deprivation of the widows in Varanasi and Vrindavan in order to study the nature of deprivations, renunciation – both forced and voluntary – and formation of social-self among them. It will examine the specific contexts in which they had to opt for asceticism or renunciation, and the nature and degree of their attainment of it. We will try to find out if the widows who were sent to Varanasi and Vrindavan were interested in their role-reversal in terms of remaining householder after the death of their husbands or not. Alongside, we will enquire into their perception and formation of social-self and the extent they make use of the various strategies in the formation of such a self. Finally, we will analyse the relationships among their deprivations, renunciation and formation of social-self, and the societal responses to their present condition and to their social-self. The study is based on an analytical survey of the widows living in Varanasi and Vrindavan. At the initial stage, an attempt was made to prepare a Census of the resident Bengali widows with the help of the city administration and the large number of voluntary organizations working in the city. But we could not succeed since neither the city administration nor any of the voluntary organizations, including a few philanthropic ones that have been working there since long, maintain any authentic records of the total number of widows, living permanently in the cities. Even the District Census Office does not have any classified enumeration of the widows. The District Gazetteers give some clue about a few widows who were repatriated decades ago from the prominent families of the undivided Bengal, Maharashtra, Rajasthan and the southern states. However, since the process of coming of the widows from different parts of the country to the city, either temporarily or permanently, has been continuing till the recent time and quite a few women born and brought up here have become widows over a period of time besides the dead ones who had come here earlier, preparing a Census of widows living in the cities became a difficult task.

The present study attempts to assess the conditions of widows in religious places. The study has been planned in eight chapters. Chapter 1 is introductory one which provides theoretical perspective of ageing of population and widows. Chapter 2 deals with status of widows in India. Chapter 3 is concerned with socio-cultural profile of Varanasi and Vrindavan. Chapter 4 is on research methodology. Chapter 5 focuses on social reforms movements. Chapter 6 deals with condition of widows and social change. Chapter 7 concerns social security and rehabilitation of widows. The last chapter provides main findings, conclusion and policy measures for rehabilitation of widows.

Bindeshwar Pathak
Satyendra Tripathi

Acknowledgements

The study has been an outcome of the constant support, encouragement and cooperation of officials, academicians, friends and relatives. Therefore, it is our obligation to express gratitude towards them. We place on record the sincere appreciation of Sulabh International Social Service Organisation, New Delhi, for entrusting the study and providing financial support to carry out the study. We are highly grateful to the concerned officials of widow ashrams for extending all kind of support to carry out the study smoothly.

We are thankful to Professor A.K. Srivastava for providing valuable suggestions and Dr. P.K. Gupta, Department of Sociology, Lucknow University for extending support in data entry in computer and tabulation of data. We are grateful to Dr. A.K. Singh, Assistant Director, Regional Centre for Urban and Environmental Studies, Lucknow University, Lucknow, who assisted us in analyzing the field data and drafting the report. We are thankful to Mr. Sunil Barar for giving the manuscript the present shape.

We express gratitude to the persons of Founder's secretariat namely Ms. Aarti Arora, Ms. Anita Agrawal, Ms. Vinita Verma, Ms. Nigar Imam, Ms. Tarun Sharma and Mr. Akhilesh Kumar Thakur for providing the infrastructural facilities for completing the study. We are also thankful to the District Magistrate of Mathura and Varanasi and other officials for extending the help in conducting the survey of the widows.

Bindeshwar Pathak
Satyendra Tripathi

1

Introduction

Eliminating gender discrimination and empowering women are among the paramount challenges facing the world today. Despite the international community's commitment to gender equality, the lives of millions of women and girls throughout the world are affected by discrimination, disempowerment and poverty. Gender equality is central to realizing the Millennium Development Goals. Eliminating gender discrimination and empowering women will require enhancing women's influence in the key decisions that shape their lives. In India, the plight of women is no better than that of women in other developing countries. Despite the honour and reverence accorded to them as deities in religion and mythology and tribute paid to them as personified in historical monuments, the ground realities have a very different tale to tell. Women constitute half of the segment of population in India and cannot be afforded to be kept out of the mainstream. Secondly, women are vital and productive workers in India's national economy, and make one-third of the labour force. Thirdly, the poorer the family, the greater is the dependence on women's economic productivity. Fourthly, there is a significant gap between women's potential and actual productivity. Therefore, women will gain proportionally more if investment allocation and development efforts are shifted in their favour. Fifthly, women's earnings have a positive correlation with children's health, nutritional levels and education.

Indian women are at the crossroad of their destiny. There is a great upsurge in their consciousness about their rights among all sections and classes of society in all regions of the country. There has been a tremendous increase in developmental activity for women since 1980. Gender equality and women empowerment are crucial for mainstreaming gender in development. The rhetoric of gender equity and women's empowerment has become common place in government policy, non-governmental advocacy, media and academic research. However, gender discrimination has been identified as one of the most pervading forms of institutional deprivation. The national government of India has initiated important steps to improve the status of women. National perspective plan for women (1988–2000), national plan of action for girl child (1991–2000), national draft policy for women (2001) are some of the key policy initiatives. Besides, government has initiated woman's centred and specific programmes for the development and empowerment of women.

There has been paradigm shift from a welfare orientation to an empowerment approach. This has further led to the emerging concept of engendering development in order to ensure gender equity, gender mainstreaming and women-centric governance. Although, India is among the most complex democracies in the world, with a long history of commitments to women's welfare and empowerment through constitutional provisions, legislation, policies and plans, yet deep levels of structural gender bias persists within families, societies and economies. There are formidable opportunities and challenges, including continued high rate of economic growth in the phase of declining sex ratio, decreasing energy and natural resources, increasing income inequality and an urban rural divide. Thus, gender equality has become a core prerequisite for sustainable and equitable economic growth. Women are major contributors to the India's economy and therefore, empowerment of women is essential for distributive justice and national growth. Engendering growth model and development plans may create opportunities for women in their mainstreaming in development process and governance. The growth models and development planning requires the suitable mechanism which is able to address the gender concerns at all stages and policy commitments along with budgetary support for them.

The 12th Five Year Plan has recognized the primacy of India's women and children who constitute about 70 per cent of population. The Plan envisages the engendering of development planning and making it more child-centric. High priority has been given to women and children from the poorest communities, from the most deprived socio-religious communities, such as Scheduled Castes, Scheduled Tribes, particularly vulnerable Tribal communities and others. The key elements for gender equity to be addressed in the 12th Five Year Plan include economic empowerment, social and physical infrastructure, enabling legislations, women's participation in governance, inclusiveness of all categories of women, engendering policies and programmes, and mainstreaming women through gender budgeting.

Ageing of population is a universal phenomenon. The changing structures of societies, patterns of family interdependence, family structure, and demographic, social and economic trends have affected the relationship between generations across the globe. India is also heading towards the similar demographic pattern like other developing countries. The proportion and population of the aged (60+ years) is gradually increasing which has long-term implications on society and particularly inter-generational relations in the family system. In traditional Indian society older people lived within a multi-generational extended family comprising one or more adults, children, grand children and other kin. The aged enjoyed honour, respect, legitimate authority within the family, community and society. They had decision-making responsibilities in economic, religious, social and political activities of the family. However, with the change of time, the socio-cultural value system has been degraded besides declining of traditional family structure. The nuclear family has emerged in Indian society where the living of family members has shrinked to one family without proper space for older persons. The changing living arrangement and functional responsibilities of the family have also affected the inter-generational relations with a little respect and honour to older persons. Thus, the older persons are being neglected, abused, exploited and isolated to some extent. In view of the changing demographics and socio-cultural change in the Indian society, the government has made attempts to provide proper care and protection to older persons and also provide them with rehabilitation services. A number of aged homes and other age-well centres have been set up by the government, non-government organizations, private and corporate houses for the rehabilitation of the aged. The Ministry of Social Justice and Empowerment, Government of India, has launched scheme of Integrated Programme for Older Persons for the welfare and rehabilitation of the aged persons in India. Under the scheme, old age homes, day care centres and mobile medical units have been set up by the non-government organizations/voluntary organizations.

Destitution

A destitute person is usually homeless as well, but homelessness is just one of the many visible manifestations of destitution. In moving away from the term 'homeless' to the broader term 'destitute', the researcher attempts to place the focus on the various different problems that together make a person destitute, as opposed to homelessness which may draw attention towards a narrower understanding of 'being without a home/shelter'. The Merriam-Webster Online Dictionary (http://www.m-w.com/) defines destitute as 'not having or possessing, entirely lacking with, of, being in want, extremely poor, desolate, forsaken without food, shelter etc., completely impoverished, lacking'. The Readers Digest Word Power Dictionary adds to this definition in the words 'extremely poor and lacking the means to provide for one down and out, forsaken, broken down'. In sum, destitution is referred to 'people who are lacking the basic means of human existence, and are therefore wanting, because they are extremely poor. This condition is being the result of (1) personal factors such as wrong choices, underdeveloped coping skills, family situations etc., or (2) social factors, where society abuses people etc., in the process breaking them down, deserting and abandoning them, or because they are marginalized, once again resulting in their being extremely poor'. In addition, the condition of being 'destitute' causes a whole range of personal and social problems, ranging from a breakdown in self-image, to the inability to break out of the vicious circle of poverty.

Reasons for Destitution

People become destitute because of various reasons that interact dynamically. The deduction follows that a variety of possible reasons, causes or problems lead to destitution. The theory is that some causes and problems are external, meaning they originate from outside the person, an occurrence which is mostly outside the control of her or him. Simultaneously, there are causes that are internal, functioning within a person to motivate certain choices above others. These 'external' problems can usually also be classified as 'social' or 'structural' in nature, while 'internal' problems are also termed 'individualistic'. These issues are dynamically interactive, and cannot really be separated. This chapter does not attempt to exhaustively explore the possible problems, causes, issues and factors contributing to destitution, but is intended merely to provide an overview of the immensity of the problem of destitution. It also serves as a starting point which following chapters will build upon. It seems reasonable to assume that few individuals aspire to be destitute – yet many still are! The reasons are often unclear, and often poorly articulated. One popular perspective has been to identify major social problems, such as unemployment. Another perspective focuses on the personalities of destitute people, which are presumed to be defective. Morse (Morse in Robertson and Greenblatt, 1992) reacts to this by stating: 'Blaming individuals is a narrow, grossly distorted oversimplification of the factors that lead to homelessness destitution'. On the other hand, explanations identifying only social forces are also inadequate. Destitution remains a complex, multi-determined phenomenon. In literature, as well as in the common view, destitution is seen as primarily a problem of poverty. Several writers have stated that at least one originating source of destitution can be found in the existence of poverty (Morse, 1992; Baxter and Hopper, 1981; Wood, 1992). Yet, even though the destitute can be perceived as the poorest of the poor, destitution is also an issue having to do with personal choice and characteristics, as well as a social, cultural, organizational and institutional problem. In dealing with the reasons for destitution, all the different issues, and the way they dynamically interact, will need to be taken into consideration.

Theories of Destitution

Meyers et al. (1999: 82) states that 'our understanding of the causes of poverty tends to be in the eye of the beholder. If care is not taken to understand our unwitting biases, our understanding of the causes of poverty tends to be an outworking of our place in the social system, our education, our culture and our personality'. When talking about destitution, and the reasons people are destitute, the real question should be: 'Why do people become so poor that they lack the basic means of human existence?' There are many theories as to why people become destitute; together these different viewpoints should offer a sound understanding of the factors involved in causing destitution. It would also seem that while some factors are more directly involved in causing destitution, others appear to function indirectly by contributing to destitution, while perhaps not directly causing it. In exploring causes for destitution, a number of theories, models and viewpoints are considered. These must be seen as complementary, each adding something to the other. They also often overlap. From these different theories, a new theory emerges.

Morse (cited by Robertson and Greenblatt, 1992) divides the factors causing destitution into six categories, namely cultural, institutional, community, organizational, group and individual factors. According to Morse (1992), cultural factors would include racism, racial discrimination and racial prejudices. Cultural factors also include prejudices against the poor because they are judged by the common public as being lazy, or weaklings with alcohol problems. Apathy and the lack of involvement that characterizes the dominant social position regarding destitute people also play a role: usually resulting in fewer social resources and services being devoted to addressing destitution. Institutional factors include macro-economic issues that promote and cause poverty, such as a lack of affordable housing, of appropriate social assistance, of mental health care and policies, of adequate substance abuse treatment, of integrated care for previous convicts (who become destitute upon leaving justice systems and prisons), as well as of coordination and cooperation between institutional systems.

Community factors concern the breakdown in communities, where communities become poor and marginalized, leading to destitution. Such factors also refer to urban redevelopment policies that adversely affect certain communities and cause them to become poorer. Organizational factors have to do with the fact that destitute people often struggle to gain 'entry' into organizations that could help them, because of issues such as needing a permanent address to qualify for services such as grants, or organizations that will not accept people with a history of mental illness or violence. Amongst organizational factors one comes across service delivery problems that contribute to destitution, because services are often not available, or accessible, or appropriate. Service withdrawal also contributes to destitution: where services are withdrawn from poor communities because people cannot pay, or grants for the delivery of those services are withdrawn. Family factors are concerned with a person's dysfunctional early family experiences, or disconnected current family experiences that subsequently cause destitution by isolating people.

Morse (1992) defines individual factors as individual characteristics that tend to contribute to destitution, such as alcoholism and drug abuse, poor physical health, mental disorders and defective personalities. These factors contribute to destitution because (1) they tend to limit a person's coping abilities; (2) diminish social supports and resources (owing to overuse or abuse of, for instance, family help); and (3) consequently make the person more dependent on social institutions and organizations. Another aspect of individual factors (Morse, 1992) is that of adaptation. At some point after a person becomes destitute, a process of adaptation to destitution begins. Gradually the person adjusts to the status of destitution. Much of this adaptive process revolves around daily activities. As Hopper et al. (1982) note, the destitute life is a difficult, demanding exercise where survival is an uncertain, demeaning and full-time occupation. 'Daily activities are geared towards meeting important basic needs for food, income and shelter while also attempting to assure one's personal safety from physical harm and harassment.'

This term is associated with Oscar Lewis, a well known anthropologist, and was first used by him in his book *Five Families: Mexican Case Studies in the Culture of Poverty* (1959). The basic thesis of the 'culture of poverty' explanation holds that some people are poor because their culture or way of life is faulty. This 'culture' is then passed down from generation to generation along family lines. According to this theoretical perspective, people are poor because of certain personal or cultural defects. Lewis writes that: Poverty becomes a dynamic factor which affects participation in the national culture and creates a subculture of its own. One can speak of the culture of the poor; for it has its own modalities and distinctive social and psychological consequences for its members. In another work, Lewis (1966) contends that the 'culture of poverty' is a 'subculture of Western society with its own structure and rationale, a way of life handed on from generation to generation along family lines ... a culture in the traditional and anthropological sense that it provides human beings a design for living'. Lewis feels that conditions of poverty generate a set of values and behaviour patterns that are unique to the poor and inclusive of such characteristics as fatalistic attitudes towards life, lack of initiative and deferred gratification, strong feelings of alienation, helplessness, dependence, and inferiority. Lewis's theory is controversial and has been widely debated and adequately critiqued, most notably by Valentine (1968, 1971) and Leacock (1971). Critics claim that the behaviour associated with the poor is the result of poverty, not its cause.

According to Valentine (1971), one of the serious shortcomings of this theory is its limited application. The culture-of-poverty theory also assumes an overly uniform view of culture and values in societies (Gang, 1972). The poor may differ in some respects, but so do many groups in their society. Contrary to this theoretical view, the poor do not constitute a homogenous group because most of the poor are not poor for life nor stem from generations of poor ancestors. Valentine (1971), in criticizing Lewis, 'reformed' the culture of poverty theory into five propositions: (1) lack of participation in the larger society by the poor; (2) different values; (3) no local organization among the poor beyond the family, unstable family life and weak identity; (4) weak character and (5) weak development of a worldview. His critique centres on the claim that these propositions are more the result of poverty than the cause of poverty. In spite of the criticisms above, the said theory has been widely accepted, at least to some degree. As Landon (2006) puts it, 'at least some of the conclusions reached in the culture of poverty theory about some poor people seem evident to even the casual observer of poverty'.

'Ethos' is defined here as society's way of thinking, a general understanding of what is true and good in a society. Harrison (1985) develops 'economic ethos' as a theory where certain social attitudes would lead to economic development, and the lack of those attitudes would, then, obviously lead to a society where poverty develops easily. These attitudes are: (1) an expectation of fair play; (2) an educational system that provides basic skills, promotes problem solving and nurtures inquisitiveness, creativity and critical thinking; (3) a good health care system; (4) an environment that encourages experimentation and criticism; (5) freedom to match skills, desires and jobs; (6) rewards for merits and achievements; (7) political and social stability and continuity.

Nida (1974) discusses economic ethos in a much more individualized way, and almost blames personal inadequacies among poor people for economic failure that would perpetuate destitution and poverty. Another aspect of a dysfunctional economic ethos would be that of corruption, which would obviously undermine a healthy economic ethos. Various theologians have also blamed institutional factors such as a dysfunctional economic ethos for causing and contributing to destitution. In this explanation, it is the individual's actions that cause or do not cause poverty, not the whole society's worldview and values (Landon, 2006). Its basic argument is that people are poor because they are irresponsible: make mistakes of judgment, get themselves in jams, are injured through carelessness, etc. The critical point is that these people 'knew better', yet took irresponsible chances, or even chose to do wrong. This explanation implies that there is something pathological about the individual, his/her thinking and behaviour, which could be repaired if he/she would simply imitate good folks. This concept links closely to that of 'individual factors' as part of Morse's theory explained above. Even if it is true (which is debatable: because people are often pushed into irresponsible behaviour simply because they are trying to survive), it is still too narrow a viewpoint to explain the whole problem of poverty and destitution.

Christian (1994) has stated that poor people are embedded in a complex framework of interacting systems. For Christian, these systems include a (1) personal system (including psychology); (2) a social system; (3) a spiritual-religious system, which is both personal and social; (4) a cultural system that includes a worldview; and (5) a biophysical system. He defines the way in which every one of these systems contributes towards entrapping people in poverty. The social system, including socio-economic-political realities, reinforces the powerlessness of the poor by means of exclusion and exploitation. This is driven by an undisclosed and often unrecognized attitude amongst non-poor people who see themselves as superior and therefore meant to rule. They consequently start to play god in the lives of the poor, using religious systems, the law, media, government policies, and people occupying positions of power (Christian, 1994). The spiritual-religious system refers to the impact of the fall and sin on individual human beings, as well as the additional impact of deception by principalities and powers. The powerlessness of the poor is reinforced by the fear and deceit created by 'the god of this world that has blinded the minds of unbelievers' and the 'trap of the devil who has taken them captive to do his will' (Christian, 1994). In this way Christian affirms that it is not simply human beings, and the systems in which they live, which create and sustain poverty. There is a cosmic adversary that works against life. For Christian (1994), cultural system encompasses inadequacies in worldview. This signifies a culture that conditions people to accept certain convictions, such as those that the 'Blacks must serve and Whites must rule' culture which dominated the apartheid years. Biophysical system (body-mind-spirit) includes the body, mind and spirit that are weakened by hunger, illness and lack of education, thereby disabling people from lifting themselves out of the poverty trap (Christian, 1994). The personal system, as Christian (1994) perceives it, refers to the 'marred' identity of the poor. Impoverished people suffer from marred identities in two ways: (1) they see themselves as 'damaged goods', a perception affirmed by the powerful who treat the poor as people with nothing to offer, while (2) a lifetime of suffering, deception and exclusion is internalized by the poor in a way that results in their no longer knowing who they are or why they were created, without value and without gifts.

Chambers (1983) describes the poor as 'living in a cluster of disadvantages', where people are poor, physically weak, isolated, vulnerable and powerless, and where these dimensions of poverty interact in a system called the poverty trap. He specifically names the following dimensions of poverty: (1) Material poverty (lack of physical goods), (2) Physical weakness (lack of health), (3) Isolation (lack of access and information), (4) Vulnerability (Few buffers against emergencies), (5) Powerlessness (poor people possess very little influence to change their world), (6) From the work of Meyers et al. (1999), spiritual poverty can be added.

One of the greatest challenges for destitute people is the extent to which they are disaffiliated or marginalized from society. There are different perspectives as to 'why' disaffiliation and destitution with concurrent marginalization occur in today's society. In the 1980s, two polarized perspectives were offered. One, expounded most strongly by Baum, Burnes, and Lamb (1993), is that people become disaffiliated of their own doing. Personal problems such as mental illness, substance abuse, and legal issues challenge a destitute person's ability to attach, or remain attached, to the rest of society. Others argue that structural changes in the economy and housing market have created more poor people and less low-income housing, making destitution inevitable for some proportion of the population. According to this second view, society abandoned the destitute.

Impact of Destitution

It is difficult to measure the impact of destitution on the voluntary sector in a quantitative way. Voluntary sector help is often the only form of help that destitute asylum seekers can access. The impact can be seen on:

Strain on Services: Most voluntary sector agencies working with destitute clients will have other functions that come under strain because of the extra workload.

Pressure on Limited Resources: The amount of time and resources spent on helping destitute clients can be a real strain on voluntary sector organizations. Agencies find it difficult to fundraise for this client group.

Staff: Staff will often spend long periods of time trying to access basic food and shelter. They may often be left feeling inadequate, frustrated and angry at a system that leaves vulnerable clients on the streets. It is demoralizing and depressing to have to face clients on a daily basis that you cannot help.

Volunteers: Many asylum seekers volunteering with agencies will drop out once their support stops. This affects the quality and consistency of volunteering that can be offered. Many volunteers feel the same pressures of staff and frustration in not being able to help, but may also feel increased pressure to provide more as the boundaries may not be so well defined.

Perception of an Organization: How do stakeholders perceive an organization that cannot assist? Many organizations feel they are not in a position to help because of the high numbers of destitute clients.

Concept of Death of Bereavement

The post marital family consisting of widow or widower is a widely known feature of every society. Facing loss of one of the marital partners is a sad event. Death is an extreme shock. It may come suddenly and without previous warning. It can be a crisis for the family and for the individual. The very term death is enough to create panic among most people. It robs a loved one and, thereby, destroys the strong ties and close relationship that binds a family. It changes the habits of eating, sleeping, dressing and conversing, habits of sex, and ego support that makes the surviving partner numb and bewildered. Reorganization is often very painful for it involves adjustment and readjustment to a new situation which often comes suddenly. Hence, death can be viewed as social, not biological. The unique qualities of each relationship make the universal experience of death peculiarly painful. No one can truly replace the person who has died. The death of one's spouse is a traumatic event. Loss of the husband is felt more than any other loss and disorganizes a woman's life deeply. The death of the husband is a devastating blow. For the widow, life may not seem worth living and she may look forward to her own early death.

Somerville mentions that death is a significant and universal family experience. However, many people and many families treat bereavement, crisis, death and widowhood with extreme brevity. It is considered a major shock, often requiring physical or medical care like any other illness or accident with time for recovery. Psychologically, bereavement is a major type in the general class of traumatic frustration-situation. Arrested impulse or thwarted habit is the root of all sorrow. Sociologically, bereavement is the dismemberment of an affectional group by death. It is, thus, a problem in intrapersonal conflict, accommodation and/or assimilation-disorganization and in interpersonal accommodation and group reorganization disintegration.

Bereavement and grief represent a crisis and critical transition for the family of the deceased. This is particularly so for the widow who has to face the crisis of not only losing the spouse but also stepping into the status of the head of the family. She has to bear the onus of being the bread winner. Waller, while studying the social aspects of bereavement, points out that bereavement may be the loss of a mate, partner, child, sibling or other close relative or associate and that its effect necessarily varies, with the age of the bereaved, his emotional involvement with the deceased, the manner of death, the other relationship of the bereaved and the degree of emancipation of the bereaved person.

Eliot, while making a deep and significant analysis of bereavement, classifies some of the ways in which families and their members respond to the crisis of bereavement. He classifies the effects of bereavement into immediate and later or primary and secondary, and among them he noted several as typical:

There can be many effects of bereavement on different levels. They can be individual effects of bereavement:

- *Total failure to readjust:* like suicide, early death, insanity, moral disintegration, and obsession.

- *Partial Failure:* for instance, eccentricities, physical illness or prostration, aboulia, purposelessness, isolation, embitterment, misanthropy, cynicism, reversion to or recurrence of grief, self-blame or personal hates, fears, and loneliness.
- *Partial Success:* like, resignation, God's will, stoicism, stereotyped formula of immortality, misery escaped, sentimental memorials, effective repression of memories, intensification of affections, extension of affections, deliberate absorption in distractions or duties, new or fantasized love objects.
- *Conspicuous Success:* like, new love object, thoroughgoing religious rationalization, spontaneous forgetting, relaxation of tensions, devotion to life work, identification with role of the deceased, creation of constructive memorials, transmutation of the experience into productive reintegration of the personality.

Thus, bereavement is a compound crisis. It is a painful emotional shock, a sharp change in social status, often an economic catastrophe and usually a philosophical challenge. It calls for reorganizing the habits and routines and ways of a life time of married living.

Parkes Murray observes, in his study on bereaved people in London, one-third of them had no contact with a clergy man apart from the funeral service, whereas three-quarters consulted a general practitioner during the six months following the bereavement. He noticed a sharp increase in consultations after bereavement, the reason for seeking advice being different at different ages. Young widows suffer from psychological difficulties whereas old widows suffer from physical symptoms. He further describes the phases, characteristics of grief and mourning, during which the widow was initially shocked or numbed and then suffered from pangs of intense pining. In the final stage there was revival and gradual return to normal life. Thus, bereavement is a compound crisis. It is a painful emotional shock, a sharp change in social status, often an economic catastrophe and usually a philosophical challenge (Duval, 1971).

State of Widowhood

Widowhood is unique and its most basic features are as follows:

- One must have been married.
- Widowhood is not welcomed because most people wish marriage to continue.
- The loss is irreplaceable and widowhood cannot be avoided (Brubaker, 1985)

Widowhood is a crisis in a woman's life, involving new social adjustments for the family as well as for herself. It is an event that constitutes the greatest and saddest change in the life of a woman. It also leads to the loss of status resulting in a state of helplessness and hopelessness. Widowhood hits women, particularly, harder than men. A widower, being economically independent, does not feel the stigma, and the loss of the spouse, as much as a woman. Widowhood is, primarily, a female phenomenon (Rosow, 1967). It is rightly said that widowhood, at all ages, changes the basic self-identity of many women. This is especially true of traditionally oriented women for whom the role of wife is central to their lives. Millions of women experience this misfortune and generally bear its burden for many years. Widowhood is an event that brings about the greatest change in the status of a widow, for it is often accompanied by deleterious consequences. This is not only because of the loss of the husband, but also because of the lack of clear-cut cultural expectations regarding the proper role of the widow. The plight of widows is indeed miserable for, almost inevitably, it carries with it, problems of ill-health, insufficiency of money, unemployment and strained social relations with one's children and one's friends for both men and women.

Widowhood in Different Religions

Hindu Tradition

Indian society, unlike American or Western society, is not voluntaristic where the involvement of an individual in various social activities is dependent on his/her own initiative. In our traditional society, involvement in social roles, social relationships, and support systems, etc. is not determined by choice or through life events but by family, caste and social norms. A widow's life is dependent upon her in-laws, her parents, siblings, and relatives.

At the time of the 1991 Census, the total number of widows in India was more than 33 million and India ranks among the highest in the world, in the incidence of widowhood. This was due to several inter-related reasons: marriage in India is stereotyped, husbands invariably are older than wives and since male mortality rates are rather high, and women begin to outlive men after their reproductive years. Another reason is that so many women are married at a very young age. Even now, in some communities in India, girls are married before they reach the age of puberty. As a result, there are still child widows in India. In spite of their large numbers, little is known about the widows. They are rarely mentioned in literature, in public debates on social policy or even by the women's movements. We hear the occasional public outcry only when the treatment of widows takes a sensational form, such as that of *Sati;* there is a striking lack of public concern for the quiet deprivations experienced by millions of widows. In this chapter, an attempt is made to highlight the historical perspective of the institution of widowhood.

Widowhood in India among the upper castes is a state of social death. The widow's social death stems from her alienation from reproduction and sexuality, following the loss of her husband and her exclusion from the functioning social unit of the family. Once a women ceases to be a wife, she ceases to be a 'person'. She is no more a daughter or daughter-in-law. The problem posed by Brahmanical patriarchy therefore is this: since the wife has no social existence outside of her husband, then as a widow who or what is she? The texts and the rituals attempt to work the problem out. The problem simply stated is that although the widow is socially dead she remains an element in society. The question then remains how to incorporate her in the social system. One way could have been to constitute a separate community of widows, a non-sexual community such as that of the female ascetics. Another could be to retain her in society but place her on the fringes and then institutionalize her marginality. This is what Brahmanical patriarchy did with the widow. The widow's institutionalized marginality, a liminal state between being physically alive and being socially dead, was the ultimate cultural outcome of the deprivation of the widow of her sexuality as well as of her personhood.

From the evidence of the classical texts, it is clear that the upper caste Hindu widow was an anomaly in traditional Hindu society since she had no place and no function in the Hindu social order. In Vedic period, a widow was allowed to remarry if she so desired. This is evident from the verse *(sloka)* in Rigveda in which the widow who lay on the pyre by the side of her dead husband was asked to rise and come to the world of the living:

> Oh lady, get up, come back to the world of living; you are lying by the side of a dead person. As far as thy wifehood to thy husband, who had seized thy hand (in marriage) is concerned, you have lived it out completely.

The Atharvaveda also lays a ritual for a woman marrying a second time to secure the union of the new couple in heaven. The *Dharmasutras* (400 BC to 100 AD) allowed remarriage even when the death of the husband was only presumed and not proved. Vasishtha has said:

> Even a Brahmin lady with living children need wait only for five years if her husband has gone out on a journey and does not return. If she is unwilling to go to him, she should marry a near relative; only she should not wed outside the family if there is an eligible person within it.

Altekar has maintained that widow remarriage came into disrepute during the period 300 BC to 200 AD. Duryodhana, when urged to make peace during the last days of the war, is reported to have said:

> I am disinclined to enjoy the earth as a man is to marry a widow.

The opposition to widow remarriage began to grow steadily and stronger from 200 AD owing to the growing influence of the ascetic norms, which were discriminatory and oppressive for woman. Manu was resolute in his attitude towards the remarriage of widows. Manu put some restrictions on widows in the form of certain duties. Some of these were:

- A widow should never remarry.
- Even after the death of her husband, she should not think of other man.
- After the death of her husband, she should remain chaste and be patient with hardships.
- If her husband left no son or daughter, she should not go to another man to have an offspring.

From about 1000 AD, the prohibition of remarriage began to be extended even to the cases of child widows. From about 1100 AD, widow remarriages disappeared almost completely in the higher sections of the Hindu society, though in the lower strata, remarriages continued to be practised. It was only in the nineteenth century that out of a desire to increase their respectability, some lower castes began to impose upon themselves the prohibition of widow marriage. Today, however, the tendency appears to be disappearing.

The wife who becomes a widow creates an anomalous situation in the Brahmanical prescriptive texts. It is significant that there is no widow in traditional mythology except Kunti. But although she is important, she is not central to the narrative in the Mahabharata. The only woman who comes close to such a position is Savitri. But she fights for his husband's life and gets it. By implication the narrative lays the groundwork for the widely-held belief that women who are widowed fall into that state because they bring it upon themselves. To that extent, they are responsible for the death of their husbands.

In brief, the Brahmanical tradition, especially after circa AD 700, outlines only two models of widowhood: that of Sati who mounts the pyre, rejects widowhood, and proves herself to be the best follower of *Stridharma,* and that of the living Sati who becomes the ascetic within the home, remaining celibate and steadfastly devoted to the husband till she dies.

The two models – the Sati who mounts the pyre and the ascetic widow who mortifies the body – are repeated throughout the centuries in all the later texts of the Brahmanical tradition. Of the two, the first remained the more ideal for a variety of reasons. The devotion of Sati who mounted the pyre and the merits that such an action brought to her relatives was no doubt perceived to be greater than that of the ascetic widow.

The passage of a woman from the position of a wife and *Sahadharmini* or one who shares her husband's religio-social duties to that of a widow was marked by various rites. The texts do indicate that soon after the death of the husband, the appearance of the widow was dramatically altered in order to segregate her from other women, as she had to give up all forms of adornment as well as those customs or symbols that were associated with marriage of a woman. These include the *kumkuma,* the vermilion mark on the forehead, the *sindoora* applied in the parting of the hair in certain parts of India, and the use of *haldi,* or turmeric among other banned items.

Other customs not specifically mentioned in the texts are also widely prevalent such as the breaking of glass bangles and the breaking of the *mangalsutra,* the sign of a married woman in many parts of India. Two other markers of widowhood are the white, ochre and occasionally maroon coarse garment prescribed for widows, and among the high castes in southern and western India, the tonsured head. The colour codes of red are banned and white prescribed as this symbolizes asexuality. In the place of the red *kumkuma* banned for widows, it is customary for them to use *vibhuti* or white ash, associated with the funeral pyre, and the exclusive use of this colour by widows among women indicates their continued association with asexuality and death.

The ritual of the tonsure marks a more extreme resolution of the asexuality of the widow. The idea underlying it was to make the outward appearance of the widow in harmony with the ideal of renunciation *(sanyas)* that she was expected to follow. It was hoped that this would help in creating an ascetic atmosphere around her, necessary to lead a celibate life. It is difficult to say when the custom of tonsure originated. Even in the *Smritis* which describe the duties of widows, the shaving of head does not figure. There is every possibility that widows of the royal families kept it unbound during the period of pollution and mourning. Unbound hair appears frequently as the sign of widowhood in the Mahabharata. When Draupadi kept her hair unbound for 12 years she was symbolically proclaiming a state of widowhood and mourning. There is, thus, no reference to this custom up to the ninth century. We find reference to it in the writings of the twelfth century, like those of Madhava and Anantadeva. Thus, the custom perhaps became general from about 1200 AD amongst the Brahmins first and was then gradually extended to the rest of the society. It was, however, more common in southern than in northern India.

During Buddhist period, a widow did not suffer any social and moral degradation due to widowhood. No stigma was attached to her by the society. There were no restrictions on her dress or good habit and she did not have to shave her head. She used to participate in socio-religious functions (Shrankhayans Grahe Sutra I, II, 5, 2) as in the later period. Widow enjoyed the same status as in pre-widowed days. In the nineties of the nineteenth century, some Hindu reformers launched a most determined attack against this custom. Society began to realize that the custom, far from protecting widows, was often exposing them to the exploitation of most unscrupulous persons. The custom began to disappear in the first quarter of the twentieth century. At present, it has practically ceased, especially in the urban areas. Symbols and rituals of marriage and widowhood, along with material arrangements affecting widows were linked together to form a structure that governed the lives of upper caste widows, which survived into the nineteenth and twentieth centuries. This structure has a complementary set of relations, which applied to lower caste widows.

In Hindu tradition, widowhood represents the last and lowest stage in life for women. Caton and Merielli conceptualize Hindu widowhood as a life of agony, pain, suffering and austerity. It is a life which has been inflicted by social customs. Cormck asserts that there is probably no aspect of womanhood that has received more sympathy than that of widowhood in India. For the majority, widowhood is certainly an unhappy and miserable state. It is observed that throughout India, Hindu women regard widowhood as a punishment of some horrible crime or crimes committed by them in their previous birth, such as disobedience or disloyalty to the husband or having even killed him. Widowhood, and its accompanying miserable existence, is considered as an atonement for some sin committed in a previous birth.

In India, widow remarriage is not encouraged, though it is legalized. In the light of such conditions, Mahatma Gandhi rightly remarked, 'Enforced widowhood upon little girls is a brutal crime for which we Hindus are daily praying. Widowhood imposed by religion or custom is an unbearable yoke and defiles the home by secret vice and degrades religion, whereas voluntary widowhood consciously adopted by a woman who has felt affection of a partner adds grace and dignity of life, sanctifies the house and uplifts religion itself.

An exploration into the folklores of different regions of India widens our awareness about the condition of widows. In the folklore of West Bengal, women considered widowhood as a great curse. Tamil folklore mentions that the condition of the widows in all cases is miserable. Her presence was considered inauspicious and, hence, a widow was discouraged from appearing at any social and cultural function. She lived an unseen existence. In the folklore of Orissa, widowhood is considered much more sorrowful than even the death of a loved daughter, for the misery over the loss of a daughter can be overcome, but widowhood dogs a woman till her own death. In all cultures, widowhood is a crisis in a woman's life. But cultures differ significantly among themselves in their ways of overcoming crises. Some cultures allow their widows to remarry, some allow it only in exceptional cases; some do not allow it under any circumstances. The last cause has been adopted by orthodox Brahmanic Hindu culture. A culture that allows widow remarriage does not necessarily become inferior to the one which disapproves of it. But what may bring about the real difference between one culture and another is their reordering of marital values.

Islamic Tradition

In Islam, widowhood, like divorce, is a non-issue. Its acceptability in society should be free from inhibitions and taboos but Muslims in Africa have mixed the values of Islam as per local customs and practice of tribal societies. In the case of northern states of Nigeria namely Abia, Anambra, Enugu, and Imo where the ethnic groups are animist, Muslim and Christian, in general, widows are denied inheritance to land particularly, and to chattels to a lesser degree. In most Nigerian families, daughters are not regarded as permanent members of their husbands' families. So the widow is disinherited in both her natal and her husband's family. Customs are far more influential than modem law, and in all the ethnic groups, matrilineal as well as patrilineal, widows are deprived of inheritance rights. Whatever the modern law may say on paper, a widow's rights are, in general, completely ignored by the deceased husband's relatives who regard his estate as their birthright. Very rarely does a widow attempt to claim her rights in a court of law.

Drinking the water in which the dead husband's body was washed is to prove that the widow is innocent of murder. She is untouchable and defiled and so must not receive gifts, pick up items from the floor, or receive a handshake. She must not speak out or make a noise unless she is required to cry. Some rites insist that the widow must be fed by others and her meals should be reduced in number. Scarification (scarring) of face with a knife or razor, sleeping with the corpse as a symbolic last sexual act with dead husband, sleeping on the bare floor, prohibition on bathing are some of the prohibitions for widows. This could last from 28 days to eight months, even when the widow is menstruating, restrictions on movement. Widow is prohibited from leaving the home for 28 days. She cannot go to work, or meet people, fetch water, cook, go to market or farm. The widow must weep for long hours even when she does not feel able; eating in unwashed dishes and plates for the duration of mourning from 28 days to three months. Sitting for long hours on the floor for many days to demonstrate her dethronement is also observed. Sometimes her hands are padded so she cannot scratch herself and sexual relations with family members, brothers-in-law, father-in-law to 'cleanse' the widow of evil spirits. This ritual of cleansing is the worst taboo of all. Its purpose is to sever the links between the living and the dead. These customs are not only degrading and harmful to women's health and status but they can also be life-threatening in the modern context of AIDS. Unhygienic instruments to shave hair or scar the skin can be carriers of virus. Widows are susceptible to scabies, diarrhoea and typhoid. Those who are raped risk infection by STDs, HIV and pregnancy as well as internal lacerations. The 'naked' rites may bring on attacks of pneumonia.

Widows are coerced to comply with mourning rites irrespective of their educational or social status. A female medical doctor (colleague of the Director of a Widows' NGO) had all her hair shaved off with the jagged edge of a broken bottle, after which all the possessions she and her doctor husband had acquired together after their marriage were seized by the brothers-in-law. The health implications are not just physical but also psychological. Psychologically many widows suffer depressions and fear. Physically, they are vulnerable to a variety of skin diseases because they cannot wash, and from food poisoning from eating off dirty plates. Many widows become seriously ill from observing such rites, but few neither dare moke a complaint nor resist compliance.

Christian Tradition

The paradox of Indian Christian Widowhood is very striking. Christianity does not condemn widowhood. There are several instances in the Bible where Jesus glorifies and sympathizes with widows. The Canonical laws concerning widows in the Old Testament refer mainly to the question of remarriage. If a man died without children, his widow was obliged to marry her deceased husband's brother. In primitive Christian times the support of the widows was made a special duty of the apostles, who collected alms for them and gave care of them to the deacons. This support of the needy widows has always been considered a particular charge of the ministers of the Christian church, and many decrees of Popes and councils make mention of it as especially incumbent on bishops, parish priests and holders of benefices. In apostolic times, widows were employed in certain capacities in the ministry of the church.

But this ideal got corrupted and women were accorded a lower status. It all stems from the mythical concept that man is made in the image of God and woman made out of the rib of a man, which is not a very significant organ of the human biological system, thereby suggesting that man is physically, intellectually and morally superior to woman whom God created as his helpmate. One should not overlook the fact that the writers of the Holy Bible, the scholars and the theologians, until the early twentieth century, and the makers of Canon laws were all men.

Sociological studies have shown that the way gender and gender boundaries are constructed in time and space, determining women's status in social hierarchy and influencing wide spheres of social action in private and public life, is closely connected to the incidence of two principal variables: the degree of female participation in economic activity and the degree of control women exert on economic resources. Likewise, gender studies in India have shown the fundamental role of these variables in explaining the women's social value and status and, consequently, gender inequality, with a strong discriminatory power between India and other world regions. In the north, control of economic resources by women is non-existent and the influence of patriarchy is persistent and pervasive. The patriarchate institution shows a close link to the structure of production processes, to the way this structure determines the degree of female participation in production and the consequential social respect of women.

2

Status of Widows in India

Widowhood in India is a complex institution. The lives of widows in India do not conform to the projected ideals of widowhood. In the Indian society, widowhood is a factor which serves to isolate a particular section of women from the mainstream of life and with age their condition deteriorates. There are numerous factors which influences the stressful nature of the transition to widowhood include the nature of previous relationships, availability of support from others, health facilities, loss of income and anticipated loneliness. In addition to their plight, restrictions are imposed upon their food and clothing habits, participation in social functions and remarriage has been prohibited for them. Widowhood exposes the gap between cultural and social realities, between precept and practice. Apart from human rights issues, there are other consequences of widowhood one of which is migration. Many widows in rural areas who are unable to cultivate their land or manage business without male assistance and often in debt after incurring the medical expenses of the dead husbands are forced to migrate to towns in search of livelihood. In many cases, this migration is fraught with risks of trafficking, physical and sexual assaults etc. and many young widows end up in the brothels.

Widows are more affected by the sin of omission all over the globe. In many developing countries, the exact number of widows, their ages and other social and economic aspects of their lives are unknown. Almost world-wise, widows comprise a significant proportion of all women, ranging from 7 per cent to 16 per cent to all adult women. However, in some countries and regions, the proportion is far higher. In developed countries, widowhood is experienced primarily by elderly women, while in developing countries, it also affects young women, many of whom are still rearing children. In some regions, girls become widows before reaching adulthood. Today, millions of world's widows, of all ages, endure extreme poverty, ostracism, violence, homelessness, ill health and discrimination in law and custom. A lack of inheritance and land rights, widow abuse and the practice of degrading and life threatening mourning and burial rights are prime examples for human rights violation that are justified by reliance on culture and traditions. Higher mortality rates among men leave many women living alone in their later years, especially since most widowed women do not remarry. Widowhood for women aged 60 years and above is most prevalent in Northern Africa and

Central Asia. In India also, majority of widows are from higher age group, i.e. 60 and above years. In the state of Uttar Pradesh, about 60 per cent widows are from the age group of 60 and above years while the proportion of widows was reported 59 per cent from the corresponding age group at the national level during 2011. It is to be noted that widowhood has been reported higher in the higher age group due to high mortality rate among aged men as compared to aged women and also because of the fact that girls are married to their male counterparts corporately from higher age. The proportion of widowhood was reported 57 per cent among the age group of 65 and above years while about two-fifth women were found widowed in the age group of 60–64 years. Thus, majority of the widows are senior citizens. Therefore, it is pertinent to discuss the status of aged in India and also to examine the policy perspective related to rehabilitation and welfare of senior citizens. It is to be noted that if we consider women widows as senior citizens, they may be provided government benefits which are entitled to senior citizens.

Status of the Aged in India

Ageing is a natural and universal phenomenon. India too is fast on the path of ageing. Biologically, the concept of ageing refers to the progressive changes that take place in cell, in an organ or in the total organism over the passage of an entire life time. Ageing is primarily concerned with the changes from maturity until death. Psychologist are of the view that there is functional declination in the performance of major organs of the body with the advancement of age resulting either from cellular loss or due to loss of enzymatic potency for which cell die. In humans, this decline begins long before the age of 60 years and becomes perceptible from age of 40–45 years. The number of older people in India has been on the increase due to the growth in population and advances in medicines. The rapid strides in industrialization and urbanization and the tendency towards dissolution of the joint family system have resulted worse conditions for older people. The growing problems of the aged in India are a cause of concern for policy makers, administrators and academicians.

Population ageing is rapidly emerging as the problem of developing countries. Ageing was not only an Asian trend up until 2000, but it is going to continue to dominate Asia in the next century as well (UNFPA, 1999). Old age presents its special and unique problems but these have been aggravated due to the unprecedented speed of socio-economic transformation leading to a number of changes in different aspects of living conditions. The needs and problems of the elderly vary significantly according to their age, socio-economic status, health, living status and other such background characteristics (Siva Raju, 2002). For elders living with their families – still the dominant living arrangement – their economic security and well-being largely depends on the economic capacity of the family unit (Alam, 2006). In traditional Indian society, the informal support systems of family, kinship and community are considered strong enough to provide social security to its members, including older people. Urbanization, industrialization and the ongoing phenomenon of globalization have cast their shadow on traditional values and norms within society. Gradual nuclearization of the joint family, erosion of morality in economy, changes in the value system, migration of youth to urban areas for jobs or work and increasing participation of women in the workforce are important factors responsible for the marginalization of older people in rural India. As a result, the elderly depend on 'money-order economy' and their intimacy with their children is only from a distance (Kumar, 1999). The many physiological, economic, emotional and interpersonal facets of ageing influence the social functioning and well-being of individuals in different ways. Changing traditional values, mobility of the younger generation, changes in family structure and role of women have contributed to a 'crisis in caring' for the elderly (Prakash, 2004). Many facets of the generation gap contribute to marginalization of older persons and their wisdom by the younger generation, leading to conflicts, lack of respect and decline of authority, neglect and sometimes even exploitation or abuse.

The availability of improved medical services, better awareness regarding health and nutrition and comparatively better overall standard of living have resulted in the delayed onset of ageing and associated problems with an ultimate increase in life expectancy at birth. Consequently, the population of the elderly persons has been increasing over the years. In India, the population of older persons (60+) has constantly been increasing ever since the advent of planning and the first census in independent India in 1951. In 1951, the proportion of the aged (60+) in the total population of India was around 5.5 per cent, which increased to nearly 6 per cent in 1971 and above 7.5 per cent in 2001. In absolute terms, the magnitude of such population has increased from nearly 2 crores in 1951 to 7.2 crores in 2001 (Table 2.1). Ageing population constitutes about 7 per cent of country's population. The proportion of aged population (60+years) has been reported high in rural areas and among females. There has been increasing trend of the ageing population in India as the proportion of aged population against the total population of country has shown significant increase over the period from 1981 to 2001.

Table 2.1

Proportion of Aged Population (60+years) in India

Area/Year	*Male*			*Female*			*Persons*		
	1981	*1991*	*2001*	*1981*	*1991*	*2001*	*1981*	*1991*	*2001*
Rural	6.8	7.2	7.4	6.8	7	8.1	6.8	7.1	7.7
Urban	5.1	5.6	6.2	5.7	6	7.2	5.4	5.7	6.7
Total	6.4	6.7	7.1	6.6	6.8	7.8	6.5	6.8	7.4

Source: Ministry of Social Justice & Empowerment, Government of India, Delhi.

The rate of growth of population of the elderly has been higher than the overall growth rate of the total population. This phenomenon of growing population of senior citizens has been the result of the recent success in the achievement of the better health standards and a longer span of life for our citizens. The life expectancy at birth for both males and females has doubled during the last half century of independent India, while an enormous decline in the crude death rates and infant mortality rates has been registered during the same period. In 1951, life expectancy at birth was recorded as low as 32 years, which has more than doubled to 65 years in 2002. All the same, crude death rates which has been as high as 22.8 in 1951 declined to as low as 8.5 (SRS, 2000), while the infant mortality rates registered a low of 68 (SRS, 2000), as against 146 per thousand live births in 1951. These positive trends in the crucial health indicators have naturally resulted in constantly increasing not only the total population of the elderly but also their proportion to the total population of India. The Indian population has increased from 361 million in 1951 to 1.027 billion in 2001. Simultaneously, the number of older people has increased from 19 million (4% of total population) to 77 million (7.5% of the total) during the same time span (Registrar General of India, 2001). In order to study the implications of an aging population in India, the changing Indian demographic configuration needs to be highlighted first. That will help us assess the challenges to be met in the future (Bhattacharya, 2005). The projected population aged 60+ and their percentage share in the total projected population of the country for the year 2006 to 2026 is shown in Table 2.2. During 2006, about 7.5 per cent of total population, 7.1 per cent of total male population and 8.0 per cent of total female population were aged 60 years and above. These figures are projected to go up to 12.4 per cent, 11.7 per cent and 13.1 per cent respectively in 2026.

Table 2.2

Projected Population of Senior Citizens in India

Year	*Projected Senior Citizens Population (Crore)*			*As per cent of total population*		
	Persons	*Male*	*Female*	*Persons*	*Male*	*Female*
2006	8.36	4.07	4.28	7.5	7.1	8.0
2011	9.85	4.81	5.03	8.3	7.8	8.8
2016	11.81	5.81	5.99	9.3	8.8	9.8
2021	14.32	7.06	7.26	10.7	10.2	11.3
2026	17.32	8.46	8.86	12.4	11.7	13.1

Source: Annual Report (2011–12), Ministry of Social Justice & Empowerment, Government of India.

State-wise projected senior citizens population by gender is shown in Table 2.3. In the state of Bihar, senior citizens constituted 5.8 per cent in the total population. It is likely to increase by 11 per cent in the year 2026. In the state of Gujarat, the proportion of senior citizens population is likely to increase by 9.2 per cent in 2026 from 5 per cent in 2006. In the state of Madhya Pradesh, senior citizens population is likely to constitute 10.4 per cent in 2026 while in the state of Rajasthan; it will be about 10.8 per cent in the corresponding year. The proportion of senior citizens population in Uttarakhand would be about 11.7 per cent, comparatively higher for female population (12.9%) during 2026. In the state of Uttar Pradesh, senior citizens population will constitute about 9.8 per cent in 2026.

Table 2.3

State-wise Projected Senior Citizens Population by Gender (As % of Total Population)

All India		*2006*	*2011*	*2016*	*2021*	*2026*
	Persons	7.5	8.3	9.3	10.7	12.4
	Male	7.1	7.8	8.8	10.2	11.7
	Female	8.0	8.8	9.8	11.3	13.1
Bihar	Persons	5.8	6.5	7.6	9.1	11.0
	Male	5.7	6.5	7.6	9.2	10.7
	Female	5.8	6.5	7.5	8.9	11.3
Gujarat	Persons	5.0	5.6	6.4	7.6	9.2
	Male	4.3	4.8	5.7	6.9	8.3
	Female	5.7	6.4	7.3	8.5	10.2
Madhya Pradesh	Persons	6.7	7.1	7.8	8.9	10.4
	Male	6.2	6.6	7.3	8.4	9.8
	Female	7.2	7.7	8.3	9.4	11.1
Rajasthan	Persons	6.7	7.3	8.2	9.4	10.8
	Male	6.0	6.6	7.5	8.6	9.9
	Female	7.3	8.0	9.0	10.2	11.9
Uttar Pradesh	Persons	6.6	7.1	7.8	8.7	9.8
	Male	6.5	6.9	7.5	8.2	9.2
	Female	6.8	7.3	8.1	9.2	10.6
Uttarakhand	Persons	7.9	8.5	9.3	10.4	11.7
	Male	7.5	7.9	8.7	9.6	10.6
	Female	8.3	9.0	10.0	11.3	12.9

Source: Annual Report (2011–12), Ministry of Social Justice & Empowerment, Government of India.

During the year 2001, senior citizens population constituted 7.45 per cent at the national level while this was found higher in the state of Uttarakhand (7.71%) and Uttar Pradesh (7.01%). In the rural areas, the proportion of aged population against the total population constituted higher share in Uttarakhand (8.29%) while this was found low in Bihar (6.68%). In urban areas, the population of senior citizens constituted 6.7 per cent at the national level and it was recorded high in Madhya Pradesh (6.36%) and Gujarat (6.23%). The population of female senior citizens constituted higher share in rural areas as compared to urban areas. This was found more pronouncing in Uttarakhand (8.36%) and Gujarat (8.08%) (Table 2.4).

It is expected that during the next five decades the size of the population will grow by about 50 per cent, but the number of older people will increase fourfold. The proportion of older people in the population will grow at a higher pace than the other groups. The Indian policy makers must take a critical note regarding the cresting wave that may be observed through a receding trend of the younger people, in addition to the incoming age wave. Such developments will not only adversely affect the supply of youths in the

Table 2.4
Percentage Share of Aged by Gender and Residence

All India		*Total*	*Rural*	*Urban*
	Persons	7.45	7.74	6.70
	Male	7.10	7.43	6.25
	Female	7.83	8.06	7.21
Bihar	Persons	6.63	6.68	6.17
	Male	6.76	6.84	6.06
	Female	6.49	6.51	6.29
Gujarat	Persons	6.91	7.31	6.23
	Male	6.17	6.57	5.52
	Female	7.70	8.08	7.04
Madhya Pradesh	Persons	7.09	7.36	6.36
	Male	6.65	6.95	5.85
	Female	7.57	7.80	6.94
Rajasthan	Persons	6.74	6.99	5.95
	Male	6.22	6.47	5.41
	Female	7.31	7.54	6.55
Uttar Pradesh	Persons	7.01	7.31	5.86
	Male	7.05	7.41	5.69
	Female	6.96	7.20	6.06
Uttarakhand	Persons	7.71	8.29	6.03
	Male	7.55	8.22	5.77
	Female	7.87	8.36	6.33

Source: Annual Report (2011–12), Ministry of Social Justice & Empowerment, Government of India.

job market, but also cause strain on the resources due to more inactive people. Indian demography will be gradually swinging to a grayer one by the next few decades. It predicts that the median age of the population will increase gradually from 23.4 years in 2000 to 30.3 years in 2025 and, finally to 37.9 years in 2050. Similarly, the old age dependency ratio will go up from 13.0 per cent in 2000 to 32.8 per cent in 2050, while the young dependency ratio is expected to come down from 58.5 per cent to 30.4 per cent by that time. Consequently, the index of aging (aged child ratio) will increase from 22.1 per cent to 108.1 per cent. Therefore, every three working Indians may have to take care of one elderly person by 2050 as compared to about eight working Indians at present. Advancement of medical science, better nutrition, and increased order of awareness among the general masses, successful implementation of the public health policies vis-à-vis social and economic developments may be considered the main reasons behind such an achievement (WHO, 1999). It has been estimated that an Indian of age 60 years today is expected to survive another 15 years. Hence, adequate savings are required to sustain an individual for a longer post-retirement period to have a decent lifestyle (Table 2.5).

Table 2.5

Projected Change of Aged Population in India

(Million)

Particular/Year	*2000*	*2015*	*2025*	*2030*	*2035*	*2040*	*2050*
Population of 60+years	77	119	167	195	223	248	308
Percentage of Total Population	7.55	9.56	12.22	13.76	15.30	16.70	20.14
Total Population	1017	1246	1369	1417	1455	1485	1531
Median Age (India)	23.4	27.2	30.3	31.4	33.5	35.0	37.9
Median Age (World)	26.4	29.5	31.9	33.0	34.0	34.9	36.8

Source: World Population Prospects, 2002.

Table 2.6

Old Age Dependency Ratio by Gender and Residence

All India		*Total*	*Rural*	*Urban*
	Persons	13.08	14.11	10.75
	Male	12.45	13.59	9.93
	Female	13.77	14.65	11.67
Bihar	Persons	12.96	13.22	10.96
	Male	13.33	13.70	10.64
	Female	12.57	12.71	11.35
Gujarat	Persons	11.47	12.60	9.76
	Male	10.23	11.34	8.61
	Female	12.83	13.93	11.08
Madhya Pradesh	Persons	13.11	14.08	10.73
	Male	12.20	13.22	9.76
	Female	14.11	15.02	11.84
Rajasthan	Persons	12.76	13.65	10.18
	Male	11.74	12.66	9.19
	Female	13.86	14.72	11.31
Uttar Pradesh	Persons	13.56	14.55	10.25
	Male	13.69	14.86	9.88
	Female	13.43	14.22	10.67
Uttarakhand	Persons	13.83	15.44	9.77
	Male	13.72	15.72	9.25
	Female	13.95	15.19	10.41

Source: Annual Report (2011–12), Ministry of Social Justice & Empowerment, Government of India.

Old age dependency ratio by gender and residence is shown in Table 2.6. Old age dependency ratio was recorded high in rural areas as compared to urban areas. Again, it was recorded significantly high for the females as compared to males. Overall, old age dependency ratio in the selected states was recorded high in Uttarakhand (13.83%) followed by Uttar Pradesh (13.56%) and it was recorded low in Gujarat (11.47%).

Changing Social Structure

As theory of motion can also work on social structure, every structure remains in balance till any component of change does not introduce so as about the population structure population structure change by the development in the field of medical sciences. This increases the life of a person, so implied leads to rise in population of aged. Rising trends in population of the aged create number of changes in the social structure, as described by Bhat and Dhruvarajan (2009: 337). India has been experiencing considerable change in its social structure and institution. Such a change can be seen especially in the changes and their implications for older people; we need to look at the traditional Indian society as a functioning unit.

The traditional structure of the mainly Hindu society in India was a patriarchal system based on the institutions of caste and the joint family. The economy was based on agriculture and the family structure basically based on joint system. The joint family is not only a social unit it is was an economic unit. The family structure was patriarchal – the oldest male member controlled all social and economic affairs and, on the other hand, senior female member exercised authority in all household matters and influenced general matter as well. Every one earned according to his or her capacity and every one received according to his or her needs. Actually this particular type of social system provides social security to its members. As Gangrade (1999) puts it, the Joint family performs the tasks of national insurance, guaranteeing basic subsistence for all the orphans, the disabled, the aged, the widows as well as the temporarily unemployed. The joint family owned land in common and all income went into a common pool. Economic transactions were made between families and not between individuals. The son inherited his father's occupation, ensuring continuity. Society was divided according to a hierarchical caste system, marriage within sub-caste kept economic differential within caste to a minimum. Thus, the social institutions of caste, kinship, and the joint family were the basic building blocks of society. In a traditional Indian society, great honour and respect to older persons is given, as the Hindu scriptures proclaim: *Matra devo bhava, Pithru devo bhava*. This is not only the duty of children but also a sacrament for them to take care of their elders. Failing to pay back *Pithru Rina* (filial debt) would have dire consequences in after life. This feeling reflects from all Indian religious literature the epics, folklore, and in tradition.

Indian society has been under the impact of rapid transformation, industrialization, urbanization technical change, education and globalization. These forces have negative impact on traditional values and institutions, so they are in the process of erosion and adaptation, resulting in the weakening of inter-generationalties. Industrialization has replaced the simple family production units by mass production and the factory (Dandekar, 1996). Individual jobs and earnings give rise to income differentials within the family. Push factor such as population pressure and pull factor such as wider economic opportunities and modern communication cause young people to migrate especially from rural to urban areas (Kumar, 1999; Jamuna, 1998). Advancement in technology in all spheres of social life challenged the utility of knowledge and skills of older persons. Supportive social systems in daily life reduced the role of older persons. Old widows are no longer indispensable for nursing sick relatives, helping ladies in childbirth or taking care of infants. There role is taken by hospitals, *ayahs*, and baby sitters.

Nowadays materialistic value or conspicuous consumption works as a pull factor, which attract people to go for work to far places. This lessened the family ties and disrupted family togetherness. Increasing urbanization due to migration and the compulsions of the city have further weakened the family. Modern education system, technological change and economic development is promoting individualism and also questioning authority. Nuclear households characterized by individuality, independence and desire for privacy are gradually replacing the joint family which emphasizes the family as a unit and demands deference to age and authority (Bhat and Dhruvaranjan, 2009). Children who migrate often find it difficult to cope with city life and elect to leave their old parents in the village causing problem of loneliness and lack of care givers for the old parents (Government of India, 1999). Parents in this circumstance cannot always count on financial support from their children and may have to take care of themselves.

Another aspect which badly effected the position of older people in society is double caring couple. Now this is a trend as well as an impact of government policies that number of females also became working. Female participation in economic activity either as a worker or as an entrepreneurs has increased considerably in the recent past in the urban informed sector and the middle class formal sector as well as in rural areas. National Policy on older persons also highlight this issue as 'due to shortage of space in dwellings in urban areas and high rents, migrants prefer to leave their parents in native place. Changing roles and expectations of women, their concepts of privacy and space, desire not to be encumbered by caring responsibilities of older people for long periods, career ambitions and employment outside the home implies a considerably reduced time for care giving'.

This quest for better lifestyle has deteriorated status of elderly in the transient Indian family structure. In this regard, D'Souza (1989) observes that change in living arrangements, family structure and sudden retirement adversely affect the old, and further that the old people are in increasing proportions losing the status and security which they enjoyed in the traditional Indian family structure. The Dak and Sharma (1987) study indicated that the headship in the households used to get transferred to the next eldest member after a certain age is attained. With regards to the feeling of the elderly staying in nuclear family, Nandal et al. (1987) finds that elderly in nuclear household have a feeling of helplessness. The aged are looked upon as burden in barely sustainable households in which each and every member contributes to the family earning and, therefore, households' support towards elderly become very difficult among the poor. An examination of intra family relations of urban elderly by Shah (1993) finds that satisfactory, intra family relations are somewhat higher among the evidences than the widowers and somewhat lower among those living in joint families compared to those living in nuclear families. Further, elderly having no substantial assets or a fairly good source of income and who are economically dependent, find the attitude and behaviour of their family members as unsatisfactory.

National Sample Survey (1987–88) of the elderly finds loneliness to be one of the major problems among the aged India. It is found that the aged feel to have lost their status due to old age and a few others comment to have lost status due to their retirement from work. This conclusion does not co-relate when tested on women. Females never had the feeling of having retired from work as against the males whose status feeling was associated with their job which they enjoyed for long.

Kaur, Grover and Aggarwal (1987) also emphasized the fact that the present generation treated the old people as a burden and their presence in the family irks most of the family members. According to Dak and Sharma (1987) the status of the aged in the changing social structure has been investigated by social scientists from different perspectives. Such investigations have more or less concluded on the breaking down of kinship and family organizations which has put the elderly in a state of helplessness, isolation and economic dependence. A further reiteration is made as regards the disappearance of the traditional form of familiar support for the elderly which need to be replaced with some policy measures. A traditional convention in the Indian family system is that parents are supposed to be taken care of by their offspring. But the burgeoning of the nuclear family and the separation of the offspring from the parents creates a situation where the old parents have to stay on their own. On some occasions, the economic security is provided by the children but not the emotional requirements of the elderly. In this context most of the primary surveys have investigated on the preference of the aged regarding their place of stay and it is found that a majority of them prefer to stay with their children or own family members in old age (Nandal et al., 1987). With the lack of familiar support, the elderly resort to stay in old age homes in case they are economically affordable. In India, there are few old age homes run by the state and central government for the deprived and poor elderly. A survey of old age homes in the state of Maharashtra by Dandekar (1993) shows that the prime reason for the aged moving into old age homes is due to the lack of proper care for them within family set-ups. The inmates of the old age homes expressed satisfaction with their own homes. This finding gives the impression that old age homes are serving as alternative care giver to those who are unable to obtain familial care. Another study on the inmates of old age homes in the state of Gujarat (Shah, 1993) finds lack of homely care as the prominent reason cited by the elderly towards their preference to stay in old age homes. Besides economic reasons, family quarrel and handicaps were found to have induced the elderly to move into old age homes (Rajan, Mishra and Sarma, 1999).

The old age leads to complications in health and deterioration of one's immunity system and, thus, creating a need for special attention and health care for the aged people. The population of Indians in the age group 60 years and above, i.e. the elderly, is increasing more rapidly than the population as a whole. The current population of elderly in India is 60 million which is expected to grow to 75 million by the year 2001 and 160 million by the year 2025 (Shah, 2004). As the elderly suffers from chronic diseases, they need long term care and they also need help to maintain activities of daily living. In the changed scenario, care providing has itself become a big question. Women's role as primary care providers has changed a lot owing to their acceptance of paid work outside the preview of the household. Poverty and illiteracy worsen the health status and impact of health care of an aged person (Nasreen, 2009). The health care services in India available for the elderly can be classified into formal and informal support systems (Shah, 2005). Formal support systems are provided by the central and state government agencies. Health is a state subject. Every Indian has an access to free health care service. The health care services are formally constituted in a referral tier system for rural areas involving the state through district hospitals, community centres/hospitals, primary health centres and sub centres. The issue of quality and quantity of their service available for the elderly needs consideration (Rao, 1999).

The family still constitutes the most important part in respect to elderly health support. The family still provides them financial support for medicine cares during illness, psychological support, etc. but these are somehow true in the sense of rural family structure. As for as urban family structure is concerned, these supports are not by and large visible. So, this is one lacuna in terms of elderly health. Secondly, India is still grappling with efforts to decrease infant mortality, childhood deaths and young adult deaths due to infections. The bulk of resources available to these institutions are utilized to meet these service demands. While medical specialists are available at district headquarters, none are trained in geriatric specially. These hospitals and centres do not provide for any separately earmarked clinics or beds for the elderly (Bali, 1999).

Economic status or economic independence is vital for a person during his/her social life. The sound economic status of a person develop a complex net of social relations while weak economic status can thickly relate kins with a person. For elderly people, economic status or independence is very important, because their body has not so much strength as younger one's has. So they slowly develop their dependency on other people. Economic security during the working years provides an opportunity for its continuation into later years through appropriate investment. An old person faces several difficulties in regard to arranging daily needs. Absence of regular and steady income generate other complexities like lack of money for food, shelter, medicine or to fulfil other social requirements. As such in the modern industrial society economic insecurity has greatly increased particularly for the retired persons. In rural communities, there is no set pattern of retirement and the old people continue to work as long as their physique allows them to. Yet, in rural areas too, when they quit working, face the same type of problems as their urban counterparts (Randhawa, 1991).

Expectations of care direct the elderly people to invest upon their children. The children also take care of them. But in the present modern society, changes in terms of technology and attitude toward individualism has changed the mindset of younger generation towards care giving. The state is not in a position to provide financial assistance to older people for their maintenance, as the cost is prohibitive. Unfortunately, the current scenario is such that a majority of older people today are not financially sound in terms of their saving and investments (Ramamurti, 2003). In view of health problem and its co-relation with economically active population in recent years, WHO worked out the concept of active ageing. The new concept of active ageing began to emerge in the 1990s under the influence of WHO which not surprisingly emphasized the vital connection between activity and health and the importance of healthy ageing (WHO, 1994, 2001). Given the link with health and the European context in which it was developed, this approach to active ageing has focused on a broader range of activities than those normally associated with production and the labour market has emphasized health and the participation and inclusion of older people as full citizen. The thinking behind this new approach is expressed perfectly in the WHO dictum 'years have been added to life now we must add life to years'. This suggests a general lifestyle strategy for the preservation of physical and mental health as people age rather than just trying to make them work longer. Thus, the essence of the emerging modern concept of active ageing is a combination of the care element of productive ageing with a strong emphasis on quality of life and mental and physical well-being. The active ageing is a new way to find a way-out of the low economic status.

Intergenerational relations are the matter of study for social scientists. Several Indian studies are available on intergenerational interactions (e.g. Anantharaman, 1979a, 1979b, 1984; Biswas, 1987; Bhingradiya and Kamala, 1997; Chadha and Singh, 1996; Jamuna, 2001; Nayar, 2001; Ramamurti, 2001, 2002). Intergenerational relations within the family have a profound influence on the older persons in the family. Whether this relationship is going to be conflict free and congenial would largely depend on how the older persons and the younger individuals perceive each other. They belong to different generations and were conditioned by social context of the two different time periods (Ramamurti, 1992). Now, elderly people have to cope not only with the changing family structure but also with changing role relations within the family. In an agriculture-based traditional society, where children followed their parents' occupation, it was natural that expertise and knowledge of each generation were passed on to the next, thus, affording older persons a useful role in society. However, this is no longer true in a modern society, in which improved education, rapid technological changes and new forms of organization have often rendered obsolete the knowledge, experience and wisdom of older persons. Once they retired, elderly people find that their children are not seeking advice from them anymore and society has not much use for them. This realization often results in a feeling of loss of status, worthlessness and loneliness. The growth of nuclear families has also meant a need for changes in role relations. Neither having authority in the family, nor being needed, they feel frustrated and depressed. If the older person is economically dependent on the children, the problem is likely to become even worse (Bhat and Dhruvaranjan, 2009). Batra and Bhaumik (2007) studied intergeneration relationships between three generation (i) elderly (ii) core giver (iii) grand children. They selected six component for this research like (i) Loss position (ii) Loss of authority (iii) Lack of support (iv) Feeling of isolation (v) Loss of respect (vi) More responsibility. From their study they find that elderly people want that their children to be more understandable and accommodating.

Problems of the Aged

Though ageing is a natural stage of human life, it brings with it enumerable problems for the people who have grown old. A detailed analysis of the major problems of the aged in the light of the findings from various studies has been attempted as under:

Economic Problems

As far as economic problems are concerned, the age issue is very basic to all the other problems faced by the aged. With the superannuation, a person has to retire from service, which not only results into loss of employment and social status but also a substantial reduction in his income levels. A study by U.K. Anand (2001: 87–88) reveals that within five years of their retirement, people exhaust their savings and they are forced to depend on their children or relatives. M. Kabir (1992) also observed that majority of the elderly, covered under his study, faced acute financial problems. This makes older persons economically insecure. The feeling of financial insecurity has been found to be the highest among the elderly women followed by those old people who lived in nuclear families. In many cases, the elderly are pressurized in myriad ways by their grown-up children to transfer all the properties immediately, if the old person hesitates, he/she invites a lot many problems, including physical torture, etc. If they smoothly transfer their properties and bank balance, etc. in the name of their children/relatives, there is hardly any assurance that their needs and aspirations would be properly taken care of.

Physiological Problems

With the growing age, the older persons experience various anatomical and physiological changes. These changes bring many psychological, behavioural and attitudinal changes in them. Consequently, they have to suffer varied sorts of physiological problems such as loss of physical strength and stamina, which becomes more acute as a person grows older. These problems become still more acute if the older people suffer from nutritional deficiency coupled with lack of medical and health care available to them. On the one hand, the elderly have a higher incidence of falling ill and due to economic dependency they are not in a position to avail quality health and medical services, on the other hand. It naturally results in their more quickly becoming infirm who need to be looked after more carefully. Various studies (Narang, 1968; Sandhu, 1978; Oberoi and Dey, 1991) observed that the older people were not getting regular treatment due to such factors as lack of medical facilities, lack of funds, lack of faith in allopathic treatment and also because they did not consider their disease as serious.

Psycho-Social Problems

Older persons experience 'reversal of roles' which qualitatively refines their status and role in their own family. The individual suffers the loss of status from the breadwinner to a neglected one in his family. The socio-psycho-physiological losses transform the aged from an independent self-supporting individual to a dependent helpless individual. Additionally, on account of the loss of economic status due to retirement, growing dependency on family members, relatives, friends and the society, a feeling of uselessness, worthlessness and insecurity creeps into the mind of the elderly. Many times the elderly find if difficulty to adjust to the changing environment, status or situation, more so when they come across the harsh reality that they were just being tolerated and were not being treated well in their family. If the older persons are not duly respected in their family, in case they are in a position to afford, they prefer to live alone which leads to the problem of loneliness. Many times, the youngsters leave their old parents to fend for themselves and establish their nuclear families. Naturally, it comes as a psychological blow to the elderly.

Overall, the elderly living alone face more problems than their fellow-beings living with families. K. Oberoi and S. Dey (1991: 11–21) observed in their study that the old people whose children and family members did not meet or visit them frequently, had been psychologically more upset and felt lonely. This loneliness, naturally, makes them psychologically depressed and they persistently face such psychological problems as old age worries, emotional instability, lack of proper response, etc. The psychological stress faced by older persons has quite serious implications. A study by S. Srinivas and B. Vijailakshmi (2001) reveals that out of the 140 older persons covered, around 29 per cent (37% females) reported suicidal tendencies. Though the sampled respondents had been living with their family, 24 per cent male and 55 per cent female elderly were not happy at all. An alarming proportion (73%) of them (85% of the older females) reported disturbed sleeping patterns, while majority of them (56%) reported poor appetite (it was 65% in case of female respondents). Thus, the severity of psycho-social stresses and problems had been much more in case of the elderly females. The problem of falling and failing health further adds to their psychological stress. As K.G. Desai (1985) puts it, 'he fears becoming psychologically vulnerable and that pushes him to loneliness. Being subjected to stress and anxiety over his future, failing health, reduced financial resources, decreasing mental abilities, and care and attention, he thinks, he will have a tough time at death'. Thus, old age turns into a nightmare.

Problem of Isolation

The experience of isolation or loneliness occurs in all human beings but it is a complex problem in old age. Isolation is associated with number of physical, social and psychological conditions. Generally, it is believed that older persons living alone or with their spouses feel isolated but today older persons living in nuclear or joint families also feel loneliness or isolation due to various reasons particularly due to lack of social integration, less or no interaction amongst family members, etc. A major national research study, covering the sample of 10,000, conducted by Agewell Foundation (2010) highlighted that over 93 per cent aged are living in complete isolation. More than three-fourth respondents in the age group of 60–70 years reported that they are going through a phase of isolation. The proportion of respondents complaining of isolation and loneliness was reported high among the age group of 70–80 years as compared to the age group of 60–70 years. The level of isolation in old age was reported high in urban areas (89.8%) as compared to rural areas (77.62%). About two-fifth aged persons reported that no/less interaction with family members or within society is major cause of their state of isolation or loneliness. About 38 per cent elderly people were found isolated because they are living alone or with their spouse only. The types of isolation were mainly social and emotional isolation. Social isolation is due to their physical and social conditions while emotional isolation is reported due to their strained inter-personal relationships of circumstances. Due to isolation and loneliness, the aged are facing the problem of depression, while on the other hand, their health is deteriorating. The problem of isolation and loneliness has also created other problems like nervousness and anxiety; panic and aggressive nature; eating disorders; addictions and substance abuse; feeling of insecurity and financial imbalance.

Housing Related Problems

Housing for the aged should be suitable not only to the living pattern which they have established in optimum health, but also to conditions of failing health and illness, commonly associated with later years of life such as, failing eye sight or hearing, slowing and unsureness of step, diminishing energy and more acute disabilities, such as blindness, forgetfulness, etc. (Anand, 2001: 91). On this pattern, the housing available to a majority of the senior citizens may be found inappropriate and unsuitable to their requirement. M. Deva Sahayam (1988: 261–69) observed that even though cultural and familial ties are quite strong in India, a greater proportion of male dependents without their spouses lived with their sons and daughters than the proportion of older widows living with their children as dependents. This reflects that sizeable populations of older widows as well as the older males have been facing the problem of 'where to live peacefully'. In the West, construction of three-generation houses is quite common, which to a great extent takes care of the housing needs of the aged.

Problem of Elder Abuse

Elder abuse is usually defined as any ill treatment to an older person (Tinker and McCreadie, 1998). It refers to 'infliction of physical, emotional or psychological harm on an older adult' (Prakash, 2001: 447). The National Elder Abuse Incidence Survey uses the term 'elder maltreatment' to cover seven general types of behaviour which include physical abuse, sexual abuse, emotional or psychological abuse, financial or material abuse, abandonment, neglect and self neglect (United Nations, 1998). Though family violence is not a new phenomenon, abuse and ill-treatment of older person in the family as well as in the institutional settings by others, has become more pronounced during the last two decades of the twentieth century. Elder abuse, though a global phenomena, remains largely hidden because it happens mostly within the privacy of the home or inside the four walls of an institution. Older persons, who are abused, are often reluctant to share their experiences with the outside world mainly due to their dependency on the abusers themselves.

S. Srinivas and B. Vijailakshmi (2001: 272–75) observed that around 81 per cent of the elderly persons, covered under their study, had faced the problem of verbal abuse, while 53 per cent of them had faced neglect followed by material abuse (37%) and physical abuse (23%). However, most of the male elderly (61%) reported material abuse than their female counterparts, while a greater proportion of the older women faced the other three forms of elder abuse reported above than their fellow males. Thus, with the degeneration of joint family system, dislocation of familiar bonds and loss of respect for the aged, the family in modern times should not be thought to be a secure place for them. Rosamma Veedon (2001) reported that elder abuse is widely prevalent in the metropolitan areas, such as Mumbai. If this situation goes on unchecked, it may have serious implications. The status of ageing in India reflects that the issues pertaining to socio-economic and demographic profiles, living arrangements, problems of and services to the elderly, interpersonal relationships, especially of the urban elderly, are highlighted to a great extent. No doubt, concerted efforts made by researchers have so far led to a better understanding of ageing issues. However, the diversity that has emerged in the ageing process necessitates our research efforts to focus on different ageing issues in society. This, in turn, is expected to promote development of effective age-related policies and programmes.

The review of the earlier studies reveals that many scholars view the elderly as passive receivers of care. Further, the problems of the vulnerable elderly like widowed females, disabled, fragile older persons and those from the unorganized sector are inadequately covered. Most studies conducted to assess various issues of the elderly are exploratory and descriptive. Ageing needs multi- and inter-disciplinary perspectives. The development of social gerontology reveals that disciplines like sociology, demography, psychology, anthropology, geography, law, social policy and administration, management, economics, nutrition, as well as varied professional training like social work, nursing, counselling and clinical psychology focus on various ageing issues. However, no single disciplinary focus gives a holistic understanding. A combination of qualitative and quantitative approaches is required for a more comprehensive understanding of ageing issues. The wide variation in levels of development and socio-economic status of people living in different geographical regions make national level studies on elderly essential. Analysis of both secondary and primary data needs to be attempted, wherever necessary, which in turn will help to focus on ageing issues, both at micro and macro levels. The focus of social gerontology is not only concerned with people in later life but also the social institutions which particularly affect that period such as retirement, pensions and welfare policy. Given the changes in the socio-economic profile of the elderly, there is a need to recognize them as a resource group and to develop suitable policies and programmes for their integration into the development process. A majority of the studies conducted so far in India are localized and based on sample surveys on specific segments of elderly with a specific disciplinary focus. However, the fact that India's elderly are a heterogeneous group necessitates proper stratification of the group. Variations in living situations need to be viewed in the context of factors like age, gender, and marital status, and region, educational and occupational status of the elderly. A holistic approach toward the ageing population, taking social, economic and cultural changes into consideration, is needed to effectively solve the emerging problems of the elderly.

Rehabilitation of the Aged

Social support and physical health are two important factors which help the overall well-being of the individual. Physical health of an individual can be greatly affected by social support system and the level of social support. As older people have physical disabilities due to deterioration in health and biological and psychological changes, rehabilitation of the aged is imperative. In order to address the emerging problems of the aged, the government and non-government organizations have made efforts to provide them protection, social security and services; however, problems of the aged cannot be addressed effectively. The institutional service for support and rehabilitation to the aged are grossly inadequate and requires policy interventions.

Scheme of Integrated Programme for Older Persons

Under the Scheme, financial assistance up to 90 per cent of the project cost is provided to government/non-governmental organizations/Panchayati Raj Institutions/local bodies, etc. for establishing and maintaining old age homes, day care centres and mobile medicare units. The Scheme has was revised in 2008. Besides increase in amount of financial assistance for existing projects, several innovative projects have been added as being eligible for assistance under the Scheme. Some of these are:

- Maintenance of respite care homes and continuous care homes
- Running of day care centres for alzheimer's dementia patients
- Physiotherapy clinics for older persons
- Help-lines and counselling centres for older persons
- Sensitizing programmes for children particularly in schools and colleges
- Regional resource and training centres
- Training of care-givers to the older persons
- Awareness generation programmes for older persons and care-givers
- Formation of senior citizens associations etc.

The eligibility criteria for beneficiaries of some important activities/projects supported under the Scheme are:

- Old age homes – for destitute older persons
- Mobile medicare units – for older persons living in slums, rural and inaccessible areas where proper health facilities are not available
- Respite care homes and continuous care homes – for older persons seriously ill requiring continuous nursing care and respite

Physical and financial performance of Integrated Programme for Older Persons is shown in Table 2.7. There has been an increasing trend in budget allocation and amount released during the 2009–2010 to 2011–2012; however, the number of NGOs assisted and number of beneficiaries has shown fluctuating trend during the corresponding period. There are 728 old age homes in India. Out of these, 325 homes are free of cost while 95 old age homes are on pay-and-stay basis, 116 homes have both free as well as pay-and-stay facilities and 11 homes have no information. A total of 278 old age homes all over the country are available for the sick and 101 homes are exclusively for women. Kerala has 124 old age homes.

Table 2.7

Physical and Financial Performance of Integrated Programme for Older Persons

Particulars	*2009–10*	*2010–11*	*2011–12*
Amount Sanctioned (BE) (₹ Crore)	22.00	40.00	40.00
Amount Sanctioned (RE) (₹ Crore)	22.00	22.00	25.00
Amount Released (₹ Crore)	19.72	20.67	19.99
Number of NGOs Assisted	362	359	348
Number of Projects Assisted	559	595	615
Number of Beneficiaries	33,100	38,785	34,630

Source: Annual Report (2011–12), Ministry of Social Justice & Empowerment, Government of India.

State-wise grants released under Integrated Programmes for Older Persons are shown in Table 2.8. During the year 2007–08, the larger amount under the scheme was released to the state of Uttar Pradesh while it was recorded low in the state of Bihar. Similarly, the largest share of grants was released to Uttar Pradesh during 2012–13. There has been significant increase in the amount of grants from 2007–08 to 2012–13 in the state of Bihar while others states have shown declining trend.

Table 2.8

State-wise Grants Released Under Integrated Programmes for Older Persons

(₹ Lakh)

State	*2007–08*	*2008–09*	*2009–10*	*2010–11*	*2011–12*	*2012–13*
Bihar	2.76	2.76	4.88	1.73	2.44	10.68
Madhya Pradesh	18.02	9.00	13.20	7.25	14.79	7.72
Rajasthan	13.15	7.48	16.66	14.89	8.89	—
Uttar Pradesh	53.52	40.31	87.09	18.66	39.29	43.38
Uttarakhand	3.63	5.34	—	12.01	5.87	9.31
India	1612.72	1772.10	1972.10	2067.42	1999.01	559.31

Source: Annual Report (2011–12), Ministry of Social Justice & Empowerment, Government of India.

Scheme-wise grants released and expenditure for older persons in India is shown in Table 2.9. Assistance to voluntary organizations under the scheme of Integrated Programme for Older Persons has an increasing trend of budget allocation and expenditure. However, the proportion of expenditure against the budget has been found significantly low. During the 11th Plan, ₹ 146 crores under the scheme were allocated while budget was curtailed under the revised estimates and only ₹ 94.23 crores were spent under the scheme during the plan period. Surprisingly, during the plan, ₹ 129 crores were allocated under the scheme of assistance for establishment of old age homes for indigent citizens. However, no expenditure was reported by the Ministry in its Annual Report, 2011–12.

Table 2.9

Scheme-wise Grants Released and Expenditure for Older Persons in India

(₹ Crore)

Years	*Assistance to Voluntary Organizations Under the Scheme of Integrated Programme for Older Persons*	*Scheme of Assistance for Establishment of Old Age Homes for Indigent Citizens*
2007–08		
BE	22.00	1.00
RG	20.00	—
Expenditure	16.13	—
2008–09		
BE	22.00	13.00
RG	22.00	13.00
Expenditure	17.72	—
2009–10		
BE	22.00	15.00
RG	22.00	—
Expenditure	19.72	—
2010–11		
BE	40.00	100.00
RG	30.00	1.00
Expenditure	20.67	—
2011–12		
BE	40.00	—
RG	25.00	—
Expenditure	19.99	—
XI Plan		
BE	146.00	129.00
RG	119.00	14.00
Expenditure	94.23	—

Source: Annual Report (2011–12), Ministry of Social Justice & Empowerment, Government of India.

Budget allocation and expenditure for older persons during the 12th Plan in India is shown in Table 2.10. During the 12th Plan, ₹ 665 crores was allocated for the older persons. Out of this, a large chunk of amount (₹ 440 crores) was allocated for assistance to NGOs under the scheme of Integrated Programme for Older Persons.

Grants-in-Aid to NGOs under the scheme of Integrated Programme for Older Persons in the selected states are shown in Table 2.11. During the year 2010–11, Uttar Pradesh received ₹ 25.11 lakhs for the establishment of 15 old age homes while ₹ 14.18 lakhs were released for the establishment of day care centres in the state. Similarly, Madhya Pradesh has set up four old age homes with the grant of ₹ 14.79 lakhs. Rajasthan and Uttarakhand each had set up two old age homes while only one old age home was set up in Bihar during the year.

Table 2.10
Budget Allocation and Expenditure for Older Persons during 12th Plan in India

(₹ Crore)

Sl. No.	Programme	12th Plan (BE)	2012–13 (BE)	2012–13 (RE)	Expenditure
1	Assistance to NGOs under the scheme of Integrated Programme for Older Persons	440.00	40.00	18.00	18.20
2	Scheme of Assistance for Establishment of Old Age Homes for Indigent Senior Citizens	—	80.00	0.01	—
3	Awareness generation for Maintenance and Welfare of Parents and Senior Citizens Act, 2007	50.00	—	—	—
4	Setting up of Help-line for senior citizens at national level	2.00	—	—	—
5	Setting up of Help-line for senior citizens at district level (in 120 districts @ ₹ 16 lakhs per District)	18.00	—	—	—
6	Setting up of a National Commission for Senior Citizens	70.00	—	—	—
7	Creation of National Trust for the Aged	70.00	—	—	—
8	Implementation of the National Policy on Senior Citizens	15.00	—	—	—
	Total	665.00	12.00	18.01	18.20

Source: Annual Report (2011–12), Ministry of Social Justice & Empowerment, Government of India.

During 2011–12, funds could not be released to eight states, namely Goa, Gujarat, Jammu & Kashmir, Jharkhand, Arunachal Pradesh, Meghalaya, Nagaland and Sikkim and six Union Territories, namely, Andaman and Nicobar Islands, Chandigarh, Daman & Diu, Dadra & Nagar Haveli, Lakshadweep and Puducherry, either due to no proposals or incomplete proposals received from the state governments. The Ministry of Social Justice and Empowerment being the nodal Ministry for the welfare of senior citizens observed the International Day of Older Persons on 1 October 2011 at the national level with a series of programmes, which included organization of an inter-generational walkathon at the India Gate lawns, New Delhi, and a cultural programme in New Delhi, wherein distinguished senior citizens and institutions working for the cause of senior citizens chosen from all over the country were felicitated with *Vayoshrestha Sammans* under different categories. State Governments were also requested to observe this occasion in a befitting manner right up to the Block levels. The International Day for Older Persons, 2011, was observed with a theme 'Health Care for Senior Citizens'. The Ministry also for the first time in 2011 organized an inter-generational walkathon on 1 October 2011 in five state capitals, namely Chandigarh, Guwahati, Bhopal, Chennai and Mumbai in collaboration with Help Age India. It proposed to allot 10 per cent of the houses constructed under government schemes for the urban and rural lower income segments to the older persons on easy loans. The policy mentions: 'The layout of the housing colonies will respond to the needs and life styles of the elderly so that there are no physical barriers to their mobility; they are allotted ground floors; and their social interaction with older society members exist.' Despite all these attempts, there is a need to impress upon the elderly about the need to adjust to the changing circumstances in life and try to live harmoniously with the younger generation as far as possible.

Table 2.11

Grants-in-Aid to NGOs under the Scheme of Integrated Programme for Older Persons

State	Projected Assisted				Grants Released (2010–11) (₹ Lakh)			
	OAH	DCC	MMU	Others	OAH	DCC	MMU	Others
Bihar	1	—	—	—	2.44	—	—	—
Madhya Pradesh	4	—	—	—	14.79	—	—	—
Rajasthan	2	1	—	—	7.48	1.41	—	—
Uttar Pradesh	15	6	—	—	25.11	14.18	—	—
Uttarakhand	2	—	—	—	5.87	—	—	—

Source: Annual Report (2011–12), Ministry of Social Justice & Empowerment, Government of India.

Programmes and Support Services for Older Persons

The National Social Assistance Programme (NSAP) came into effect from 15 August 1995. NSAP is a social assistance programme for the poor households and represents a significant step towards the fulfillment of the Directive Principles enshrined in Article 41 and 42 of the Constitution of India, recognizing concurrent responsibility of the Centre and the state governments in the matter. The National Old Age Pension Scheme (NOAPS) covers older persons/destitute having little or no regular means of subsistence from his/her own source of income or through financial support from family members or other sources. The age of applicant must be 65 years or above. At present, 50 per cent of the older persons under Below Poverty Line (BPL) destitute, are covered under NOAPS. The Centre contributes ₹ 200 per month per to the beneficiary. The state (provincial) governments are advised to add matching amount or more as their contribution in the federal set-up. During the 10th Five Year Plan (2002–07), a total of 1,10,793,860 elderly were covered and US $ 1002.20 million approximately was incurred on this count (Prakash, 2007). Annapurna Scheme covers all the other elderly below poverty line who are not covered under the NOAPS. A provision of 10 kgs of rice or wheat is provided to the needy elderly. Under the scheme, US $ 56 million was incurred and 43,03,491 elderly were covered in the 10th plan (2002–07).

Presently, persons of 60 years of age are entitled for 30 per cent concessions in train fare in all classes. There are different airlines providing 45 per cent to 50 per cent concession in air journey to senior citizens. Older persons who are above 65 years of age also enjoy income tax rebate upto ₹ 15,000 of actual tax with provision for deduction of ₹ 20,000 spent on account of medical insurance premium and ₹ 40,000 spent on account of medical treatment from taxable income. Senior citizens are exempted from Income Tax up to ₹ 1.95 lakh as per the Union Annual Budget, 2007. Banks are providing 0.5 per cent-1 per cent additional interest to older persons of 65 years and above on fixed deposit. The public facilities for the elderly are initiated by the government which includes reservation of seats for elderly in the public transport, railways and airways, etc.

Some of the public sector insurance companies provide life insurance coverage up to 75 years of age and many private insurance companies have 55 years as the last entry age. The Insurance Policy Schemes announced for older persons include Jeevan Dhara (18–65 years), Jeevan Akshay (30–75 years), Jeevan Suraksha (25–60 years), and Senior Citizen Unit Plan (18–54 years). In addition, Health Insurance Schemes covering Mediclaim Policy and other individual and Group Mediclaim Policies are also offered by nationalized as well as private insurance companies. The government is taking steps to enforce a uniform policy on all insurance companies as regards entry age of senior citizens. The government has launched a Reverse Mortgage System for senior citizens to extract value out of their property and lead a hassle free life by securing a regular income as loan against their existing property (Prakash, 2007).

Ministry of Social Justice & Empowerment, Government of India, is implementing an Integrated Programme for Older Persons with an aim to empower and improve the quality of life of older persons. The basic thrust of the programme is on older persons of 60 years and above particularly the infirm, destitute and widows. Under the scheme, financial assistance is provided to non-governmental organizations, autonomous bodies, educational institutions, cooperative societies, etc. up to 90 per cent of the project cost for setting up and maintenance of day care centres, mobile medicare units, old age homes and non-institutional service centres. During the 10th Five Year plan, the Ministry provided financial assistance to voluntary organizations to the tune of US $ 18.6 million. The scheme for Assistance to Construction of Old Age Homes provides one time grant to local bodies, NGOs, etc. for construction of old age homes or multi-service centres for older persons. The Ministry also incurred an expenditure of US $ 70,000 for construction of old age homes during 10th Five Year Plan.

Growing old is also marked by failing health and advancing age may bring with it enumerable health complications. Restricted physical mobility coupled with crippled health makes it difficult for older persons to access the health facilities if they do not enjoy the support of the family or have a care institution within their easy access. Realizing the real situation wherein the older persons live, Para 36 of the National Policy envisages covering of health insurance and financial security towards essential medical care and affordable treatment process. Some of the initiatives by the government are enabling separate counters/OPD in hospitals and free medical services under Central Government Health Scheme, in government hospitals to facilitate easy accessibility to the elderly including Geriatric Units in the hospitals (Prakash, 2007).

Pension Scheme

In our country, the government is the biggest employer. Till today people prefer government job instead of a job under private employer, though government is paying less employment and perks as compare to that in a private sector job. People still have great attraction for government jobs. There are two main reasons behind this attitude – security of job and social security. Security of job is not in the preview of this study. So we will not discuss this issue. We are concerned here with social security. Every government job is provided with a social security in form of assured pension after retirement. Provision for pension for the government servants was initiated by the Royal Commission on civil establishment in 1881. The Government of India Act 1919 and 1935 made further provisions.

The Constitution of India accepted the privative provision and further made some other beneficiaries masseurs for their employees. Relevant provisions are made in part XIV and Article 309 of the Constitution which relate to the recruitment and conditions of services of persons serving the Union or a state. Under these articles, various rules and regulations have been framed by the government from time to time which lay down the conditions of service, including retirement/terminal benefits to its employees. For a government employee there is not only provision of regular income through pension but also some other retirement benefits are made:

- Any government servant retires before a minimum of 10 years of qualifying service are not entitled to any pension. But such employees are entitled for service gratuity.
- On retirement, a government employee can get one-third of the amount for lump sum payment on the basis of a commutation table.
- There is a provision of injury/disable pension for those government employees who get injury or disability to work during their official duty.
- Invalid pension may be granted if a government servant retires from service on account of any bodily or mental infirmity which permanently incapacitates him/her and forbids from active service (Rajan, 2001).

Contributory Provident Fund

Industrial staff in government departments, persons employed on contract basis for a specified period and scientific and technical personnel entering government service at a relatively advanced age, are generally covered by the contributory provident fund scheme. This is governed by the Contributory Provident Fund (India) Rules 1962. Now these schemes are spread to all government employees who came in job after 2005.

Privileges and Benefits for Older People

Under National Old Age Pension Scheme, Central Assistance is available on fulfillment of the following criteria (1) the age of the applicant (male or female) should be 65 years or more, (2) the applicant must be a destitute in the sense that he/she has no regular means of subsistence from his/her own source of income or through financial support from family members or other sources. The amount of old age pension is ₹ 75 per month. This scheme is implemented in the states and Union Territories through Panchayats and Municipalities. Both Panchayats and Municipalities are encouraged to involve voluntary agencies as much as possible in benefitting the destitute elderly for whom this scheme is intended.

Annapurna

A new scheme called Annapurna has been recently initiated by the Government of India under which free foodgrain up to 10 kg per month is provided to such destitute older persons who are otherwise eligible for old age pension under the National Old Age Pension Scheme but are not receiving it and whose sons are not residing with them.

Widowhood in India

Widowhood is a universal phenomenon. It is a special case of mortality where the husband dies earlier than the wife. The rate of widowhood varies from country to country and within countries from time to time. In addition to natural factors relating to general mortality, man-made factors like wars and terrorism also can increase the incidence of widowhood in a population. Thus, in the last century, the two World Wars, the Korean War, the Vietnamese War, civil wars and armed conflicts in many countries including Myanmar, Cambodia, Sub-Saharan Africa and several Latin American countries, ethnic conflicts and several other internecine killings have resulted in large-scale massacre of men resulting in widowhood. Afghanistan is a case in point in very recent times. It is estimated that in Afghanistan where conflicts and wars were going on for more than a decade in the past, the incidence of widowhood is as high as 70 per cent. The same is true of the African state of Rwanda where the Genocide of 1994 had decimated a large part of the male population. The civil war in Mozambique and ethnic cleansing in Bosnia, Kosavo and East Timor have wiped out thousands of men. The consequence of terrorism and large-scale violence is more on women because more men are killed in these uprisings and families are left without male support. A natural phenomenon that has added to the rate of increase of widows in recent years in developed countries is increased longevity of women. As women live longer than men by at least 5 years, they are destined to live without husbands during the extended years of their lives. However, this is an old age phenomenon and as such its impact on widowhood has a different dimension. This is, of course, a matter for concern but the problems of old widows are different from those of young widows.

Widowhood in India is characterized not only by the pangs of separation of spouse by the widow but also the consequent mental agony and economic dislocation. There is a huge social cost involved in widowhood, the like of which has no comparison in the world except perhaps in some African countries. The Indian widow in traditional society was a virtual non-entity: widowhood brings her social death but being biologically alive, she suffers from all the physical and mental agonies that this kind of life brings to her while being socially dead.

The most formidable problem that a widow faced in traditional culture was the set of cruel and inhuman customs and practices that society had imposed on her and that divested her of all her social roles. She was reduced to the position of a living non-entity. The scourge came after the Puranic age. It originated in the centuries preceding the law-giver Manu, who speaks of the marginalized role of a widow, Manu approved the prevailing code and incorporated in his 'Smriti'. However, he had in mind a young widow without children. A woman with children was to be under the control of her sons in old age. In the case of young widows a severe, Draconian Code was framed and imposed by the society. A dress code de-robbed her of all colours and deprived her of all her jewellery including the *mangalsutra* and the *bindi* or any make-up. She was to wear only plain white robe and smear ash (*vibhuti*) on her forehead. In extreme cases she was also required to tonsure her hair. A food code denied her all tasty and spicy food which was supposed to make her lustful. She was to eat frugal food, cooked by her, twice a day, on all impotent days, she was supposed to fast. A food behaviour code required that she should not go out of the home. Even inside the house, she was not allowed to come out of her cloistered room or meet and talk to other members of the family except minimally and when absolutely needed. Even where some freedom of movement within the household was permitted, she could not see male members, let alone talk to them for fear of enticing them for forbidden acts. Her presence in festivals and religious functions was a taboo. Finally, a moral code prescribed that she should devote the rest of her life in prayer and observance of religious rituals involving fasting. Prayer was considered the only way for her to atone for the sin of causing the death of her husband. The cold irony was that when society established and legitimized such codes, even her parents and siblings found themselves helpless and compelled to enforce these codes on the bereaved wife.

The Manu Code regulates women's position within marriage and especially within widowhood. The ideological justification and the normative cogency or institutionalization of husband devotion (or *patryvata*) goes back to the sacred and to the principle of the relationship between dharma and reincarnation. Religious sanction in case of disobedience to the duties of chaste and faithful wife before and after the husband's death (endless cycles of reincarnation into vile beasts) and the collective contempt from the community ensure women's social compliance. According to 2001 Census data, India had 34 million widows, 8 million more than in the 1991 Census; whereas, according to 2011 Census, there are around 43 million, about 8 per cent of the entire Indian female population (Census of India, 2011). The 2001 Census (latest available figures) shows a consistent number of young widows aged 15–24 years from 1971 to 2001. The 1991 Census showed that the 15– 19 year age bracket had a total of 65,590 widows with as many as 28,828 in 10–14 year of age (Census of India, 1991). In 2001, there was 0.68 per cent of young widows out of the 20–24 year old female population and 20 per cent out of the 15–19 year old female population. Beyond any religious justification, the various strategies of social contempt and marginalization used by the community against widows are aimed at solving the problem of their social sustainability. Once the husband dies, the widow becomes a heavy burden on the husband's family, a threat for the inheritance and, therefore, an unwanted insider (Srivastava, 2002). For the widows who remain within the husband's family, which happens in the majority of cases in the South, but nevertheless in a condition of severe social and family marginalization which even prohibits physical contact because widows are considered untouchable and inauspicious, there are other widows who live by begging and praying in the temples and ashrams of Vrindavan or Varanasi, the two Uttar Pradesh cities where widows are most likely to be abandoned by their husband's family. It is significant to note that Vrindavan or Varanasi widows come above all from the North, West Bengal, Rajasthan, Bihar, Uttar Pradesh and Andhra Pradesh (Chen, 1998; National Commission for Women, 2009). Specific behaviour, feeding and dress codes (little or poor and standardized feeding, strictly subject to fasting regulations and, above all, devoid of any appealing element, which surrogates physical death) have the function to annul widow identity in order to stifle any potential for social or sexual claim. These self-reduction practices enter into mechanisms whose effectiveness has been pointed from sociological theory. To the extent that people invest a sense of self in what they possess, these mechanisms consist in the systematic loss of any personal possession emphasizing individuality, including own name (Goffman, 1961). The systematic process of de-personalization which widowhood implies for women consists as well in total loss of the woman's usual look (the personal façade) which is sacrificed to homologation criteria such as shaving of the head, erasing the *bindi*, breaking the bangles, the white sari imposition, losing the female pronoun she which is substituted by the new style of life pronoun it, highlighting a no longer acknowledged social identity. In the end, widows are mutilated in their identity, de-sexualized, no longer individuals but things, non-entities – nothing, 'confined within a circle of the zero' (Chakravarty, 2002), marginalized, 'tolerated but never welcomed' (Khanna, 2002). Thus, while the government has failed in checking the phenomena, society has succeeded in placing the widow at its edge, putting her in a condition of being physically alive but socially dead and ultimately institutionalizing her social marginality.

According to Uma Chakravarti, the reason for all these restrictions was the fear that the sexuality of the young widow was a threat to the entire society. Hence, she had to be 'neutered' and 'un-sexed'. Young widows were considered sexually dangerous and earned the potential to disrupt, pollute and desecrate the dead husband's lineage and hence she had to be emasculated of all her sexuality. There was also another objective in sending the widow to oblivion. This is to prevent her from making any demand on her lost husband's property or a share in the parental property. In a cloistered life, property is of no use and even if she has property she is not permitted to administer it or draw benefits from it. It cannot be said that this cruel practice existed universally in all parts of India. Since the Brahmins were the custodians of morality, this was more strictly applied by them than by other communities where property and patriarchal values were not much in vogue. Certainly it found no acceptance among the socially lower categories who had to survive on their labour. They cannot afford to maintain a non-productive widow in the family for long: neither was there physical space for such secluded surroundings. Studies among the lower castes found that while in non-manual jobs the number of widow was smaller than non-widows, in agricultural and outdoor field activities, the number was equal.

As per 1981 Census data, there were 27 million widows in the Indian population. This works out to be 8 per cent of the female population and 14 per cent of the married women. The 1991 Census showed an increase in the absolute number of widows (to 33 million) though the rate of widowhood was more or less the same (8.77%). Figures for 2001 are not available, bit projecting the 1991 rate to 2001 Census data will put the figure to a staggering 40 million. Among the married females, the rate of widowhood will work out to be around 17 per cent. The data indicated that while the proportion of widows in the female population of all ages and marital status is 8 per cent, that in the population of ever-married females it is 14.8 per cent. The proportion of widowers in the total male population during this period was only 2.4 per cent and among ever-married male it was 5.4 per cent. The incidence of widowhood is more than double of that existing among women. It will be seen that in 1981, in every age group, widows were more than widowers and that it increased steadily as the age increased. The increase was quite steep at higher ages and reached 77.2 per cent in the case of 70+ populations. Here again the contrast in the case of men is obvious. As per 2011 Census, widows in India were reported to be 43 million. Out of total widows in India, only 0.45 per cent widows were from the age group of less than 20 years. However, 58.18 per cent widows were from the higher age group, i.e. 60 and above years. Slightly less than 10 per cent widows were from the age group of 80 and above years. In the state of Uttar Pradesh, 4.86 million widows were reported. Majority of the widows were from the higher age group of 60 and above years (60.85%). About 1.6 per cent widows were young, from the age group of less than 25 years (Table 2.12).

Table 2.12

Widows in India and Uttar Pradesh

Age Group (Years)	*Uttar Pradesh*		*India*	
	Number of Widows	*Percentage*	*Number of Widows*	*Percentage*
0–9	—	—	—	—
10–14	10,896	0.22	63,647	0.15
15–19	22,949	0.47	1,30,484	0.30
20–24	42,382	0.87	3,11,452	0.72
25–29	70,768	1.46	6,42,498	1.48
30–34	1,16,089	2.39	10,96,010	2.53
35–39	1,99,774	4.11	18,39,357	4.25
40–44	2,75,300	5.67	25,69,153	5.94

...Cont'd

...Cont'd

45–49	3,36,310	6.92	32,69,711	7.56
50–54	4,19,024	8.63	39,72,473	9.18
55–59	4,08,111	8.40	39,96,475	9.24
60–64	7,82,369	16.11	65,71,107	15.19
65–59	6,39,774	13.17	58,13,953	13.44
70–74	6,98,744	14.39	57,55,159	13.30
75–79	3,00,980	5.20	29,42,010	6.80
80 and above	4,96,277	10.22	41,44,457	9.58
Age Not Specified	36,441	0.75	1,43,532	0.33
All Ages	48,56,188	100.00	4,32,61,478	10.00

Source: Census, 2011

As per 2011 Census, widows, divorcees and separated women (20 and above years) constituted 8.2 per cent. This was reported high in Tamil Nadu (12.6%) followed by Kerala (12.4%), Karnataka (12.3%) and Andhra Pradesh (11.5%). In the state of Uttar Pradesh, widows, divorcees and separated women from the age group of 20 and above years accounted for 5.7 per cent. As per Sample Registration Survey, persons below 10 years of age are being treated as unmarried. Widows, divorcees and separated women constituted more than 10 per cent of the population. This was found more pronouncing in Tamil Nadu (14.8%), Karnataka (14.7%), Kerala (14.5%), Andhra Pradesh (13.6%) and West Bengal (11.4%). In the state of Uttar Pradesh, it was recorded at 7.1 per cent (Table 2.13).

Table 2.13

Percentage Distribution of Widows, Divorcees and Separated Women in India

State	*Percentage of Widows/ Divorce/Separated (20 and above Years)*			*Percentage of Widows/ Divorce/Separated (10 and above Years)*		
	Total	*Male*	*Female*	*Total*	*Male*	*Female*
India	5.2	2.3	8.2	6.4	2.8	10.1
Andhra Pradesh	7.0	2.6	11.5	8.3	3.1	13.6
Assam	4.9	1.7	8.2	6.1	2.2	10.2
Bihar	3.5	2.3	4.7	4.6	3.1	6.2
Chhattisgarh	5.6	2.6	8.7	7.1	3.3	10.9
Delhi	3.6	1.9	5.6	4.4	2.3	6.9
Gujarat	5.3	2.7	8.0	6.5	3.4	9.8
Haryana	4.4	2.2	6.8	5.4	2.7	8.4
Himachal Pradesh	5.9	2.5	9.2	7.0	3.0	10.9
Jammu and Kashmir	4.1	2.4	6.0	4.9	2.9	7.1
Jharkhand	4.0	1.9	6.3	5.1	2.4	8.0
Karnataka	7.0	1.6	12.3	8.4	2.0	14.7
Kerala	7.2	1.5	12.4	8.5	1.8	14.5
Madhya Pradesh	4.7	2.6	6.9	5.9	3.3	8.7

...Cont'd

...Cont'd

Maharashtra	5.7	2.0	9.5	6.9	2.5	11.5
Odisha	6.0	2.5	9.5	7.3	3.1	11.5
Punjab	4.8	2.7	7.1	5.7	3.2	8.5
Rajasthan	4.2	2.0	6.6	5.3	2.6	8.3
Tamil Nadu	7.6	2.5	12.6	9.0	3.0	14.8
Uttar Pradesh	4.1	2.8	5.7	5.3	3.5	7.1
West Bengal	5.5	1.6	9.6	6.6	1.9	11.4

Source: Census, 2011.

According to 2001 Census, India had 34 million widows, 8 million more than in 1991; whereas, according to 2011 Census, there are around 40 million constituting 8 per cent of female population. In 1971, about 1.24 per cent women in the age group of less than 20 years were widows while in 2001, this declined to 0.88 per cent. Similarly, percentage of widows from the age group of 65 and above years has declined from 74.11 per cent in 1971 to 56.62 per cent in 2001 (Table 2.14).

Table 2.14
Percentage Distribution of Widow by Age in India

Age Group	*1971*	*1981*	*1991*	*2001*
15–19	0.34	0.21	0.18	0.20
20–24	0.09	0.69	0.59	0.68
25–29	1.85	1.5	1.15	1.37
30–34	3.95	3.12	2.32	2.59
35–39	6.99	5.42	3.94	4.45
40–44	14.19	10.86	7.71	7.71
45–49	20.42	15.96	11.16	11.31
50–54	36.55	29.72	21.93	20.18
55–59	41.07	31.79	23.76	21.95
60–64	62.55	56.07	45.24	40.0
65 and Above	74.11	70.34	59.83	56.62

Source: Census, 2001.

As per information available from National Commission for Women, there were 2,957 destitute women during 2001–02 while during 2005, the number of widows, destitute and abandoned women were recorded to be 3105. There has been significant increase of destitute women in Vrindavan during the corresponding period. Out of total destitute women in 2005, 90.18 per cent destitute women were from West Bengal, Odisha, Rajasthan and Madhya Pradesh. Out of total destitute women, most of the women were widows (90.18%). Majority of the widows were from the age group of 60 and above years (71.43%). Out of total destitute women, most of the women were illiterate (86.96%) and regularly visiting Bhajan Asharams (80.51%). Less than one-third destitute women were receiving widow/old age pension. There has been significant change in the age composition of destitute women, education level and receiving of benefits under various schemes during the surveys of NYK (2001–02) and surveys of Nagar Palika Parishad (2005) (Table 2.15).

The National Legal Services Authority, which had filed social justice litigation before the Supreme Court of India for protection and amelioration of the different problems faced by a large number of old destitute widows, informed that the Sulabh International Social Service Organisation, New Delhi, is willing to make arrangement for supply of food to the destitute women living in different homes in Vrindavan. The National Legal Services Authority also listed the following homes run by the government and the different NGOs where widows are living: (1) Mahila Ashray Sadan at Ramanuj Nagar, (2) Mahila Ashray Sadan-I at Chaitanya Vihar, Phase-II, (3) Mahila Ashray Sadan-II at Chaitanya Vihar, Phase-II, (4) Meera Sahbhagini Kendra (established by Government of U.P.), (5) All India Women's Conference (Tarash Mandir) and (6) Amar Badi now Maa Dham. As per information available, there are 645 women inmates living in these ashrams against the capacity of 927 women inmates.

Table 2.15

Widows, Destitute and Abandoned Women in Vrindavan

Particulars	*Survey by NYK (2001–02)*	*Per centage*	*Survey by Nagar Palika Parishad (2005)*	*Per centage*
Total Destitute Women in Vrindavan	2,957	100.0	3,105	100.00
Widows	2,678	90.60	2,800	90.18
Other Destitute Women	140	4.73	137	4.41
Abandoned Women	145	4.90	141	4.54
Number of Women in the Age Group of 15–20 years	27	0.91	30	0.96
Number of Women in the Age Group of 60 and above years	1,883	63.68	2,000	71.43
Number of Illiterate Women	2,661	89.54	2,700	86.96
Number of Women who go to Bhajan Asharams	2,528	82.11	2,500	80.51
Women Who Get Widow Pension	227	7.68	235	7.57
Women Who Get Old Age Pension	729	24.65	740	23.83
Women Who Benefitted by Annapurna Scheme	71	2.40	100	3.22

Source: National Commission for Women, 2009.

The direction of the Supreme Court was carried out by Dr Bindeshwar Pathak, Founder, Sulabh Sanitation and Social Reform Movement, along with a team of social workers, on 11 August 2012 in Vrindavan. The widows residing at Maa Dham did not require any financial help for food and, thus, excluding the number of inmates of the ashram, 552 women inmates were identified for financial help for food by the Sulabh International Social Service Organisation. The women inmates were provided regular payment of ₹ 25 per day to each widow. Most of the widows living in Mahila Ashrams are not covered under social security benefits. A significant proportion of destitute women belong to higher age group, i.e. above 60 years. Thus, they need care and protection besides regular support for food, cloth and shelter. A large number of widows are not able to cook food due to old age (Table 2.16).

Table 2.16

Widow Inmates in Asharams of Vrindavan

Particulars	*Mahila Ashram Sadan, Ramanuj Nagar*	*Mahila Ashram Sadan-I, Chatanya Vihar Phase-2*	*Mahila Ashram Sadan-II, Chatanya Vihar*	*Meera Sahbhagini Kendra*	*All India Women Conference (Tarash Mandir)*	*Gild of Services (Maa Dham)*
Installed Capacity	62	250	250	135	30	200
Number of Inmates	62	171	152	135	30	95
Number of Widows Receiving Widow Pension	32	69	12	40	30	06
Number of Widows Receiving Old Age Pension	30	68	04	73	—	50
Number of Women Receiving Mahamaya Pension	—	02	36	27	—	—
Number of Women Having Ration Cards	62	171	—	135	30	83
Number of Women Receiving Support for Food	62	171	124	135	—	—

Source: Sulabh International Social Service Organisation, Delhi.

The last NCW Report, commissioned by the Indian Supreme Court (National Commission for Women), dates back to 2009. Its aim was to explore the situation of women and the thousands of widows who throng the holy city of Vrindavan. Of the 216 women interviewed, widows (as much as 78% of the sample) lived in temples and in ashrams, forsaken in Vrindavan and left in miserable conditions by the deceased husband's relatives or their own children. About 30 per cent had resided there for over 20 years; 20 per cent for 10 to 20 years and another 30 per cent, for less than 5 years. In 74 per cent of the cases, widows came from West Bengal, and their widowhood for the most part began in adolescence, age 15–16, after a child wedding (even as young as 10 or 12) with men at least twice their age. Two out of five widows got married before the age of 12 and almost one out of three was widowed by the age of 24. Moreover, it is estimated that in the subcontinent, one out four women marry before the legal age of 18, and almost one out of five marry under the age of 10. Widows generally live in very oppressive conditions, depending mainly on begging and prostitution for survival (National Commission for Women, 2009).

Widowhood in India is a complex institution fraught with contradictions in meaning and practice. The lives of many widows in India do not conform to the projected ideals of widowhood. Equally, the ideals of widowhood have been redefined over time and place. There are numerous factors, which influence the stressful nature of the transition to widowhood, including the ego-strength of the survivor, the nature of previous relationships, availability of support from others, health facilities, loss of income and anticipated loneliness. To add to their plight, restrictions are imposed upon their food and clothing habits, participation in social functions and remarriage is prohibited for them. Perhaps more than any other social institution in India, widowhood exposes the gap between cultural and social realities, between precept and practice. To begin with, nearly 10 per cent of all women and 55 per cent of women over 50 years are widows: this social reality undermines the projected ideal that all women should remain devoted, chaste wives.

Recognizing the presence of widows in society, the orthodox Hindu lawmakers formulated a set of rights as well as duties for the Hindu widows. In principle, a widow is entitled to the share of her late husband's property or to maintenance by his extended family. In return, the duty of the widow is to uphold the propriety – the honour and purity – of the husband's family and lineage. If her husband's extended family fails to support her, a widow has certain residual rights in her natal home. In real life, the duties of widows are more widely enforced than the rights of the widows are honoured. This is so for a variety of reasons but mainly because the rights of widows are contingent on the duties or obligations of others, mainly male kin, which they cannot enforce. The link between cultural ideals and social reality are the marriage, kinship and caste systems, which organize and structure women's daily lives. In very real everyday ways, these institutions and the underlying ideology of gender relations interact to restrict the capacity of widows to make individual choices and to take individual actions. These restrictions often have dire consequences for widows and their children, both those who manage on their own and those who live as unwanted dependents. The widows live lives of enforced asceticism, prayer and abstinence. Lord Krishna whose play with the *Gopinis* of Vrindavan is treated in Vaishnava philosophy as unison of *Jeevatma* (mortal) and *Paramatma* (divine) and who is worshipped in Hindu religion as the perfect and ever-encompassing divine male figure (*Purushottam*) and protector of *Dharma* represents the call of the divine for the individual souls. As the Bhakti movement spread, *Radha* became the inspiration for supreme devotion to Lord Krishna with the popularization of the epic *Geet Govindam*. For the widows, in absence of their husband, the patriarchal society asked them to worship Lord Krishna as their divine husband. Perhaps this could be a key historical reason for which Vrindavan, the holiest site for the Vaishnavas for being the birthplace of Lord Krishna emerged as the most popular destination for the widows all over India. Vrindavan occupies a special position in a Bengali Hindu's heart since the days the Bengali Vaishnavite mystic, Sri Chaitanya Maha Prabhu, who in 1515, more or less founded the town of Vrindavan by reclaiming it from wilderness. Later Vrindavan was dotted with Krishna temples and for generations, widows have made a pilgrimage to Vrindavan. It is another story that a substantial number of them are either admonished by the families of their former husbands or are literally dropped off by relatives that no longer want them.

The following basic problems could be witnessed in the life of an aging woman/widow:

Medical issues: With advancing age, women go through menopause and attendant health issues such as a higher likelihood of osteoporosis, but few Indian medical college syllabi pay enough attention to Geriatrics. In addition, there is lack of home-based health care and assisted living and hospital care for elderly women who are poor and marginalized. The reproductive and sexual health of the widows are extremely neglected and considered a taboo. Even in case of non-consensual sex (mostly by the in-laws and other family members), the blame is squarely put on the widow.

Economic/Financial issues: The widows have to face many kinds of deprivation: economic, social, cultural and emotional. Of all the deprivations, the economic deprivation is the most harmful. Earlier researches show that household headed by widows suffer dramatic decline in per capita income and that the mortality risk of widowhood was higher for women than men. Among basic causes of their vulnerability are restrictions on the residence, inheritance, remarriage and employment opportunities of widows. With women living longer, they are more likely to outlive their husbands. A bulk of these women does not have training and assistance to manage their financial affairs independently like pension and other savings of the husbands. The situation is grimmer for the women in the unorganized sector where basically 95 per cent of Indian population live. With little or no saving, no steady stream of income, the poor women live at the mercy of other members of the family.

Social & Psychological issues: With the increasing urbanization and employment in organized sector, Indian family system is moving to a nuclear family structure, the age-old support systems that sustained the older generation are being dismantled while new social structures are not yet widow friendly. Schemes like Widow Pension Schemes and National Old Age Pension Scheme are inadequate compared to the demand on ground. Psychological issue is routinely faced even by the widows of the so-called higher echelons of the society. Till date, widows are accused of being 'responsible' for the death of their husband and described as the curse of the family. They are forced to obey restrictive dress code and behaviour and have bland food, observe fasting on particular days, etc. These practices are mainly observed by the widows belonging to higher caste.

Legal issues: Unaware of her rights (especially under Hindu Succession Act, 1956) and incapable of asserting herself, a woman has no recourse to judicial help. Chen (1994) has reported that about 30 per cent of the widows suffered serious and sometimes violent conflicts over inheritance, movable and immovable assets, etc. They are often cheated by their in-laws and near and dear ones. Apart from human rights issues, there are other consequences of widowhood one of which is migration. Many widows in rural areas, unable to cultivate the land or manage the crop without male assistance and often in debt after incurring the medical expenses of the dead husbands are forced to migrate to towns in search of livelihood. In many cases, this migration is fraught with risks of trafficking, physical and sexual assaults, etc. and many young widows end up in the brothels. One study found that inheritance laws often served to entrap women. Their husbands'/families, intent on preventing division of land and homes, frequently forced them to remarry back into the family (which has been reported mostly from north India).

Plight of widows at religious places is worse and, therefore, it requires urgent attention of policy makers, development professionals and administrators to empower the widows so that they may live in dignity. There have been efforts by government and non-government organizations for improving the lives of widows at religious places. However, the institutional arrangements for their shelter, food, health medical care are grossly inadequate. Widows at religious places are facing severe problems in terms of shelter, food, health and medical care, besides their living conditions being worse. Due to old age and lack of social security measures, the misery of widows has grown manifold. Widows need care, protection and dignity of life besides praying and worshipping gods and goddesses at religious places.

3

Socio-Cultural Profile of Universe

A large number of widows are living in religious places such as Mathura–Vrindavan, Varanasi–Kashi in Uttar Pradesh and Puri in Orissa. Most of the widows living in Varanasi and Vrindavan are from West Bengal, Orissa, Rajasthan and Madhya Pradesh. Varanasi has been a place of Shaiva sect while Vrindavan–Mathura has been a place of Vaishnav sect of Hindu religion and therefore widows are coming from various places to live here. It is believed that death in Kashi–Varanasi gives *moksha* to the deceased person, it being the city of Lord Shiva. Similarly, widows who are devotees of Lord Krishna and Mathura being the birth place of the Lord, prefer to live in Vrindavan to worship Lord Krishna. In this part of the report, an attempt has been made to narrate the cultural profile of both the cities.

Socio-religious Profile of Varanasi

In this part of the chapter, we shall discuss the origin and the socio-religious profile of Varanasi city, the ascetic traditions in the city, the world-view of the householders and of the renouncers, the socio-demographic composition of its population, including permanent migrant residents from different parts of the country, the literacy rates with educational level and occupational pursuits of the people in general and of the Bengalis in particular, and an interplay of their both material and spiritual life in the city. While analysing all these, we shall also look into the nature, reasons and periods of migration of the Bengalis, including their widows, to Varanasi city. More precisely, we shall discuss in detail the life of the Bengali widows – how have they been able to manage their material as well as spiritual or ascetic life in the city. But before doing that we shall briefly look at the origin and the socio-religious profile of the city, and the socio-demographic composition of its population.

In Hindu mythology, the old city of Kashi or Banaras or the present day Varanasi has enjoyed the status of being the purest, the most pious and the highest degree of religious spiritual centre on this earth. It has been regarded as the city of Lord Shiva, who is naturally agreed upon as being the most powerful of the trio of gods – Brahma, Vishnu and Mahesha or Shiva or Shankara. Mythologically, the city is also said to be resting on the *Trishula* (trident) of Lord Shiva. Interestingly, of the three forms of Shiva – destroyer, protector or kind-hearted, and the ascetic or renouncer – (with the highest degree of rejoice in the renunciation of materialism) Varanasi has always symbolized his latter two forms. Lord Shiva's form of being protector is also evident from his protecting the city of Varanasi when it was broken by the *Chakra* (discus) of Vishnu *(Vishnu Purana,* Book, V, Chapter, XXXIV cf. in Sherring, 1868, reprinted in 1975). For his protective role and kindness to human-beings, Shiva has been incarnated in the famous Vishwanath temple in the centre of the city. However, all the three forms of Lord Shiva have concretely manifested in both the religious-spiritual and the material life of the people living in the city.

Yet, another myth portrays Varanasi as the centre of truthfulness and a firm commitment to a life of truthfulness. The myth of Raja (king) Harishchandra of the *post-Ramayana* period is still remembered by the people in the city and elsewhere in the country. According to the myth, Raja Harishchandra of Ayodhya (now in Faizabad district of Uttar Pradesh) was put to test for his truthfulness and *dana* (offering) after an agreement between Vashishtha and Vishwamitra, the two notoriously rivalrous Brahmin and Kshatriya priests. Vishwamitra in the disguise of an impoverished Brahmin took away Harishchandra's kingdom in *dana.* To pay the *dakshina* (supplementary gift or fee to be paid on top of the *dana),* Harishchandra sold himself as a funeral attendant to Kalu Dom – the then Dom Raja (the head of the funeral attendants who used to collect *kar* (tax), in lieu of preparing pyre, for incinerating the corpse and providing fire to ignite it). To supplement the remaining amount of the *dakshina,* he sold his wife Taramati also to a malevolent and grasping Brahmin (Vishwamitra himself in disguise) in the Varanasi city. Vishwamitra, in his next disguise as a snake, bit Rohit, Harishchandra's son, who was staying with Taramati. Taramati took the corpse of her son to the *ghat* (the river bank) for cremation where she was asked by her husband on duty to pay the *kar* to cremate the corpse. In fact, he refused to cremate the corpse without levying the *kar.* In absence of any belongings on her to pay the *kar,* Taramati offered her *sari* wrapped around herself. At that point both Vishwamitra and Vashistha, raining petals of flowers, swooped down on the *ghat.* They took Harishchandra, Taramati, their revived son and Kalu Dom to heaven. But later Rohit came down to earth and ruled Ayodhya for many years as the true son of his truthful father.

The message of this myth has been adopted as a living reality and is well integrated in the socio-religious tradition of Varanasi. It is not only eulogized by the construction of the well-known Harishchandra *Ghat* on the bank of the river Ganges but even in the daily conversation of the people living in the city, vows are taken in the name of Raja Harishchandra to honour their promises. In some cases, they even fulfil these at the cost of undergoing all sorts of miseries and inconveniences. This also shows that the socio-religious tradition of the city adopted and accommodated significant elements drawn from the places located hundreds of miles away from Varanasi; in this case, from another geo-political territory of Ayodhya. Yet another significance of this myth is exemplified in the well-pronounced presence of Vaishnavism in the city. In Hindu mythology, Lord Rama has been described as an incarnation of Lord

Vishnu. Since Harishchandra fell in the line or lineage of Lord Rama as mentioned above, he might have been instrumental in introducing Vaishnavism in the city.

The city also has a sizeable population of followers of the Shaivite sect but there has not been a single case of conflict or contradiction in the known history of Varanasi between these two sects. Not only this, but the role of Vishnu as a destroyer of the city is not perceived even in the faintest memory of the people of the city. In fact, both the sects have been accepted as being complementary to each other. Besides these two major religious sects, each with their own symbols and preaching and with their distinct set of followers and monasteries, the city has maintained several other sects of Hinduism such as Ravidas Panth, Kabir Panth (though there could be disagreement on its being a *panth* or sect of Hinduism because Kabir had maintained equal distance from both Hinduism and Islam), Dadu Panth, and several cults such as those of Chaitanya Mahaprabhu, Ballabhacharya, Ramanujacharya, Radhaswami, Ma Anandmayee, Arya Samaj, Sanatan Dharma, Ramakrishna Mission, Ma Sharada, the cult of Ghazi Miyan (Searle-Chatterjee, 1998: 145–58), etc. (for details see Sherring, 1975; Saraswati, 1973; Motichand, 1985; Vidyasagar, 1986: 107–10; Parry, 1998: 33–38). According to Sinha and Saraswati (1998: 51), there were a total number of 1,284 (1,187 males and 97 females) ascetics or *sanyasis* of numerous denominations of Hindu sects, and of Sikhism and Buddhism, living in the *ashramas, mathas, viharas,* etc. in Varanasi city in 1968. 'Among the ascetics of all kinds, the Shankara School of *Sannyasis,* which includes Dandi (239) Naga (91) and Paramhansas (296) are in majority (48.8%), and then come the Vaishnava *vairagis* (36.6%) of all varieties including Kabir Panthi, Dadu Panthi, Gareebdasi, Gheesa and Swaminarain. This establishes the numerical importance *of* the Shaiva *sannyasis* in the ascetic population of Kashi. The Vaishnavas are only next to the Shaiva ascetics. Considering the sub-section of a *sampradaya,* the Paramhansas (296) outnumber the Ramanandis (258) by a narrow margin; the Dandis have the third place in this order' (ibid., 51–52).

Sometime in the sixth century BC, according to Saraswati (1975: 7), Lord Buddha delivered his fist sermon in Sarnath near Varanasi. Since then, Buddhism continued to flourish in the city. In the ancient Buddhist *fatakas,* Kashi has been described as an independent kingdom or princely state and Banaras, including Kashikhand as a city. Buddha's association with Kashi is described in several *Jatakas* also in which he is named as Brahrnadatta who had taken numerous births for the welfare of the people of Kashi and of the adjoining areas. In the recent times, Buddhism – both with its Hinayan and Mahayan sects or schools of thought – is especially present in the world famous Buddhist monastery at Sarnath which has come almost within the vicinity of Varanasi city. Buddhism as interpreted by Dr Ambedkar in the latter part of the twentieth century is also practised and propagated by the people, especially the lower castes, through constructing a number of Buddha *Viharas* (Buddhist monasteries) and installing the statues of both Buddha and Ambedkar at various places in the city. According to Saraswati (1975: 7), the seventh Jain Tirthankara was born in Kashi, although the exact date or even approximate period of his birth is not known. The 23rd Jain Tirthankara was also born in Kashi sometimes in the eighth century BC. It may, thus, be surmised that Jainism as a religious tradition might have come to the city sometime later. Although the exact period is not specifically known, but 'Huien-Tsang (who had visited Kashi in the seventh century A.D.) was struck by the scholarship and devotion of the Brahaman students, and the Jain and the Buddhist ascetics of Kashi (Varanasi) in the seventh century' (1975: 9). The number of ascetics of other religions such as Jainism and Buddhism was not very significant.

Several other religious traditions such as Islam, Sikhism, Christianity, etc. came to the city during the medieval period of the history of Varanasi city. According to Saraswati (1975: 8), Akbar had defeated Jaichanda, the king of Kashi, and established a mint there in 1567 A.D. Similarly, in 1722 A.D., the Nawab of Oudh had ruled Kashi. This simply means that Islam as a religious faith, through its various symbols such as mosque, cultural styles of life, etc., came to Varanasi city during the sixteenth eighteenth century A.D. During the last part of the fifteenth and the first half of the sixteenth century, Guru Nanak – the founder Guru of the Sikhism – had also visited Varanasi (Saraswati, 1975: 7–9). Although the East India Company gained controlled over Varanasi during the mid-fifteenth century, the Christianity came in some form to Varanasi in the second half of the nineteenth century, as the Church Missionary Society was established in 1888. What is important to mention here is that Islam, Sikhism and Christianity as religious traditions or belief systems came to Varanasi city much later. It is neither easy at this stage to find out the specific date(s) about their entry into the city nor is our intention to do so here. Instead, what may be said here is that these religions, besides Hinduism, are very much present in the city and the tensions especially between the Hindus and the Muslims, resulting into communal riots, have also been witnessed during several periods in the city.

All these religious traditions such as Jainism, Buddhism, Islam, Sikhism, Christianity, etc. may, in certain ways, be termed as little traditions, and of the Hinduism inclusive of its various religio-philosophical principles and practices, besides those of its sects or *sampradayas,* as a great tradition (for details, see Singer and Redfield, 1959; Saraswati, 1973; Singh, 1974). This analogy, strictly speaking, may not hold much ground in the present time particularly in view of the fact that the followers of at least Hinduism and Islam – the two prominent religions in the city, especially the latter one – would not accept it though the former would invariably insist for it. Then, what can appropriately be said is that the people of Varanasi city live with multiple traditions (Dube, 1965, 1968) which consist of the religious traditions of the literati (the Sanskritic Pandits), the priests and of the laity* (the commoners like professionals, traders, service class people, rickshaw-pullers, drivers, hawkers, milkmen, etc). A large number of the latter have not yet shelved their relations with the beliefs and the cultural practices of their native places. Hence, they maintain their oral traditions, which could be termed as little traditions (Singer and Redfield, 1959; Saraswati, 1973). In other words, the socio-religious life of the people living in Varanasi is characteristically distinct, which may not easily be found in other cities in the country.

Going by the socio-economic profile of the city, we find that right from its early days, Varanasi has remained a centre of affluence because of being the kingdom of numerous *rajas* or kings. It has also been the place of stay for rich merchants engaged in trade of indigenous products. According to Bayly (2000: 229–30), 'For the (East India) Company and the European private traders, the most important developments in north India's pre-colonial commercial geography were the consolidation of Banares as the main money market for eastern India, and the growth of Mirzapur (its neighbouring district) as the key commodity mart between Bengal, Hindustan and central India … . Its (Varanasi's) position athwart the trade routes, its status as a centre of pilgrimage, and its relatively stable hinterland laid the foundations for a growing importance. The creation of a mint there in 1734 and the decline of the Jagat Seths in Bengal after their fatal quarrel with the Nawab of Bengal in 1756 further increased the commercial significance of (Banaras or Varanasi) the up-country city'. He further says that, 'The city was the natural entry point because some of the greatest buyers were the Maratha chieftains who came to Banaras for pilgrimage, and the sellers were often north Indians or Central Asians' (Bayly, 2000: 232). As a result, several *rajas* and *nawabs* of the neighbouring as well as of the far off princely states such as Netore, etc. in Bengal; Betiah in Bihar; Gwalior and Indore in Madhya Pradesh; Vijayanagaram of south India; etc. and a number of chieftains, landlords and *rats* (noblemen) had built their palaces and *kothis* (palatial houses) in the city. During the colonial period, Varanasi remained one of the important imperial centres of north India.

Interestingly, perhaps since the medieval period, the city has also accommodated a number of *akharas* (wrestling grounds), which promote not only physical fitness but even competitive spirit among a section of the people living there. It has also maintained a number of *gharanas* – centres of classical vocal and instrumental music. Thus, since a long time, the city has remained a unique combination of two cultures or cultural traditions – the classical or Sanskritic one, and the modern ones. In other words, it is a city of the *moksha* and of the *bhoga* – spiritualism and material well-being, though the former is anchored in the core of the mindset of the people living in the city and its vicinity. While the former incorporates learning and teaching of the religious scriptures, practicing spirituality and asceticism, the latter includes the *masti* (enjoyment), the *phakkarpan* (detachment from excessive possession) and the *akharapan* (rusticism). According to Saraswati (1973: 107), these terms are often used by the people of Varanasi. In their 'self-identification' as a cultural group or as a distinct community, the people of Kashi address themselves by the term 'Banarasi'. He further says, 'Nevertheless it is true that such attributes of 'Banarasis as *Masti, Phakkarpan* and *Akkharpan* are more often assigned to Siva, the God of bliss, and the city of Kashi is allegoricaliy known as *Mahasamasan* (the great cremation ground) – the playground of Siva, the god of destruction' (Saraswati, 1973: 108; for details, see Eck, 1983: 303–06; Kumar, 1995; Simon, 1998: 245–68).

Tradition of Kashivas

Contrary to the great tradition and little traditions (Redfield, 1955; Singer, 1955; Singer and Redfield, 1959; Marriott, 1961) and to the multiple traditions (Dube, 1965, 1968), Hinduism has also a unique tradition of *Kashivas* (living religiously in Kashi). Such a tradition is very much rooted in the mindset of Hindus living in different parts of the country, and is based on their belief that living in Kashi or Varanasi leads them to earn *punya* (bliss) and get their all sins committed in whatsoever forms and degree while living elsewhere, washed away. Saraswati (1985: 107–20) has considered the *Kashivas* as a 'useful institution that helps avoid many tears of domestic life'. In his opinion, 'In the contemporary Hindu society, family life is getting more and more difficult. With the increasing generational conflict in values and aspirations, the Hindu joint family system is cut to the quick. Disintegration stares it in the face. The problems of the old people are mounting; the old values that once used to sustain them in the family have now become feeble in the modern mind. The old people suffer the neglect of their sons who were traditionally supposed to look after and saccour them. The irony of the circumstances is that no alternative system has yet evolved for their security and care. Kashivas is the only institution which gives them some relief' (Saraswati, 1985: 118). In fact, the tradition of the *Kashivas* is much older and deeper than being merely an institutional tradition which provides some relief to the old people. It is, rather, a cultural tradition in the sense that it has a number of social-structural units or elements found in the forms of *mathas* or mutts, *ashramas, dharmashala,* etc. which have distinctive material and man-power supports, specific codes of conduct, social relations, interaction patterns and so forth. Besides, this tradition has also a number of cultural symbols such as taking holy dips regularly in the river Ganges, offering regular prayers and chanting *bhajans* or religious songs, performing numerous rituals and rites with the help of the *Pandas,* giving or receiving *danas* or *bhikshas* (offerings or alms in begging), etc. All these are the important inherent parts of the *Kashivasis* and of the tradition of the *Kashivas.*

Prior to the Independence, the rich people of the upper castes especially from Bengal, Bihar and eastern Uttar Pradesh, used to bring the old persons of their families to stay in Kashi, earn *punya,* wash away their sins, and calmly and peacefully die; thus to attain the *moksha* or *mukti* from taking re-birth. Such a tradition was open to both males and females of the rich families. Besides the said attributes, the tradition of the *Kashivas* has also been rooted, since early times, in a few more specific considerations. These have been the cheap living, not remaining hungry, and enjoying both the *bhoga* and the *yoga* simultaneously. This simply means that the standard of living in Varanasi in earlier times was not very high, although this could not be universally generalized. For instance, we have already mentioned that since early times till the colonial period, Kashi or Varanasi was not only the capital of many rulers but it was also the centre of stay of rich merchants, noblemen, landlords, *rais,* etc. who lived lavishly in the city. The cheap living was more applicable to the commoner or the rural-folks whose presence, either temporarily or permanently, was needed in the city for rendering various types of services to the rich people. Not only that but the rural-folks, especially from the nearby areas, on their part, preferred to migrate either temporarily or permanently, under both voluntary and compulsive circumstances, to Varanasi rather than to a city located far away, which was considered as *pardes* or a foreign country by them. This is very much supported by the folk-saying of *Kam Khaye, Kashi Vase* (eat less if more is not available but stay in Kashi or Varanasi).

In the city of Kashi or Varanasi and in its neighbouring regions, there had all along been a saying that nobody sleeps hungry while living in the city of Lord Siva. Such saying or belief had spread as far and wide as to the undivided Bengal. In fact, the belief among the people of Bengal had been that Kashi happened to be the place of the Goddess Annapurna where nobody lived without *anna* (food). Apparently *bhoga* was confined to the rich people or those who lived luxuriously, while *yoga* remained in the domain of the ascetics or the renouncers, including those who had temporally shown their detachment from the material comfort even for the purpose of learning or attaining knowledge. But the deeper aspect of both the *bhoga* and the *yoga,* in the context of the tradition of the *Kashivas,* may be understood in terms of their unique amalgamation in a single person. In other words, living comfortably in Kashi or Varanasi but at the same time being disciplined or even indisciplined in the name of Lord Siva, or not being excessively involved in material affairs, was considered to be part of the *yoga.* We have stated above that a number of rulers, landlords and chieftains especially from East Bengal, Bihar, different parts of UP, particularly the eastern region, Maharashtra, central India or Madhya Bharat, Rajputana (Rajasthan) and the southern states had built their palaces and *Kothis* in Varanasi city. They and their kinsmen used to come to Varanasi once or twice in a year to do the *Kashivas.* The requirements of the *bhoga* and the *yoga* tradition of the *Kashivas* were also very much followed by them during their stay in the city. Thus, the tradition of the *Kashivas* may be said to be based on the cultural attributes such as cheap living, not remaining hungry even without any earning, washing away one's sins, converging of both the *bhoga* and the *yoga,* earning *punya* and attaining the *moksha* or *mukti* from rebirth. Such attributes happened to be (and continue to be so even in the present time) based on a number of social institutions or at least social structural arrangements like *ashramas, mathas, dharmashalas,* etc., besides on the permanent source(s) of earning, especially in the cases of those involved in both the *bhoga* and the *yogas,* as stated earlier in this chapter. Later on, especially during the second half of the nineteenth and up to the early twentieth century, the tradition of the *Kashivas* got reduced only to the bringing of elderly persons, particularly the males who were nearing death, of the rich upper caste families, for their dying peacefully in the city and thus getting *mukti* from rebirth. This tradition, although confined to a few rich upper caste families, still continues. This tradition is very much linked with the mindset of the Hindus, as stated earlier, wherein the elderly Hindus have always desired, either on their own or in the artificially created situation, to spend their old age in Kashi and die there.

Widows and Their Kashivas

The tradition of the *Kashivas* was not only confined to the elderly males but also to the upper caste Hindu females. Both married and widows have desired or were made to desire to come to Kashi for their *Kashivas* for attaining *moksha* or *mukti*. However, according to Bhattacharya (1984: 47), 'It is worthy to think whether the widows crowd on their own in Varanasi for the *Kashivas*. In reality, although every Hindu has the desire for the *Kashivas* but there are a few other reasons for the old widows who come after leaving everything for the *Kashivas*. Some of these reasons are very much related to their real life conditions which they leave behind.' Regarding their socio-economic and regional background before their coming to Varanasi for the *Kashivas*, Bhattacharya (1984: 47) further says that the south Indian widows living in Varanasi belong to the relatively prosperous families. They come from the state of Karnataka, Andhra Pradesh and Tamil Nadu. Such widows either come frequently to Varanasi for their *Kashivas* or they live permanently in the city. Since they come from relatively prosperous family backgrounds, they do not depend on begging for their livelihood while staying permanently in Varanasi. But their number has declined over a period of time.

Interestingly, the widows from Punjab, Haryana, Rajasthan, Himalayan region, Gujarat and Orissa do not come for the *Kashivas*. The reason lies in the fact that their being widows is not considered as a burden on their families. More than that, the property right in the north Indian states has traditionally been governed by the *Mitakshara* – the Hindu customary law under which the women are entitled for inheriting the share of property of their deceased husbands only for their life-long maintenance (Carroll, 1999: 6–26; Chowdhry, 1999: 302–36). Even the Hindu Succession Act 1956, which gave equal rights to both sons and daughters to succeed the property of their father, did not reform the Hindu customary *Mitakshara* law, but it 'merely tinkered with it. The Act intervenes to providing some right of inheritance to the female relations (widows) of a coparcener at his death' (Carroll, 1991: 798). Even to deprive her of such share and control her sexuality, especially in the case of a young widow, the custom of the *Karewa* or *Chaddar Dalna* (putting a shawl or a piece of cloth on her) was in vogue during the colonial period in the erstwhile Punjab (Chowdhry, 1996: 65–82; 1999: 302–36). It is a different matter that such a custom has been contested by the women, especially the educated ones, but their protest has not brought any substantive change in the customary practice, particularly in rural areas.

The customary practice of depriving a widow from inheriting the property of her deceased husband has all along remained confined to the upper and middle level peasant castes, not only in the undivided Punjab but in the whole of north India. The young widows from the lower castes were always allowed to get remarried even if they had one or two issues from their deceased husbands. This practice still continues among them. Without raising the issue of inheritance of property by the lower castes widows, Kolenda (1992: 172–220) has stated that, 'For lower castes such as the untouchable Chuhras (of Punjab), there are ranked statuses within widowhood. (The women becoming widow after the death of their first husbands are ranked higher in the status than those becoming widow after their getting remarried). According to them, the Hindu widow is a cultural unit'. But what can be added here is that the widow, both as a cultural unit as well as a social category, loses her right of inheritance of the estate or property of her deceased husband, if being young she remarries.

Such practice of getting a young and issueless widow remarried was also very much in vogue among the lower castes in the colonial Bengal wherein the Hindu customary law of inheritance known as *Dayabhaga* enjoyed the legal sanction for a long time. This practice of widow-marriage *vis-à-vis* imposition of the Hindu customary law of inheritance among the Rajbansis of the Darjeeling Terai has quite elaborately been explained by Lucy Carroll (1999). It is a fact that the Rajbansis were a tribe but during the second half of the nineteenth century, they got inducted in the caste system prevalent in Bengal. In the case of a Rajbansi widow getting remarried or keeping a *dangua* (keeping a notional husband without undergoing the rituals of formal remarriage), Carroll has mentioned about the duality in regard to her inheritance of the share of the estate or property of her deceased husband. To substantiate her point, she has referred to a number of contradictory judicial pronouncements made on a suit filed in 1923 by the daughter of a Rajbansi father against the inheritance of his estate or property by his widow keeping a *dangua*. In her own words, 'The Munsiff of Siliguri held that the family was a non-Hindu by descent and origin and was governed not by Hindu law but by custom. He further held that among the Rajbansis, a widow may keep a *dangua* and that a widow so doing is permitted by custom to retain her former husband's property. The Deputy Commissioner of Darjeeling reversed the Munsiff's decision on the ground that the Calcutta High Court had previously held the Rajbansis to be Hindus and subject to Hindu Law. And Hindu Law, as interpreted in the strictly 'orthodox' tradition of the Calcutta High Court, divested remarried widows of any inheritance they had reserved from their first husbands, regardless of custom of remarriage among the tribe or caste concerned' (Carroll, 1999: 18–19). The practice of getting young widows remarried still continues among the lower castes in different parts of the country, although it is not applicable to the aged widows either of the upper castes or of the lower castes.

Retrospectively, the upper caste widows from Bengal, Bihar (including the Maithili and Bhojpuri speaking regions) and from Nepal used to come to Varanasi, either voluntarily or under compulsion for their *Kashivas,* irrespective of their age and the socio-economic background of their families. Being victims for a long time of the inheritance of property in Bengal, north-eastern part of Bihar and other feudatories or feudal states that was governed by the custom of *Dayabhag,* and also of a number of socio-economic factors and cultural practices prevailing in their families and in their respective regions before they came to Varanasi for the *Kashivas,* these widows, especially the old ones, were totally destitute and dependent on begging for their daily sustenance. Although the custom of *Dayabhag* was legally abolished in 1937, 'There was no distinction under the pre-1956 law in regard to the devolution of property held by a *Dayabhaga* male depending on whether the property was joint family property as well as his own separate property; his undivided interest in joint family property as well as his separate property passed by inheritance to the same heirs in the same hierarchy of preference. The absence of a rule of survivorship in *Dayabhaga* meant that a daughter might well figure as an heir to her father's joint family property, which she could never do in *Mitakshara,* unless her father were a sole surviving coparcenar' (Carroll, 1991: 804). But at the same time, since she had the chance to contest for her share, the daughter used to get compensated by getting presents at the time of her marriage, usually in the form of jewellery, clothes, etc. which were popularly known as *Streedhana.* This *Streedhana* was her own property and her husband or any member of his family did not have any right over it. By extension, her *Streedhana* was meant for her sustenance in the event of the death of her husband. But one could easily imagine that in a large majority of the cases, even the *Streedhana* of a woman in the middle and lower class families used to be spent either by her husband or his/her kinsmen or by herself during the bad days or at the time of any misery, especially after the death of her husband. In such a situation, or in the situation after her becoming a widow, she did not have any option except to take up a pilgrimage, preferably Kashi or Varanasi for *Kashivas.*

In the case of the Bengali society, the *Kulinism* started around 1500 A.D. and ended by 1850 A.D. due to the crusade launched by Raja Ram Mohan Roy, Ishwar Chandra Vidyasagar, etc. The institution of *Kulinism* was more specifically confined to the first five upper ranked clans of the Radhi Brahmins (a sub-caste of the Brahmins) and to the first three upper ranked clans of the Radhi Kayastha (a sub-caste of the Kayastha) of the present-day western and northern regions of north Bengal. 'The lower grades of clans in the Radhi Brahmin sub-caste were referred to as Srotriyas, those in the Dakhina-radhi Kayastha sub-caste as Maulika' (Inden, 1976: 1). The *Kulinism* in both the castes and sub-castes of the Brahmins and the Kayasthas was not based on their better economic condition and their enjoying political power but on their claim of pure origin or of pure blood or of ritual purity in the caste based society of Bengal. Not only were the *Kulins* worshipped by the lower clans or sub-castes of their own caste, but also by other castes in their respective area. For marriage purpose however, they were confined to their own sub-caste. According to Inden (1976: 104), 'due to the *Kulina's* superior capacity to transform inherited rank into its superior fruits, he was considered to be a human deity. An action of rank *(kula-karma),* marriage with a *Kulina,* was thought, therefore, to take the form of worship *(puja, arcana)* in which a daughter was given to a *Kulina* or escaped from him after wealth and food were offered to that *Kulina* in order to induce him to make this transforming marriage.' Because of a disproportionate ratio of both the males and females with the number of females being higher, the poor *Kulins* were bound to marry their daughters, including girl children, to the *Kulin* grooms, irrespective of whether they were already married. The majority of the *Kulin* males had to marry several times and thus they had many wives, including the girl brides, whom they never visited again in the rest of their life. The historical evidences also suggest that the poor parents were compelled to marry their daughters, including girl children, to the male *Kulin* who were either aged or on the verge of death. The custom became rigid not only for retaining the purity of the clan or of sub-caste but also because in Hinduism a girl child was considered a *paraya dhana* (other's property) and getting her married to the right person, her owner, made her parents free from the debt of the other.

This resulted into enormous number of widows, including child widows, in the rural areas of Bengal, presently western and northern regions of West Bengal. According to Desai, 'As soon as he *(Kulin* Brahmin) married the next woman, he might discard the former without incurring any liability. These discarded women either stayed with their parents or took resort to certain other illegal activities (Desai, 1970: 67–68). One may be tempted to know about the women who became widows due to the *Kulin* marriage, yet their number at this stage is neither available nor relevant for the purpose of the present study. Even if some such widows might have come to Varanasi, they would have died long back in the city itself, leaving no trace behind.

Demographic Composition of Population

The city of Varanasi is situated at the western banks of the river Ganges where it flows from south to north. The total population of the city at the 1951 Census was 3,55,777 persons, with an increase of 62.8 per cent since 1881 – the first official Census enumerated in India. There was, however, a decrease of 11.2 per cent in the city's population during the following three decades of 1891–1921. Such decrease of population of Varanasi city was part of the unfavourable growth of urban population in the country as a whole. But in the subsequent decade of 1921–1931, the population of the city grew by 3.5 per cent, which can be attributed to the immigration of people in the city. Such factors, along with other factors like steady natural growth of population, continued till 1951 Census (Singh, 1955: 55–56). The immigrant population to the city was not only drawn from the nearby villages, but also from far off places like Bengal, Maharashtra, Gujarat, a few cities and villages in UP and Bihar, and from the deep south like Tamil Nadu. The purpose of coming of the immigrant population in Varanasi city was mainly of two folds – in search of a livelihood and in search of *moksha* or salvation, including peace from the various types of miseries, tensions, excessive materialism, etc. As per the Censuses of 1881 and 1941 before Independence, the percentages of population of two major religious communities, Hindus and Muslims, in the city were 76.4 and 23.6 in 1881, and 69.4 and 30.6 in 1941, respectively. As far as the increase of population of the Hindu and Muslim communities during the said period (1881 and 1941) is concerned, it was 18.5 and 73.9 per cent, respectively (Singh, 1955: 63). The percentages of other religious communities like Jain, Buddhist, Sikh and Christian were not very significant during the said decades in the city.

There were mainly five streams along which people of different walks of life migrated to the city before Independence. These were: rule, livelihood, trade and commerce, amusement and salvation. A number of Hindu and

Muslim rulers, along with their ministers and courtiers, servants, etc. ruled the city at different points in times. Similarly, the traders and businessmen from the different parts of Uttar Pradesh, Punjab, Rajasthan, Gujarat, Bihar, Bengal, etc. came to the city and had set up their business establishments. A number of rich people from the states like Bengal, Bihar, Maharashtra, Madhya Pradesh (then Central Provinces and Berar), Rajasthan, etc. came to the city and built their *Kothis* or palatial houses, as stated earlier in this chapter. Occasionally, they themselves or their representatives and kinsmen used to visit the city and stay in these *Kothis*. They used to visit the city for both *bogha* (amusement) and to earn the *punya* (bliss) by giving *danas* (offerings) in the forms of foods, clothes, gifts, etc. to the beggars and the other needy ones (for details, see Bayly, 2000). The last stream of immigrants to the city consisted exclusively of those who came to seek liberation from the various types of miseries and to obtain *moksha* (getting rid of the numerous births or transmigration of soul). These elements of population consisted of both rich and poor who lived in the city either with self-support or with the support offered by others, including begging. Although it is not possible at this stage to know the exact number of each category of immigrants to the city, particularly before Independence, it may be mentioned that as Benares (now Varanasi) ranked highest as the religious centre of India, immigrants of all streams came to the city seeking the blessings of Lord Siva in all their endeavours. Whether they succeeded or not is a moot question which cannot be empirically verified at this stage. We can only go by the belief in the myth that all those who come here seeking blessings of Lord Siva get success in their efforts.

After Independence, there had been a dramatic increase in the total population of the city which was demonstrated in the 1951 Census when the population of the city increased from 2,66,002 persons in 1941 to 3,55,777 persons in 1951, as mentioned above. This further increased to 4,89,864 persons in the 1961 Census. Such dramatic increase in population, especially during the 1941–1951 decade, was attributed to the 'post war developments, the great influx of rural population for employment and number of refugees (settled in Varanasi) following the partition of the country' (Singh, 1955: 56). The steady increase in the city's population since then has been enumerated in the subsequent Censuses of 1961, 1971, 1981 and 1991 respectively. For instance, it has increased to 13, 22,248 persons in 1991 as compared to 9,90,798 persons in 1981 and 6,06,721 persons in 1971. In other words, the continuous increase in population of the city over all these decades might have been possible due to the overall improvements in the civic conditions, emergence of a number of educational institutions, growth of diversified occupations, trade and commerce, transport system, white collar jobs, etc.

Like all Indian cities, Varanasi also represents a masculine character since the early days. The male-female ratio in the city, as per the 1951 Census, was 811 females per 1000 males which were significantly less than the average male-female ratio in the country. Even prior to Independence, such a disproportionate ratio of males and females in the city was almost constant which, according to Singh (1955: 65), was probably due to the male immigrants to the city as workers in factories, offices and other business concerns. Singh has further stated that, 'Such men usually find it cheaper and more convenient to leave their families in the countryside to carry on the traditional occupation, while they themselves live in the town, often in unsatisfactory and crowded conditions. In Banaras, however, this factor, increasing the proportion of males to females, does not operate to the same extent since the women folk may accompany the men immigrants on account of the religious character of the city' (Singh, 1955: 65). As the character of Varanasi city has significantly changed during the last few decades, the females now accompany their males on account of the latter's getting employed and having permanent settlements in the city. Consequently, the ratio of the male-female population has increased during the last four decades. Interestingly, the number of females was more than males (2,74,043 males and 3,32,676 females) according to 1981 Census, though it largely falls in the line of the average sex ratio in the country wherein the number of females over per 1000 males has all along been less.

Community-wise Concentration of Population

The population in almost all Indian cities consists of two major religious communities: Hindus and Muslims. The population of other religious communities is found in insignificant numbers. Varanasi city is in no way an exception to this. This is evident from the community-wise population given in the 1961 Census. According to this, out of a total population of 4,89,864 persons in the city, the Hindus were 74.6 per cent and the Muslims were 24.6 per cent. Of the rest, the Sikhs constituted 0.35 per cent, Christians 0.2 per cent, Jains 0.13 per cent and Buddhists only 0.05 per cent. A fact may, however, be noted that there has been substantive increase in population of the city at 1971, 1981 and 1991 Censuses with a little increase or decrease in percentages of population *of* the various communities living in the city. Such increase in the community-wise distribution of population in the city may be attributed to the tremendous growth of trade and commerce, business, and other government and non-government services, educational institutions/ etc. as mentioned above. As far as the concentration of the people of major religious communities like Hindus and Muslims in the city is concerned, it is distinctively visible 'that in Banaras both Hindus and Muslims are not so well diffused in their distribution over the city … . In Banaras some well concentrated pockets of Muslim population have been developed … . In the northern portion of the city there are two concentrations of Muslims: (1) Alaipura and its contiguous areas in the Jaitpura wards; (2) the eastern half of the Adampura ward, north of the Maidagin – Kashi Station road. In the city's western part there is some degree of concentration (of Muslims) in and around Lallapura west of the Chetganj road. In the Dasaswamedh ward, there is a great concentration of Muslim population in Madanpura (Singh, 1955: 63–64). Though the concentrations of the people of other minority communities such as the Jains, Buddhists, Sikhs and Christians are not distinctively visible in specific wards or *mohallas,* the population of Hindus is widely spread in the city which has expanded during the recent decades towards the south-west beyond Banaras Hindu University (BHU), between BHU and Diesel Locomotive Works (DLW), and in the north-west beyond Kachahari upto Sivpur in the west and Sarnath in the north. Even among the Hindus, the different ethnic communities with their numerous castes and sub-castes are concentrated in some specific parts of the old city. For instance, the South Indians and the Maharashtrians are preponderantly concentrated in the areas called Kedarghat on the banks of the river Ganges and in the Shiwala *mohalla*. 'Bengalis are concentrated mainly in two areas, firstly, in the Dasaswamedh ward-east of the Madanpura road and west of the Ganges with Kedarghat and Kedareshwar temple as the centre. From north to south the area extends from the Dasaswamedh road to Sonarpura. Secondly, a new Bengali locality, rectangular in shape, is developed in the Bhelupura ward, north of water works (which is also known as Bengali Tola) extending up to Luxa, and hemmed in between the Kamachcha and Rampura roads. Bengalis, particularly the women-folk, are more religiously minded than most and many people, in the latter part of their lives wish to settle in such sacred places' (Singh, 1955: 64). It may not be possible at this stage to trace the history of the different immigrant groups or communities which came into the city. However, 'The Bengalis (whenever they migrated to the city) first occupied the open space south of the Dasaswamedh ghat along the Ganga and when no space was left there, their colony found a suitable location in Bhelupura ward which is not far away from the Ganga' (Singh, 1955: 64). As far as their representation in the population of Varanasi city is concerned, at the time of Independence every fifth person in the city was a Bengali. But nearly half a century after Independence, their representation has reduced to one to fifteen, that is, of every fifteen persons there is only one Bengali living in the city (Chattopadhyay, 1988: 42).

Ethnicity and Cultural Traditions in the City

Since the concept of ethnicity has been defined along with either all or any aspect such as a specific language, dress pattern, food habits, customs and beliefs, common festivals, etc. the Hindus and Muslims with some or all these aspects may not be called ethnic communities. This is also because the former are divided into numerous castes and sub-castes, and the latter into the caste-like groups. In such a case, what is important for a group or community to be considered as an ethnic group or community is that the group or community, besides the above mentioned characteristics, is to be small in population size with a strong we-feeling among its members. But such strong we-feeling may be contextual or occasional and it may refer to another group or community as its rival even if such rivalry is a notional one. Such a group or community could have continued with its distinctive cultural characteristics amidst its socio-cultural interaction with the other groups or communities. Not only that, but such a group or community should also feel proud of its distinct socio-cultural characteristics. Since the present study is concerned with the Bengali widows living in Varanasi city, it is necessary to briefly look into how the Bengalis in the city are an ethnic community. Bengalis living in Varanasi may be considered as a distinct ethnic community, although they are not only Hindus but are also divided into a number of castes and sub-castes. The mother tongue of the Bengalis of Varanasi is Bangla. Although there are both literate and illiterate, and rich and poor Bengalis, but more often than not they speak in their mother tongue. They also celebrate their common festivals such as Durga Puja, Kali Puja, Saraswati Puja, etc. and worship common gods and goddesses. More than that, they consider themselves as Bengalis and others also consider them so. Although they are Hindus, they do not consider the other Hindus living in the city as their own brethren because of the diversified socio-cultural practices of the latter.

As far as the phases during which the Bengalis migrated to Varanasi city are concerned, four specific phases have been identified. These are as follows:

- Between the seventh and twelfth century AD – for expansion of rule of the Bengali kings including the kings of Pal-dynasty, and for the trade.
- During the thirteenth to seventeenth century AD – primarily for religious learning and for trade.
- During the eighteenth century up to the 1930s AD – due to religious beliefs and practices.
- Since 1947 till date – mostly in the form of refugees after the Partition of the country into India and East Pakistan (now Bangladesh), and also for education, employment, etc. (Ramakant, 1986: 14–31; for details, see Ghosh, 1986: 119–22).

It is extremely difficult to tell how many Bengali families or individuals had migrated initially or during the early phases to Varanasi city, how had they interacted with the local people, and how were they able to retain their culture, their customs and belief system(s). It is also difficult to determine concretely whether there were some vital internal forces in the Bengali society itself which had compelled a section of the people of Bengal to migrate to or become instrumental to others' migration to Varanasi city during the different phases of their migration. However, going by each of the above mentioned phases of the Bengalis' migration to Varanasi city, it will be easier to briefly spell out the specific causes which had facilitated a section of the Bengalis to move to Varanasi and settle permanently in certain pockets in the city.

In the first phase (seventh to twelfth century), a number of persons, especially from the ruling classes and a few Brahmin families, came to Varanasi city for learning the Hindu *Dharmashastras* particularly Vedas, Sanskrit grammar, philosophy, ethics, traditional law, etc. from the learned Pandits of Varanasi city (then Kashi). However, although nothing is known authentically at this stage, it is possible that they had also entered into debates and discourses about the traditional Hindu *Dharmashastras,* and in the process, contributed to enriching the existing knowledge by incorporating their indigenous learning into them.

In the second phase, besides the merchants, several Pandits from various parts of Bengal came to Varanasi to learn the religious rites and rituals for attaining priesthood. Banaras or Varanasi city was an established centre of *Sakta* worship and since there were a number of such centres in Bengal, their newly acquired religious knowledge helped them not only in reviving the forms and vigour of the worship of the *Sakta* or *Shakti* in the forms of Durga and Kali (Mahashakti) in Bengal, but also the symbolisms of worshipping Lord Siva, which had existed there since early time. According to Bhattacharya

(1986: 16), these forms and symbols of the worship of *Sakta* were corroborated as the *Saktivad* of Rani Bhawani of the eighteenth century.

In the third phase of the Bengalis' migration to Banaras during the eighteenth, nineteenth and up to early twentieth centuries, more and more rich Bengalis not only got settled permanently here but also financed to its reconstruction. More specifically, a number of Bengali Nawabs, Zamindars, Rajas, landlords and businessmen constructed their own *kothis* (palatial houses), and also 'financed the construction and repair of streets, wells, temples, palaces, burning ghats, etc. in different places of Banaras, Rani Bhawani of Natore being the most noteworthy personality in this connection' (Jha, 1986: 22). Besides, a new rich class of Bengalis was also created in Banaras whose passion to earn virtues as well as exhibit their richness was expressed in different forms of their activities such as setting up a number of educational institutions, constructing *ashramas, dharmashalas,* etc. Writing about the Bengalis living in Varanasi during this period, Sherring (1975: 146–47) has stated that they formed a considerable community who lived in the locality of Bengali Tola and were noted chiefly for having a superior education in comparison to others. They were acquainted with the English language and were proud of their circumstances. 'Yet the uneducated portion of the Bengali community adhere to the customs of Hindu society just as vividly as other inhabitants of the city, doing with equal pertinacity to caste, and exhibit the same blind and senseless attachment to idol worship'.

Finally, the last phase of migration of hundreds of thousands of Bengalis was caused due to the Partition of the country in 1947. Interestingly, during this phase a sizeable number of Bengali families from the then East Bengal flew to Varanasi city for getting refuge in the form of getting shelter, white collar jobs, etc. Unfortunately, although Bengalis as a whole had a high socio-economic and cultural status in Varanasi, the Bengali widows in the city lived in quite helpless and miserable socio-economic conditions. A sizeable number of them can easily be seen begging, even today, on various *ghats* of the river Ganges. In the next chapter we will discuss the socio-cultural and economic deprivations of the Bengali widows living in Varanasi.

The Vrindavan Connection

Vrindavan has been celebrated in legend and song as the land of the *gopis* – the frolicsome young maidens who spent many hours in the pursuit of Lord Krishna. These legends are celebrated in the interminable *bhajans* ringing out from every alley of this temple strewn town. These *bhajans* hide the trauma of the later day *gopis* – the white-clad, sad-eyed widows who have come to Vrindavan as a last refuge from a world that has refused them a home, let alone joy or love. Also connected with Krishna is the area around Mathura known as Braja *mandala* the cultural centre of Braj *bhumi*, the land of Lord Krishna's childhood. Other sacred towns in this area are Vrindavan, Gokul, Govardhan, Barsana and Nandgaon. There are other similar places connected with different gods in South Asia. But what are the special ties that bind the Bengali widow to Vrindavan? (To a lesser extent, Banaras has also provided a similar refuge to widows.) Bengal's long connection with Vaishnavism provides part of the answer for the Bengali connection with Vrindavan. Followers of both Chaitanya and Vallabhacharya seek Krishna realization. Consequently, for them the land of Krishna's nativity is sacred. Krishna's manifestation in Vrindavan was believed to have occurred for two reasons: to relieve the sufferings of the earth and, as per the Chaitanyaite Vaishnavas' belief, to experience for himself the sweetness of Radha's love for him. This association of Vrindavan with Radha makes Vrindavan more important to followers of Chaitanya. The dedication of Vrindavan to Radha is also symbolic of the association of the place with feminine divinity. (Selflessness and devotion, which are essential components of *bhakti* in Hindu sociology, are traditionally associated with females.) It is said that the first Hindu temples that displayed an image of Radha without an image of Krishna are in Vrindavan. Pilgrims to Vrindavan aspire to be one with the divine Radha, for 'Radha's love is the epitome of devotion to the Lord'.

Sri Krishna-Chaitanya, popularly known as Chaitanyadeva, led the Bhakti movement in Bengal. The successor to this movement was the Gaudiya Vaishnava sect. (They were called Gaudiya Vaishnavas since they came from Gauda, i.e. Bengal). The birth of Chaitanya in 1486 was of great significance for the Vaishnava faith in Bengal. Chaitanya's *diksha* and *sanyas* guru were disciples of Madhovendra Puri who had earlier established a small temple in Vrindavan. The two leading men in the new form of Vaishnava worship, which set up Chaitanya as the founder, were Advaitacharya and Nityanand. Besides them, six Goswamis were acknowledged as the chief teachers. (These scholars settled down at Vrindavan or Mathura, where many of their descendants still remain, and are in possession of several temples. Other scholars from Bengal gathered around them. This Brindavan coterie of scholars became the intellectual centre of the sect. From Vrindavan, the scholars went back to disseminate their philosophy and theology to Bengal. However, the Vrindavan *gosains* themselves never returned to Bengal.) Chaitanya's followers were responsible for popularizing Vrindavan as one of the chief religious centres in north India. Till the end of the sixteenth century, the whole country was thickly forested. The Bengali Vaishnavas were responsible for conversion of this woodland into Vrindavan. Thus, the foundation of all the material prosperity and religious exclusiveness characteristic of the place was laid by direct disciples of Chaitanya. They spearheaded the total development of Vrindavan in accordance with the directions received from Chaitanya. Other sacred spots in the cultural complex of Braj, like Mathura and Govardhana, had functioned as places of pilgrimage, but Vrindavan as a significant religious centre came up solely through Chaitanya's efforts.

Women in Vaishnava Society

Vaishnavism flowered in Bengal due to the widespread impact of Chaitanya in the early part of the sixteenth century. His popularity was linked to his ability to dissociate the joy and ecstasy of God-realization from ascriptive codes of social and religious conduct and was rooted in the Bhakti tradition. Vaishnava *bhakti* laid stress on individual achievement by linking personal devotion to God. Vaishnava *bhakti* encouraged self-expression in the devotee and signified a union of implicit faith with incessant devotion. The term *bhakti* is considered as etymologically feminine and epitomises the whole religious and moral code of the sect. For the Vaishnavas, the human soul is the eternal woman in search of the eternal lover – Krishna; it seeks an eternal romance with the Divine.

By transcending caste and family distinctions, the Chaitanya movement brought about a virtual social revolution in the rigid Hindu social order. The reordering enabled scholarly men from low castes and women to benefit from the movement. The passion generated by Chaitanya signified a break from the meaningless rituals and superstition and succeeded in convening large groups in Bengal. Though Nabadwip, Puri and Vrindavan were acknowledged as centres of Vaishnavism, yet its impact was as great in the villages of Bengal. It is common to find images of Radha-Krishna in close embrace in the family shrines of most Bengali households. Even the followers of the *Sakta* tradition had such images, although they were members of the aristocracy and Vaishnavism had an association with the common people. The Vaishnavas accorded equal importance to the male and female members of their community, thus giving women an opportunity to salvage some religious esteem. Records exist of village women deserting homes to join Vaishnava ashrams.

An examination of nineteenth century Bengali popular culture reveals a vast repertoire of *kirtans, kavi* songs and other compositions dealing with the love of Krishna and Radha. The highly emotionalized group singing – *kirtan* was characteristic of Bengali Vaishnavism. The *kirtan* and *kavi* songs reveal saturation with devotional spirit and deal with the lives and times of Lord Krishna and Sri Chaitanya. *Kirtan* sessions often assume proportions of a full-length drama, describing certain aspects of Radha's love for Krishna. Metaphorically, this life on Earth is supposed to be nothing more or nothing less than the *viraha* (separation) between Radha and Krishna. These compositions emphasize that, like Radha, those who love Krishna will be united with Him. *Kirtan* singing, to the accompaniment of instruments, was a practice among all sections of society but was especially popular among the relatively lower strata of society as the emotional appeal of religion was immense in these groups. Besides the religious aspect, *kirtan* singing had a non-religious aspect also. It created a strong bonding, a feeling of community. Ordinary people often coped with crises and threats by singing *kirtans*.

In exploring the female constituency of Vaishnavism, Catherine Ojha noted that women profit from all Hindu movements that bring welfare to the lowest strata of society. This is possible because the status of women has been equated with that of the Sudra since they came to be barred from the religious culture of the higher *varna*. Radha was given a preeminent position in the worship of Krishna by Chaitanya.

For Vaishnavas, a woman was the ideal *bhakta* because devotion required both a duality of being and complete self-surrender. Vaishnavism did not differentiate between women from royal families and widows or women from socially marginalized groups. This is why important Vaishnava pilgrim centres like Vrindavan became a favourite refuge of female groups from all classes. It is recognized that Bengali Vaishnavism privileged the female devotee in many respects. A significant number of non-widows-destitutes, women estranged from their families, wives steeped in spirituality, reside in Vrindavan. Are these women victims of social exclusion? The concept of social exclusion focuses on relational issues. This is in contrast to the concept of poverty, which signifies a paucity of resources. These women are not systematically forced locked out of participation in normal family life. The pressures of poverty, the yearning for Krishna and unstable relationships within the family create a situation where Vrindavan exerts a powerful 'pull' factor and lures them into leaving their homes. Such women are often members of families that are fragmented or are in disarray.

The Bengali Widow

In commenting about the condition of the Bengali Hindu widow today, it is useful to begin from an examination of events more than a century ago. It is acknowledged that widows as a group are social outcastes. The practice in Bengal of casting women into social oblivion by sending them to Kashi and Vrindavan is more than a century old. It was a practice during the period that hailed the Bengal renaissance as a success story. While the social objective of emancipation of women in nineteenth century Bengal was being achieved, the scheme for excluding the widows was being carried out in a unique way.

All over India, patriarchy chose to marginalize the widow and rob her of her individuality. Bengalis carried this marginalization a step further. What were the reasons for this difference in the treatment meted out to the Bengali widow? The difference in the mindset of the patriarchy in Bengal was due to the early social transformation in the region. Socially and economically, nineteenth century Bengali women did not form a homogenous group. This was a period of great transition. There was some dismantling of the existing hierarchical relations as the social order was breaking down. The existing social ties binding together women of different classes were being torn apart. This transition could not create the social space necessary for accommodating widows. Deportation to a pilgrim centre was a convenient strategy and assuaged the accompanying guilt generated by the exile of widows. Towards this end, they were sent to places of pilgrimage like Varanasi and Vrindavan to live on a pittance. In this manner, the Bengali male succeeded in exercising total control over the cultural and economic life of widows.

Widows were often victims of male lust, sometimes even within the extended family. Many such victims of circumstances were socially ostracized for breaking the norms of chastity. Life-long celibacy and the other tortuous rituals designed for widows were supposed to erase desire. The ascetic lifestyle was designed to ensure male control over her sexuality. Life was a grim baffle for survival for most of these widows without any means of livelihood. The practice of *sati* ended some lives. Conversion to Christianity was one survival strategy for some widows. Others eked out a meagre living from alms in religious places.

What were other alternatives available? Through force of circumstances, such women had to seek work outside their villages. (Manual wage work by women has always been considered degrading in India; various strategies were known to be employed to make such work invisible or disguise it. In Bengal, the situation was worse.) Such wage work was generally the last option exercised by widows. This is obvious from the many pejorative terms which were in use in Bengal to designate women who joined the work force; this living, however, only gave them an existence at the base of the social pyramid. Reports show that the jute mills of Calcutta employed a large number of women and children. Yet because of their urgency to find work and association with low skill they were concentrated in the lowest paid jobs in the mills. Prostitution was another avenue that gave poor *and* young widows a livelihood. In 1853, the total population of Calcutta was about 4,00,000. The number of prostitutes was 12,419 of which 10,000 were Hindus. In 1867, their number increased to 30,000. Of this figure, 90 per cent were reportedly Hindu widows. The *Amrita Bazar Patrika* of 11 March 1869 reported that 90 per cent of the prostitutes in Bengal were widows. The chief urban centre of Calcutta had men who had not settled down but earned their livelihood in different professions. The main factors for entry into prostitution during the period seem to be economic distress and social oppression.

Bengali literature of early twentieth century has portrayed the dilemma of the widows with great sensitivity. *Chokher Bali* (1903) by Rabindranath Tagore addressed the problem of sexuality of a young and beautiful widow. The noted Bengali novelist Saratchandra Chattopadhyaya, in several novels, has portrayed women who were ostracized because of sexual transgressions. In *Pallisamaj,* he created the character of a widow who yields to desire. Despite her privileged caste and class status, she is coerced into moving to Varanasi to resolve the tension generated by her transgressions. These fictional pieces highlight how women who are thought of as having transgressed society's normatively ascribed gender roles are forced, in different ways, into silence. The silence of these widows was more eloquent than speech. The stories, which mirrored society, attempted to study this silence.

Bengali society presented the extreme example of variation in the degree of seclusion of women depending upon social class. Whereas the imitation of Western lifestyle had loosened the norms of seclusion for upper class women, for the lower caste and lower class women, there were derogatory terms used for participating in the labour force due to economic crisis. The prevalence of this upper caste ideology was responsible for the consistently low female labour force participation rate of Bengal, as revealed by figures available over more than a century. Patriarchal controls ensured the marginalization and exclusion of widows. The existence or awareness of a widow's passion and desire was totally overlooked. It was obvious that this worrisome category of womanhood had to be excluded. The severity and inhumanity of the act of sending off was cushioned by the ring of religiosity ascribed to the places of exile. The places were mainly Varanasi and Vrindavan. Varanasi is one of the most sacred *tirthas in* the Hindu religion whereas the Vaishnavas dominated Vrindavan and Mathura, the mythical abode of Krishna. The options before a widow were very clear: if she chose to live within the family, she had to create an ascetic identity. However, her labour and property were to remain at the mercy of the male authority within the family. (The arduous labour expected from widows by their own families was obvious in the common criticism of Indian families for making drudges out of widowed female relatives.) If she somehow transgressed the norms set by patriarchy, deportation to distant lands was the only option. It was surprising that in the rigidly hierarchical society of the nineteenth century, the 'exiled' widows become free electrons in the social chemistry of Bengali society. Scholars have commented about the ironical situation of the more liberal laws of inheritance in Bengal hardening attitudes towards women. An examination of the laws reveals that it was expedient to send widows away, giving the other members the right to enjoy her property.

The legal treatises – Dharmashastras (literal meaning – teaching or science of righteousness' or treatises based on *dharma)* – and the commentaries on them shaped the Hindu inheritance laws and practices. These law books provided guidelines for all men and women. The *Dharmashastra* tradition was broadly divided into two 'schools' – the Dayabhagas school was in force in Bengal while the Mitakshara school was followed in the rest of the country. (These systems applied mainly to upper caste communities.) What were the fundamental differences between the Dayabhaga and Mitakshara schools? There were differences in three respects. These are:

- the division or classification of heritage
- the nature of co-ownership in joint family property
- the mode of devolution of joint family property

According to the Dayabhaga, even the male issue of a person cannot acquire interest in the property by birth alone. Their rights in the property of their father arise for the first time on his death whether such property is ancestral or otherwise. In the Mitakshara school, the joint family property devolves by survivorship whereas in the Dayabhaga, joint family property devolves by succession in the same way as separate property. The Dayabhaga school, therefore, has developed a law of succession of a widely different kind. It gives the widow of a person dying without male issue the whole of his property although he might have been joint owner with his brother and other coparceners at the time of his death. This was unlike the rule of survivorship in Mitakshara.

To sum up, under the Dayabhaga school, a widow could inherit property under all circumstances. In cases of joint property, she could sue for partition as co-heir of the property. This right was equally available to movable and unmovable property. Succession under the Mitakshara and Dayabhaga schools operated along different principles. Mitakshara was based on propinquity or nearness of blood relationship of the deceased, and under Dayabhaga it was based on the spiritual benefit conferred on the deceased. The Mitakshara school was founded by Vijnanesvara, a renowned commentator of Mithila around 900 A.D. Dayabhaga School was known as the reformed school and extolled the position of women. It was written by Jimutavahana, a commentator from Bengal who wrote around the tenth-eleventh century. Since this school came into existence about two centuries later than the Mitakshara school, it tried to improve upon its defects. (Jimutavahana was a minister of King Vishvaksena of Bengal). Jimutavahana liberalized the law in favour of the widow. He did not include the inherited property under *streedhana* because he wanted the widow to be an heir to her husband, even when the latter was a member of the joint family at the time of his death. He undoubtedly took one step further in expansion of widow's rights. He argued that if the family was still a joint family, the husband's death did not terminate the wife's co-ownership in her husband's property. The rationale behind granting property right to the widow is clear from Jimutavahana's assertion:

The husband lives in the body of his wife even after his death. Her act of piety and virtue are equally shared by her husband as long as she lives. If half of the body of her lives in the body of her husband how can others inherit her property?

Thus, the Dayabhaga school repudiated the doctrine that property is by birth right. The right of a widow to become a co-owner and enforce a partition on her own account was realized in several instances in the eighteenth and nineteenth centuries. These showed Hindu widows from Bengal inheriting zamindari estates from their husbands, as a limited interest in the absence of sons, and managing these estates through male agents while themselves remaining in *purdah*.

Big zamindaris like Natore, Burdwan, Mahisdal, Tamluk, Midnapore, Dinajpore, Bishnupur were, at some points of time, under direct supervision of the female landlords. Interestingly, Rammohun Roy had an awareness of the far-reaching changes taking place in Bengal economy due to rise in land values and of prices in general. Probably this had prompted him to campaign for the freedom to own and dispose of property. He also championed the implementation of laws of the Dayabhaga school of inheritance and rights of females to property. However, it was mostly in elite families that widows could make use of these provisions. In middle class upper caste families, the widows remained in oblivion.

These developments revealed a situation in Bengal where joint families frequently exhibited instances of female members holding a position in all respects equal to that of males. Although her power of alienation was of a qualified character, yet so long as she lived, hardly any distinction could be made between such a female member and her male coparceners. Right from the origins of the Dayabhaga doctrine in the tenth–eleventh centuries, the situation in Bengal for widows was better than in other parts of India. However, with the passage of time, gradual erosion of women's rights was taking place. In the sixteenth century, Raghunandan had made modifications in women's property rights within the Dayabhaga school, causing considerable damage in the progressive situation of property rights for women. In the eighteenth century, the Krishnagar Raj of Bengal had spearheaded the implementation of tighter norms of austere widowhood, which had repercussions in the tightening of norms at all levels. The traditional literature of *Dharmashastras/Smritis* was used in the appropriation of tradition for the legitimization of colonial rule. The early East India Company officials were not comfortable with the scriptural sanction accorded to women's rights and its realization for many reasons. They had no direct access to the female proprietors. There were fears that their revenue might decrease due to quarrels between the female proprietors and their male family members. Accordingly, the codification and translation of the traditional literature to fulfil the administrative needs of the colonial ideologues began. By the middle of the eighteenth century, the work of codification and compilation was complete. At the beginning of the nineteenth century, legal changes were proposed which would affect the conjugal order. Along with other changes, there were new laws on *sati* and widow remarriage. The issue of *sati* and the debate over widow remarriage created schisms among the Hindu orthodoxy. The adoption of the new Dayabhaga norms, which were harsh on women, was another area causing cleavages in Hindu society. Upper caste practices and Brahmanical norms were influencing the upwardly mobile agricultural, artisan and trading castes.

The Widow Remarriage Act in 1856 was stewarded by the social reformer Iswar Chandra Vidyasagar, who used the sacred texts to provide legal sanction to widow remarriage. However, it made the widow, upon remarriage, forfeit her share in her deceased husband's estate. The Brahmin pandits and British judges connived to introduce some clauses in the Act which checked the right to maintenance and inheritance from the husband's property and granted the guardianship of children to the relations of the deceased husband.

The Hindu Women's Right to Property Act of 1937 extended the Dayabhaga principle to the whole of British India and invested the widow with the right to inherit her husband's share in the family property. This was irrespective of the consideration as to whether he had effected a separation from the joint family or not. The Hindu Women's Right to Separate Residence and Maintenance Act, 1946, and the Bigamy Prevention Act gave a wife a right to separate residence under certain circumstances. It also prevented the husband from taking a second wife without a formal dissolution of the first marriage. These Acts were consolidated and amended by the Hindu Succession Act. The Hindu Succession Act, 1956, gave full ownership in the property inherited or acquired by a woman to her. The widow, mother and the daughter do not only inherit property along with the son, but also take an equal share with him. However, it considered the location of women as being in the marital family and not the natal family. The doctrines in force earlier in Hindu society – the Mitakshara and the Dayabhaga, were only practised by the upper castes. The introduction of common laws for all groups was deleterious to the lives of the lower castes. The common laws reflected a hardening of gender norms for women in these groups.

The development and popularization of Vrindavan by Chaitanyadeva's followers began at the end of the sixteenth century. The movement of widows from Bengal to the Vaishnava centre of Vrindavan, however, began in the late nineteenth century. Two major factors accounted for the time lag between this turn of events. These were the gradual deterioration in the progressive property laws for women from the sixteenth century onwards and the extreme marginalization of widows in Bengal in the nineteenth century.

The Bengali widows in Vrindavan of the past belonged to two categories – widows from wealthy families and a small number of destitute widows. For the first group of widows, financial provisions were made for these women by their families. The sound financial status of these widows from Bengal in earlier times accounted for the fact of the residents of Vrindavan holding them in high esteem. A reflection of this situation is obtained from the structure of property holdings in Vrindavan until a few decades back. There are many temples here that were built by the aristocracy of Bengal and other parts of eastern India. They also funded *ashrams*. The second group of widows, destitute, ostensibly came to experience the intense love and yearning that Radha had for Krishna, though economic conditions at home may also have dictated the course of their actions. The widows who had limited means were attached to such *ashrams*. They would perform all the daily tasks necessary for the smooth functioning of the *ashram* or temple to pay for their upkeep. To cope with their daily needs they served at temples. With changes in the finances of the aristocracy, funds for the upkeep of these temples came down to a trickle. Consequently, for some establishments, changes in ownership had already taken place. For others, such changes are bound to occur soon. Newer temples and *ashrams* received funds from patrons of Rajasthan and Gujarat. The respect and veneration for the Bengali property owners now no longer existed. Widows from Bengal are now not held in high regard. Their poor pecuniary circumstances and the manner in which they conducted themselves was also responsible for that state of affairs. A lot of bickering and bitterness crusted within the walls of their cramped rooms. Nonetheless, it offered a refuge; so much so, when someone chose to go back home for a visit she brought back other destitute widows known to her.

It emerges that the degree of marginality, leading to social exclusion, forced upon the Bengali widow, was markedly different for different castes. As the adherence to the *Dharmashastra* tradition was generally restricted to the upper castes, the gradual deterioration in property rights of women within the Dayabhaga school of the *Dharmashastra* tradition would only marginally affect women of the lower castes. Thus, the initial years of deportation to religious centres had an impact only on the upper caste Bengali widow. Moreover, for the lower caste and lower class, there was less compulsion and more freedom of choice in the movement to Vrindavan.

The frequent natural and man-made calamities that West Bengal has suffered from have created a large floating population. Frequent floods, villages on river banks eaten up by erosion, and the large migrant population from Bangladesh – these pose perpetual problems for some parts of the state. However, it should be realized that all Bengali speaking women in Vrindavan are not from Bengal – the post-Partition period saw dispersal of the Bengali speaking population over a wide geographical area – Assam, Tripura, Orissa, Manipur, UP, and parts of central India. The continuing influx of migrants from Bangladesh, some of whom turn up in Vrindavan, create an erroneous picture of the situation in Bengal. Many of them, in their need to hide their status as illegal migrants, give their place of origin within West Bengal.

The Bengali widows of Vrindavan have received much media attention in recent years, though many of these are based on inaccurate and incomplete reports. The Report of Survey on Bengali Women in Brindaban 2000, commissioned by the Department of Social Welfare, West Bengal Government, brings to light a more complete picture of the situation. The aims and objective of the survey were as follows:

- to determine with a reasonable degree of accuracy the number of destitute Bengali women in Vrindavan and its surrounding areas
- to explore the reasons that precipitated the influx to the area
- to find out to what extent the influx still continues
- to make an assessment of the present socio-economic status of such women, to propose measures which can bring them relief in their distress

This report highlighted the need to investigate the influx of young girls brought from West Bengal and other states by middlemen active in trafficking in Vrindavan. The large number of thriving abortion centres in Mathura speaks of the sexual exploitation of these women. Many young girls may have been lured into coming to the temple town. Is this victimization partially aided and abetted by family members? The Report has also commented about the exaggeration in the figures of the numerical strength of Bengali women in Vrindavan present in most writings on the topic. It has, however, recognized the vulnerable position of Bengali women in Vrindavan and has recommended measures to ease their situation.

The Situation Today

What is the situation for Bengali widows in Vrindavan today? Vrindavan has more than 1000 temples. Additionally, every home has *apuja* room or temple where idols of the child Krishna or Radha and Krishna are adorned. Countless *dharamshalas,* guesthouses, and *ashrams* are found all over the town. The *Bhajan ashram,* an institution of some novelty, is of not much antiquity in Vrindavan. The first *bhajan ashram* reportedly came up about a century ago through the donations of Seth Janaki Das Patodia. Over time, these institutions became increasingly popular and today there are numerous *bhajan ashrams* all over the town. The donors and their trusts hope to gather spiritual merit by funding these establishments.

How do these *bhajan ashrams* function? Homeless women, mainly widows, seeking spiritual solace and sustenance are housed in these places. Chanting of Radha-Krishna's name goes on all through the day, specific shifts being allotted to separate groups of women. The women are provided with some rations and money for chanting in each shift. These *bhajan ashrams* provide an outlet for the devotion of the women in search of divine bliss. The presence of a large number of women in similar straitened circumstances should logically create a sense of comraderie within them. Such bonds did not come to the fore. The women have to rush about from their lodgings and maintain a rigorous routine to keep to their schedule of chanting. If they miss out, they do not get the rations specified for the shift. Some religious organizations donate blankets and other items at the end of each shift. The linking of daily rations to their physical presence at each three hourly shift can create problems for the widows, many of them in frail health. The daily ration given to each widow for participating in religious chants every morning in the *bhajan ashrams* is about 250 gms of rice and 100 gms of *dal*. A sum of ₹ 2–3 is given for participation in chanting every evening. This rate was the same in most parts of Vrindavan, though some informants noted that in the section of Vrindavan called Raman Reti the wages' were higher. The *bhajan ashrams* that gave higher wages' allowed only younger widows to take part in the chanting. Here only young group of widows were allowed, supposedly to ensure harmonious chanting with greater involvement. Whether these establishments act as dens for the sexual exploitation of the young widows is a question that remains unanswered. *The Report of Survey on Bengali Women in Brindahan 2000* recommended that, as the *bhajan ashrams* are the main beneficiaries of the labour of the inmates, they should be approached for financial contributions to relief schemes for shelter, medical help, etc.

The impression gathered from conversations with inmates of different *ashrams* was that some districts of West Bengal are over-represented in the numbers they send to Vrindavan. The number of inmates from Murshidabad and North 24-Parganas is reportedly very high. Further studies can ascertain the over-representation of some districts as the place of origin of the inmates of *ashrams* and find reasons for the same. Many widows are from economically weak backgrounds. According to the NSS: 50th Round (July 1993 to June 1994) calorie intake per person in West Bengal, which was below the national average in 1972–73, moved to a position above the national average in 1993–94. These reports show that the decline in the proportion of the rural population under the poverty line between 1977–78 and 1993–94 was the highest in West Bengal. It is probable that detailed macro surveys will bring these shifts into focus. It is logical to expect a substantial decrease in the numbers of widows who are from West Bengal as a result of the improvement in the nutritional status.

It is customary in Bengal (and in most parts of India) for a widowed mother with limited means to divide her time by alternating her stay with each son. Thus, for widows with more than one offspring, a home could be provided by the other offspring(s) in cases of default by one son. It is difficult to ascertain the extent of intergenerational support available to the widows. In economically challenged situations, such support often breaks down and reduces the willingness of children to provide support. The welfare of the older generation is partially dependent upon the economic position of the households in which they live. The rapid pace of social change puts a lot of strain on intra-family relationships and relegates many widows to a marginal role.

Besides the economic safety net, for what other reasons does Vrindavan continue to draw countless women year after year? The pilgrim route from Vrindavan to Bengal developed before the British rule. The connection continues to be a thriving one even today. The experience of Vrindavan is positive for those who find kindred souls and experience a measure of peace in their surroundings. Many Bengali widows who are in Vrindavan have tumultuous past-years in refugee camps, children trying to eke a living in new surroundings and the lack of intergenerational support that economic deprivation brings. Such widows are in a state of ambivalence – the pain and exclusion from the kin network is coupled with a 'corresponding heightening of the self. The agonies and anxieties of the past are balanced and a new identity comes to the fore. The orthodox ideal for Hindu widows – that of leading a chaste, ascetic and austere life is only possible for a dependent widow. With countless instances of maltreatment, psychological and financial abuse by family members, Vrindavan becomes a survival strategy for the impoverished widow. The life of piety within the Vaishnava world becomes an answer to the erosion of kin support, breakdown of intergenerational links and the lack of social security measures.

Social Profile of Vrindavan

Vanam Vrindavanam Naam Pashvayam Navkananam Gopgopigavam Sevyam Punyaditraunvirudham Srimadbhagwat (10/11/28). In ancient times, as mentioned in the *Srimadbhagwat* and in the writings of poet Kalidas, Vrindavan, located on the banks of river Yamuna, was a place of green woods and rolling meadows. It was home to Lord Krishna where he is said to have herded his cows, danced with the *gopis,* fought the evil Kansa and fallen in love with Radha. The ancient name of the city, 'Brindaban,' had been named after its ancient groves of 'Brinda,' *Ocimum tenuiflorum,* or Tulsi, with *ban* meaning a grove or a forest. Two small groves still exist, Nidhivan and Seva Kunj. It lies in the Braj region. It is about 15km away from Mathura city, the birthplace of Lord Krishna and in recent times the hub of Mathura district administration. While in the past Vrindavan was considered the most beautiful of forests in the whole of India (Kalidas) in the last 250 years it has mushroomed into a concrete jungle filled with hundreds of temples, ashrams and apartments catering to an ever increasing flow of tourists and *moksh* seekers. The roads and by-lanes choke with modern day traffic and a milieu of people from different parts of India and the rest of the world. The Radha-Krishna legend continues to be the main source of livelihood for its people and most of the income generation activities in the city depend on the functioning of its over 5,000 temples and ashrams. Vaishnavism is the main tradition followed in Vrindavan.

Nidhi means 'the place where invaluable gems are found'. This is a small grove of Tulsi. Radha and Krishna are said to have taken rest here, after dancing and other conjugal affairs. There is a small temple here known as the 'sleeping temple'. The samadhi of the guru of Tansen, is located on site. Renowned musicians of India take part in Swami Haridas Sammelan, an annual event in honour of Swami Haridas. The Seva Kunj marks the place where Lord Krishna once performed the Raaslila with Radha-Rani and the *gopis*.

Brajbhoomi – the land where Lord Krishna was born and spent his youth – has today little towns and hamlets that are still alive with the Krishna – legend. The city of Mathura, in Uttar Pradesh, the nucleus of Brajbhoomi, is located at a distances of 145 km south-east of Delhi and 58 km north-west of Agra. Covering an area of about 3,800 sq km today, Brajbhoomi can be divided into two distinct units – the eastern part in the trans-Yamuna tract with places like Gokul, Mahavan, Baldeo, Mat and Bajna and the western side of the Yamuna covering the Mathura region that encompasses Vrindavan, Govardhan, Kusum Sarovar, Barsana and Nandgaon. The land of Braj starts from Kotban near

Hodel about 95 km from Delhi and ends at Runakta which is known especially for its association with the great poet Surdas, an ardent Krishna devotee. The town included hundreds of temples dedicated to the worship of Radha and Krishna and is considered sacred by a number of religious traditions such as Gaudiya Vaishnavism, Vaishnavism and Hinduism in general. According to the locals and the administration, a survey of the place in 2000–01 revealed that there were more than 5,000 temples and ashrams in the city.

Situated on the bank of river Yamuna, Vrindavan is a heritage and tourist place in the state of Uttar Pradesh, India. It is located at a distance of 145 km south of the national capital Delhi and is accessible by road (National Highway No. 2). The nearest railway station is at Mathura located at a distance of 14 km. Built during the sixteenth and seventeenth centuries, there are more than 5,500 temples mainly devoted to life and deeds of lord Krishna and Radha Rani, his consort. In addition to temples, Vrindavan has *samadhis* (places where ashes of famous religious persons are kept), *ghats* (stepped bathing places along the river), *kunjas* (gardens), *kundas* (man-made water tanks) and institutions of religious and cultural education. There is a 10-km-long circular pathway surrounding the town called *Parikrama Marg* where, on specific days such as *Ekadasi,* the 11th day of the waxing and waning of moon, devotees, bare-footed in many cases, perform the ritual of walking and completing the *Parikrama.*

The area of the town is 4.56 sq km and as per 2001 Census of India, it has a population of 56,692. The daily inflow of pilgrims and tourists is about 10,000 and on the birthday of the lord Krishna, it reaches to its peak with one million visitors. It is said that in the year 2003, some 3.31 million devotees and 16,000 international tourists visited Vrindavan. A technical assessment report, under the *Eco-City Project of Government of India, for the city of Vrindavan* draws a fair picture of the city in its modern avatar. According to this report:

- Most of the land in the town is owned by the temple trusts and is not generally available for other uses. The town is congested (density 15,000 persons per sq km) and people suffer from lack of light and ventilation in buildings.
- The water of Yamuna River is contaminated due to lack of flow in river as a result of storage of water up-stream in the states of Haryana and Delhi. Discharge of industrial effluent and untreated sewage adds to the river water pollution. River front is neglected as the river course has shifted away from the bathing *ghats* and the land between the *ghats* and river course is heavily polluted by solid waste scattered all over or stagnant and stinking pools of water.
- A large number of 300 to 400 year old temples, built with good quality red sand stone with rich architectural style, are dilapidated and require conservation.
- Roads are narrow (3m. to 9m.) with buildings on both sides. There are no footpaths.
- Traffic is mixed and carts driven by animals (camel, horse, or bullock), cycle rickshaw, cycles, automobiles and pedestrians compete for the same road space. As a part of the 10th Five Year Plan, the Central Pollution

Control Board (CPCB) initiated the Eco-city Project, in 2002, with grant-in-aid from the Ministry of Environment and Forest (MoEF), Government of India. The German Technical Cooperation (GTZ), under its Indo German Programme on Advisory Services for Environmental Management (ASEM), extended the technical support to the project.

- Roads leading to temple entrances normally have commercial activities on either side that reduce their capacity and add further to the traffic congestion.
- Storm water drains are open and carry sewage, plastic bags and other solid wastes dumped carelessly by the people, which block them at places.

About 3000 destitute women are living in Vrindavan. Most of the destitute women, including widows, live in ashrams and homes run by government agencies and trusts. During the field survey, these women were met at the homes run by government authorities and NGOs, at their rented accommodations, at *bhajan ashrams* and in other public places such as *ghats* and temples. Their stories are presented in the form of statistical output and case studies. In addition to the direct interviews information was collected on all the women living in homes run by the government and NGOs. According to a letter by the DM of Mathura to NCW dated 17.12.09, there are six ashray sadan/short stay homes for women in Vrindavan. Two of these are run under the centrally sponsored scheme called Swadhar Yojna; two under the Meera Sehbhagini Yojna of the Government of Uttar Pradesh and two are run by AIWC and Guild of Services, respectively. The destitute women of Vrindavan, on the whole, are dependent on the state, the *bhajan ashrams and* the pilgrims that come to the town of Vrindavan. The *bhajan ashrams* are the single most important entity in their lives and are the only places where an outsider can get a quick glimpse into their lives. For the study team, the Bhagwan bhajan ashram at Patharpura and the Balaji bhajan ashram at Ramanreti were the focal point for meeting with women and following their lives. The state provides the women with shelter, pension, ration and at times health care in the form of camps, distribution of wheel chairs and spectacles. The pilgrims provide the women with cash (as alms), food, clothes, blankets, woollens and other items of need.

The socio-cultural profile of Varanasi and Vrindavan presents interesting scenario. Varanasi has been abode of Lord Shiva and thus, it is the place of Shaiv sect while Mathura and Vrindavan being the place of Lord Krishna is known for Vaishnav sect. A large number of widows from neighbouring states like West Bengal, Madhya Pradesh, Rajasthan, Odisha, Gujarat, Maharashtra and other places migrated to these two religious places to settle their life as both the places are known for *moksha* – the liberation from birth and death. Vrindavan – Mathura have comparatively larger concentration of widows and destitute women; however, their life in the city is worse.

4

Research Methodology

Women constitute about half of the population of country, however, they face disparities, inequalities, exploitation and abuse which are adversely affecting their health, nutrition, educational attainment, skills, occupational status, etc. There are a number of gender specific barriers which prevent women from gaining access to their rightful share in the flow of public goods and services. These barriers have roots in prevailing socio-cultural value system, institutional set-up and societal structure. Unless these barriers are removed and the felt needs of women are incorporated in the planning and development process, the fruits of economic growth are likely to bypass a large segment of human resources of the country. India being a democratic country cannot afford development without considering women as they are the prime mover of economy besides their significant contribution in the economy. Eliminating gender discrimination and empowering women are among the paramount challenges facing the world today. Despite the international community's commitment to gender equality, the lives of millions of women and girls throughout the world are affected by discrimination, disempowerment and poverty. Gender equality is central to realizing the Millennium Development Goals. Eliminating gender discrimination and empowering women will require enhancing women's influence in the key decisions that shape their lives.

The present study deals mainly with the various problems faced by widows in traditional Hindu society, as well as the socio-economic and demographic implications of widowhood. From a sociological point of view widowhood may be perceived as a change in the status of women caused by the dissolution of marriage and which necessitates the establishment of new ties within the family, with the kin group and the community. The importance of the study of widowhood lies in the fact that the death of one's spouse precipitates a period of crisis. It is also a traumatic experience for almost everyone within the family unit. It brings about a number of economic and social consequences both for the members of the immediate family and the community. The consequences are apt to be more serious in case of death among middle-aged spouses, who leaves a wife and young children as dependents. The most affected persons in our traditional society are young widows. The death of the husband has a serious consequence on the widow.

Apart from the severe emotional stress of coping with the loss of a husband, it often means the widow has to undertake the problems of looking after the socio-economic needs of the family. The problem becomes more acute in the case of young illiterate widows. In such cases, a woman who is herself dependent, is suddenly faced with the task of mustering resources to look after her children who now look to her for everything.

Women generally occupy a secondary position in most societies and do not enjoy socio-religious or political life. Even today, in spite of changes as those granted to married women, they are deprived of the necessities which every human being has a right to enjoy. Consequently, social norms and taboos consign the unfortunate widows to an even more disadvantaged position. They are considered a bad omen and inauspicious and thereby restricted in their socio-religious functions. Widows who are young, poor and uneducated face even more problems. Thus, when the position of widows is deplorable, the condition of Hindu widows who are governed by the age old oppressive and rigid customs is, indeed, lamentable. The position of Hindu widow is miserable and her lot is unenviable. The present study is concerned with various religion widows, living in the urban and rural areas of Vrindavan and Varanasi district.

The main focus of the study is on the problems faced by widows, the factors responsible for her predicament and the manner in which they attempt to overcome them. The major interest of the present study is to investigate the circumstances under which widows face deprivation. This study also tries to find out the consequences caused by various kinds of deprivation to the widow herself, her family and to society in general. This study of widowhood provides us not only with the adequate understanding of the magnitude of the problems and its prospects in future, but also deals with the various ramifications and implications of widowhood and the state of deprivation faced by them. So far most of the studies undertaken have examined only the socio-economic aspect of the problem. Hence, this study makes an attempt to understand the sociological implications of widowhood, particularly the deprivation faced by a widow in the economic, social psychological and cultural spheres.

The Problem

The position of a widow in society is a crucial topic which sociologists have does discuss and elucidate. The treatment which she receives is often an index to the attitudes of society towards women as a class. What is the general lot of widows? What are the problems faced by them? What are the changes in their lifestyles? Can she marry again if she so desires? Did her husband leave any property so that she could lead an honourable and independent life after his death? These are the main questions which we have to explore in connection with the position of widows. The tragic alienation of a widow today is casually related to continued loss of her status and dignity in the remote past.

From available literature on widowhood, one finds that several factors are responsible for the deprived position of widows. There is no uniform pattern of widowhood either in terms of conditions leading to such a phenomenon or in terms of the consequences pattern. There is also no uniform lifestyle for widows.

The lifestyles vary not only according to the location in the social system, be it an upper class area or a middle-class area, or the slum, urban or rural areas, but also by their own combination of characteristics. Patterns emerge when such factors as educational level of the women are compared to their social life and space. So it emerges that the more educated and trained widows are able to enter into and maintain more social roles and social relations. On the other hand, poor, uneducated, ignorant and illiterate widows face difficulties in entering and maintaining social roles and social relations.

Some of the questions which the writer has tried to take up for investigation are as follows: Are there any changes in the socio-economic conditions of women after widowhood? What are the problems faced by them? What are the factors that may be considered as responsible for their low social status? The types of treatment they received before and after widowhood? Are there any differences in the lifestyle of widow of both rural and urban areas/what are their life, remarriage of widows, future plans, for themselves and their children? Suggestions for the welfare of the widow were also sought.

The sample widows are drawn from diverse social backgrounds. Hence, the views of widows about their status and roles differ. Socio-economic background size of the family, value system of every caste, are important factors that decide the nature for the problems, which widows have to face in their life, which also may explain the diverse ways of life of widows. The present investigation considers the differences in the background characteristics of widows of both rural and urban areas as well as the difference in the nature of socio-emotional support and caste value system, in order to understand how far such differences contribute to the state of deprivation and the problems of adjustments of widows.

Scope of the Study

The problem of widowhood has elicited considerable interest in the minds of researchers in recent times. Widowhood is a complex transition, with various possible consequences, both subjective and objective. In the Indian context the problems assumes considerable importance, as the age difference between husband and wife is higher, widow remarriage is highly restricted. The influence of widowhood on fertility is higher than in modern societies An increasing trend towards the small family norm, nuclearization of families and continuous erosion of family, kinship ties even in rural areas of our society, seems to have a bearing on the problems of widowhood. It has been rightly said that widowhood is a combination of the problems of the woman and the widow. Hence, in order to understand the complex phenomenon of widowhood, a systematic study of the various problems faced by widows, the causes, the consequences and the effects on the personality of widows, the difficulties in adopting to widowhood and how they manage to overcome the problems, becomes essential.

There is a growing research literature on widowhood. Most of it is concerned with the explanation of psychological and emotional adaptations to bereavement and the socio-economic conditions of widows. Hence, the present study, which is an attempt to find out the causes and consequences of economic, social, psychological and cultural deprivation, assumes importance. The present study work is confined to the study of 732 widows belonging to Vrindavan and Varanasi districts. The field of investigation was restricted to the above mentioned areas, because of the limited resources and time available.

Most of the widows included in the study are from widow homes/ashrams established for rehabilitation of destitute and widow women. The study is focusing on profiling and rehabilitation of widow women living in religious places. Most of the women covered in the study are from Hindu communities. Though the study is confined to only two religious cities of Varanasi and Vrindavan, it provides in-depth analysis pertaining to socio-cultural and economic background of widows and their social conditions besides their participation in development programmes and schemes. The study has also attempted to review the problems of widows and their social conditions at the national level besides the analysis of the efforts made by government and non-government organizations for social reforms, welfare and rehabilitation of widows in India. It is expected that the study will be of immense importance for the policymakers, administrators and development professionals working in the field of welfare and rehabilitation of destitute women.

Objectives of the Study

The present study takes into account various problems faced by widows, causes and consequences and efforts made by them to overcome the problems. This study also takes into cognizance the opinion, attitudes of widows towards status of Hindu widows, factors that improve their status and remarriage of widows. Hence, it pertains to the analysis of relationships between background factors and the problems and the differences between the rural and urban area and between the upper, the intermediate and lower castes.

The following are some of the major aims of the present study:

- To study the changes brought about by widowhood in the socio-economic conditions of widows
- To ascertain the socio-economic background of the deceased husbands of the widows
- To ascertain the difficulties faced by widows in upbringing their children and their reasons responsible for the same
- To assess the extent of deprivation faced in terms of economic, social, psychological and cultural and the manner in which they manage to overcome them
- To elicit, their opinion towards widow remarriage, their future plans regarding themselves and their children and their suggestions for the welfare of widows
- To extract, their perception towards social activist, NGO's and other social welfare agencies working for their welfare and rehabilitations

Methods and Procedures

As mentioned earlier, the present study is an attempt to explain the state of deprivation faced by widows in the fields like economic, social psychological and cultural, the problems of adjustment of widows and the factors which have an impact on the life of widows. The requisite data is obtained through the interview method with the help of a structured interviews schedule. The interview method is considered as the basic field techniques through which the widows were approached and the responses received from them were recorded in the field itself.

The Interview

In the sociological investigations, the interview is accepted as a reliable field technique for the collection of data. The present investigation is based on the primary data, consisting of the responses received from the respondents to the schedule, collected through the personal interview method. A prior appointment with the respondents was taken. The interviews were conducted at their ashram as their convenience. The normal duration of an interview was about 80 to 90 minutes. Questions were asked by the researcher in Hindi language only and the relevant response was recorded in the schedule. Information regarding the various aspects of widow's life was also collected through discussion and observation, because a majority of them were illiterates. Most of the respondents willingly agreed to spend some of their time to answer the questions and participate in the discussions. Most of them were fully cooperative. The researcher used to listen patiently to every kind of experience, either happy or unhappy, which the widows narrated while the interview was conducted. A rapport was first established with the respondents so that they could believe that the researcher was there not only to ask questions but also to share some of their personal experiences. By and large, this procedure was effective and useful both in rural and urban areas. However, it was noticed that rural widows were freer and open minded in providing information than urban widows.

The Instrument

A pre-coded structured schedule was used as the principal instrument for the collection of data. A tentatively prepared schedule was presented in a non-sample area as a pilot study to locate the ambiguity and redundancy of questions included therein. The final schedule was drawn after making necessary corrections, with the help of which each of the respondents was interviewed in the absence of other members of their family. The interview schedule is prepared in such a way as to obtain the relevant information broadly under the following sections:

Background Characteristics of the Widows

Information is obtained regarding the socio-economic characteristics of the widow, both before and after widowhood, their caste and community affiliations, type of family to which they belonged to and the size of the family, number of members in the family, income enjoyed, reactions towards marital life, etc.

Particulars of Deceased Husbands and Children

Under this head, relevant information is obtained as regards the age of the deceased husband, their educational level, occupation, income, cause of death, nature of treatment received, reasons for not receiving treatment if valid, property left by them. In the case of children, information is obtained regarding their age, educational level, occupation, income, reasons for the discontinuation of their education if valid, persons whom they consult for advice, problems faced by the widows in bringing them up.

Deprivation Faced by the Widows

Under this head, relevant questions are included that try to ascertain from the respondents, the amount of deprivation faced by widows in social, psychological and cultural fields, the problems of adjustment of widows and the manner in which they manage to overcome them. Questions are also included to ascertain whether there are any changes in the visits of kinsmen of both sides, friends of the widows and vice versa and leisure time activities.

Attitudes and Orientation

Under this head, relevant questions are included to ascertain the respondent's orientations and attitudes toward death and widowhood, the status of widow in Hindu society, the remarriage of widows. The questions also included certain number of brief statements, the responses to which could be either in the affirmative or negative. These items mainly included either favourable or unfavourable attitudes towards marriage, and status of widows.

Future Plans and Suggestions

Under this head, questions are included to ascertain information from the respondents about their future plans regarding themselves and their children and suggestion for the state and others to work for the welfare of the widows.

Pilot Study

A pilot study was conducted before the main interview schedule was finalized in order to ensure the suitability of the questions and the sample. This study included the interview of 50 widows, 25 each from Vrindavan and Varanasi, who belonged to different religions, castes and social class. This study was carried out in Vrindavan and Varanasi cities. The sample of widows selected from both the cities varied in caste, age and income. A draft of interview schedule, which comprised structured answers, was used for the purpose of the pilot study. The pilot study helped the researcher to add a few more direct questions and responses so as to meet the objectives of the study. The responses were given codes and scores so as to make the analysis easy.

Sampling Procedure

The present study is confined to the study of 732 widows who are the inhabitants of Vrindavan and Varanasi districts. The 2011 Census of India was used to determine which wards were to be sampled and which streets constituted a given area. Next, a list of households in which widows lived was made by using the snow-ball techniques, which served as the source of the sample. Two-way stratified simple random sampling method was used for the selection of widows. Since the name and addresses of widows are not maintained either by the census or local authorities as the case may be, the researcher found it difficult to trace the widows for the purpose of the study. However, with the given objectives of the study, namely the impact of deprivation, it was decided to select a sample in such a way as to ensure adequate representation of various variables like caste, age, income, area, and education, the respondents were selected based on the following criteria:

- Respondents should be widow
- Respondents be living in either ashram or other than home

To identify the widows in the respective localities the help of leaders of different agencies/associations like Mahila Mandals, NGOs and other prominent local persons was sought. The purpose of the study was thoroughly explained to them and cooperation from their end was sought. Personal visits were made to every household to collect the basic information, and recorded on a separate paper. Only from those families where widows were present, further detailed information was collected on the pre-coded structured schedules by interview method. The same sampling procedure was used in both the areas.

It is presumed that caste, age, income and locality are some of the social characteristics which have influenced the deprivation faced. Besides, background variables like occupation, income and property left by the deceased husbands also affected the deprivation level/process. It is also considered that attitudes of the respondents are also possible variables affecting deprivation level and adjustment process.

Hypothesis

The following hypotheses are framed in order to test them in the light of the findings of the present study.

- The income of the husbands has an influence on the widow's level of economic deprivation
- Absence of father influences the children's behaviour
- Caste has influence on the level of cultural deprivation of widows
- There is a significant difference in the social deprivation level of rural and urban widows
- Husband's age at death has influence on the economic deprivation of widows
- There is a significant difference in the emotional deprivation of rural and urban widows

5

Social Reform Movements

The nineteenth century is considered as the most eventful period in the history of women's struggle for the rights of equality and freedom. During this period, the advent of western liberalism and English education made enlightened Indians conscious about the deplorable condition of society. They were particularly concerned about the miserable plight of women particularly young widows, 'sati pratha', polygamy, etc. They expressed necessity of reforms to eradicate social evils which had afflicted the society. It was the great social reformer Raja Ram Mohun Roy who appeared on the scene and provided leadership to the educated elite. He was instrumental in forming popular opinion against social evils and resolved to help women to secure rightful place in the society. The new reformists concentrated on social upliftment of Indian women through the abolition of pernicious customs of sati and child marriage and enforcement of widow remarriage. They also advocated female education. Many enlightened Muslim rulers tried their best to prohibit the practice of 'sati' but without any tangible results. The Sikhs and the Marathas prohibited the practice within their territories. The British Government, however, showed indifference in the existing laws of both the Hindus and Muslims. But the government could not remain aloof and it was Raja Ram Mohun Roy who triggered off the official reform. The then Government of British India considered the question of abolition of Sati in 1823, in the face of stiff opposition from the Hindu orthodoxy. Roy took the lead in organizing counter propaganda through the press. He submitted a counter petition to the government which condemned the rite of 'sati' as 'murders according to every *shastra* as well as common sense of all nations.'

Raja Ram Mohun Roy's most effective weapon was his intelligent use of the press and his power to argue and win over his adversaries. He wrote tracts in Bengali and his journal 'Sambad – Kaumudi' became the main vehicle of his campaign against 'sati'. In this respect he was violently opposed by the orthodox Hindus led by Raja Radhakanta Deb. He knew that the campaign against 'sati' was going to be a hard and long struggle and all he hoped to achieve was to give the widest possible publicity to this terrible social evil; to focus attention by promoting open discussion and even controversy and thus gradually mobilize public opinion in favour of practical measures against it.

Roy's anti-sati campaign was aimed at awakening the conscience of his own community. He directly organized public opinion against this barbaric social custom and ultimately the government took decision for its abolition through legislation. The campaign against the practice of 'sati' created problem of amelioration of their pitiable condition. In his 'brief Remarks Regarding Modern Encroachments on the Ancient Rights of Females according to the Hindu Law of Inheritance', Roy condemned the practice and defended the fundamental rights of women. He remarked '... in a country where the name of death makes the male shudder, the female from her firmness of mind offers to burn with the corpse of the deceased husband'. He lamented, 'seeing the women thus dependent and exposed to every misery, you feel for them no compassion, that might exempt them from being tied down and burnt to death'. With his powerful writings, he argued in favour of women's liberation from all social injustice. In his life-long battle for the betterment of women's lot, Roy upheld the theory of glorified motherhood, instead of degraded womanhood.

Increasing contact with the western liberalism, growing social consciousness among masses and numerous reform societies, discussion groups and literary activities of mid-century Bengal heralded another crusade in favour of 'widow-remarriage'. The chief promoter of this reform movement was Pandit Ishwar Chandra Vidyasagar. In 1837, while the Calcutta press took up the cause of the widows, an agitation started for this reform in Bombay also. In Calcutta Nilakanta Bandhopadhyaya and a few other gentlemen made futile attempts to introduce widow-remarriage. It was due to the earnest efforts of Ishwarchandra Vidyasagar that the question became a historic and dynamic social issue. He devoted himself with indomitable courage to further the cause of widow remarriage in the teeth of violent opposition from the orthodoxy. In 1851, he tried to prove through his writings and speeches that remarriage of widows was sanctioned by the *shastras* and advocated abolition of polygamy.

His main supporter was the Maharaja of Burdwan. His campaign culminated in the publication of his major work on the subject, 'Marriage of Hindu Widows' in 1856. In order to remove legal bar against widow remarriage, Vidyasagar presented a petition, bearing a large number of signatures, impressing on the Government of India the urgent necessity of enacting legislation. Finally, Act XV of 1856 was passed legalizing marriage of widows. The passage of the legislation on widow remarriage added a new chapter to nineteenth century's struggle for modernization and liberalism. However, it inspired educated persons to think about the position of women in the society yet nothing tangible resulted from it. Deep-rooted social customs and caste system, staunch orthodox reaction and lack of proper reformist zeal after the death of Vidyasagar limited the scope of widow remarriage. In western and northern India, this movement became quite popular due to the vigorous support of Vishnu Shastri Pandit with the active backing of reformers like Ranade, Telang and Gopal Deshmukh. While Vidyasagar had sought government sanction for widow remarriage, Vishnu Shastri Pandit desired the sanction of the highest religious authority with jurisdiction in western India, the Shankaracharya of Karver and Sankeshwar. In Ahmedabad, Gujarati reformers formed a Remarriage Association; in Madras Presidency, Viresalingam Pantulu launched his crusade against enforced widowhood. The Arya Samaj of Dayanand Saraswati also fought for this cause.

The nineteenth century reformists' onslaught was on the practice of polygamy and Kulinism which permitted the Kulin Brahmins to marry an indefinite number of wives. Vidyasagar in his writings severely condemned polygamy. In 1871, his first tract on polygamy was published and the second in 1873. His untiring energy was devoted against the evils of early marriage also. He emphasized that the age limit of sons should be 18. He strongly backed the view that infant marriage was the root cause of sufferings of Indian widows. He, therefore, advocated a minimum age limit on marriage of girls. Vidyasagar is known for his support to the cause of female education. He said that female education had been emphasized even in the past and women played an important part in the scholastic field and that there is nothing 'inherent either in the Hindu or in the Muslim religion which militates against the education of women'. However, education of girls could not make much headway during the nineteenth century due to prejudice and ignorance, practice of child marriage, 'purdah system', lack of girls' schools and women teachers. Apart from the activities of the European missionaries, it was Raja Radhakanta Deb who supported the cause of female education. Though he was the leader of the orthodox Hindus who opposed Vidyasagar's crusade against widow remarriage, yet he personally believed that to make nation progressive women must be educated.

Keshabchandra Sen supported the women's right for better position and earnestly fought for marriage reform. In his lecture delivered to an audience in London, he said, 'The people, both men and women, have fallen into a low state so much so that it is impossible to recognize, in the modern India, the noble soul *of* the Ancient Hindu. You see Brahmans who have more than 70 wives. There is another injurious custom which makes an old man of 80 marry a little girl of five years. Then there is the custom which prevents a Hindu widow from remarrying.' He also voted against the custom of early marriage and pointed to the Hindu scriptures in support of his contention. He wrote, 'Our women have elements of character which are really noble and good and these ought to constitute the basis upon which we should raise the superstructure of reformed female society.' Keshabchandra Sen's greatest achievement in the social sphere was the Marriage Act of 1872. It was a radical step with provisions like prohibition against polygamy; legal allowance for divorce; no reference to the castes of marriage partners and an age limit for marriage of 14 for girls and 18 for men.

During the century, Ramakrishna Paramahansa directly appealed to humanity to sanction a revered position for women. His worship of the Goddess Kali, the mother of 'Shakti', attracted ordinary people as well as the educated elite. He recognized the Mother in all women even in the most degraded. The ideals of Ramakrishna were carried to its logical end by his famous disciple Swami Vivekananda's liberalism. His message inspired many people to advocate social progress for women. He was of the firm view that to make India truly modern, women should be emancipated from their artificial social bondage. Swamiji pointed out, 'as a bird with only one wing cannot fly, similarly, a nation with her women in shackles can make no progress'. But unlike Vidyasagar, Vivekananda was not enthusiastic about the widow remarriage movements.

In northern India, another individualistic movement was launched by the founder of Dayanand Saraswati. He exhorted Indians to participate fully in social endeavours, the object of which was to liberate society from poverty and ignorance. Dayanand was of the opinion that 'women were equal to men in their ability to achieve emancipation and they should be educated and not allowed to marry before they reached 18, later revised to 16'. A staunch Vedantist, Dayanand held that the widows should be allowed to take other husbands and thus fulfil their role as mothers. The Arya Samaj attacked idolatry and various caste rituals, particularly marriage and funeral rites.

Malabari was concerned about the question of early marriage of girls. According to F. Max Muller, Malabari believed, 'though widows were no longer burnt as widows, their life was in many cases worse than death. Owing to the system of very early and what has been truly called child marriages, the number of child widows is, and has been for many years very large in India, and the only means of reducing their number was to prohibit early marriages altogether'.

Malabari in his book *Niti Vinod* portrayed the sorrows of Hindu widows. He appealed to the sentiments of all Indians, not only to the educated elite. Heimsath wrote, 'Malabari did not rely only on considered arguments to support his cases but allowed his pen to flow freely, sometimes into exaggeration painting a graphic picture of social evils which few could ignore. Some action had to follow.' In 1884, Malabari published 'Infant Marriage in India' and 'Enforced Widowhood' which drew attention of a wide section of people and social reformers to glaring social evils prevalent in Hindu society. The ceaseless efforts of Malabari's publicity through his newspaper Indian Spectator and Journal East and West, culminated in the passing of the Age of Consent Bill that raised the Age of Consent from 10 to 12 years. The passage of the Bill was a big step towards the emancipation of women from age old bondage. John Stuart Mill was perhaps the only thinker who applied the principles of liberty and equality to women. In 'The Subjection of Women' in 1869 he protested against the discrimination of women.

The women in India have been able to achieve right to equality after a long struggle against orthodoxy, obscurantism and superstitious beliefs. The progressive constitutional provisions and various legislative measures have bestowed on women equal opportunities in political, social, economic and cultural spheres. The Constitution of India contemplates a social revolution brought about through the use of law as an instrument of direct change. The attainment of equality of status for women is implicit in the Preamble, the Fundamental Rights and the Directive Principles of State Policy. The Preamble to the Constitution of India lays down the principles of Justice, Liberty, Equality and Fraternity for all. In India, law is regarded as the basic instrument of bringing about social change with the ultimate goal of the emancipation of women.

Women have suffered due to the heterogenous nature of the Indian society with its structure based on social and economic inequalities. These inequalities are inherent in the traditional Indian social structure. These disabilities of women particularly in the educational and economic spheres have led to halting progress in the role and status of women. Although the constitutional provisions and legislative measures for women are quite progressive, yet these have not made the desired impact on the position and status of women. This is because, on the one hand, we have adopted a democratic, egalitarian and progressive political set-up for the country and, on the other hand, we have a backward-looking traditional social structure. There is a constant and dynamic interaction between traditional social structure and modern political, social and democratic outlook.

Emancipation of women has come only after years of bitter struggle against odds led by scores of eminent social reformers, thinkers and philosophers. As late as the nineteenth century, John Stuart Mill wrote on the 'Subjection of Women'. Even in 1792 when Mary Wollstonecraft published 'A Vindication of the Rights of Women', it was still a far cry. The establishment of the USSR in 1917 opened a new vista for equality of the sexes. In India after the dawn of Independence in 1947, women have made tremendous progress in different walks of life.

Social Conditions and Deprivation of Widows

The problem of deprivation is a complex phenomenon due to socio-cultural and religious dimension. The intensity of deprivation is much due to social taboos and cultural prejudices in a traditional society. Deprivation in the nature of discrimination leads to several social problems. In the present context the term deprivation has been used to denote 'a social setting in which widows are physically, socially, economically and psychologically handicapped to fulfill their bio-social needs'. Deprivation results in a systematic exploitation and dehumanization of widows. The death of a child may be seen as a personal calamity but the death of a husband is seen as altering the social identity of a woman. Widowhood is almost always accompanied by a deep sense of shock due to the sudden, and often unexpected, death of the husband. A woman is stupefied and immobilized with extreme grief. The loss of the husband creates a deep void in her life and she immediately becomes dependent on her children or relatives, often such a wound is healed only by time.

Widowhood marks a transition from a marital to a widowed status which is not smooth, for it means not only a loss of status but also a loss of pride, privileges, prestige and independence within the family. For a man, the loss of spouse is only a personal grief but for a woman it means additionally a difficult adjustment to be made. Many women are unable to cope with such a transition. Thus, the consequences of widowhood to a woman are more hazardous than to a man. Many a time, a widow faces difficulty in adjusting to her new status because the social norms and taboos put her in most disadvantaged position, and restrict her social interactions. She is confronted with a new set of expectations after widowhood. Many studies have pointed out that the death of a husband brings about a stigma, in Hindu society and along with it, severe deprivation of status. Every phase of widowhood is critical, hard, challenging and deranging and brings about severe social, economic, emotional and cultural deprivation.

The cultural deprivation in widowhood pervades all the spheres of a widow's life and there is a drastic change in her lifestyle after widowhood. Widows have to start altogether a different life in food habits, dress, etc. The norms of widowhood are essentially the norms of asceticism in Hindu society. The basic emphasis is on simple, *Sati vie-food*, i.e. pure food which does not produce passions, whereas Muslims and Christians are not forced to lead a life of abstinence and are at liberty to enjoy life. There are no restrictions on food habits, dress and remarriage.

In general, a Hindu widow is deprived of wearing the *tali*, flowers, glass-bangles, nose ring and applying *kumkuma*. However, the life of an orthodox Brahmin widow is most pitiable. According to strict, orthodox rites, a Brahmin widow had to face, much against her will, the horrible and inhuman rite of tonsure. She is also culturally isolated and is made to spend her time in constant devotion to God, a total separation from worldly affairs and pleasures.

Remarriage of Widows

In India, widow remarriage is allowed among some of the lower castes and encouraged especially in rural areas but is in disfavour in all the castes. Census report of 1911 (Mysore) states that, 'The marriage of widows is prohibited only among Brahmins and in a very few other castes. Among the rest such marriages are allowed. In few castes like Besta and Uppar a fine has to be paid for the benefit of the caste people if a man marries a widow'. The negative attitude towards remarriage of widows is so strong that even today, people believe that this practice does not have either social or religious sanction. Katti and Nagesh, in another study in Hubli city and some neighbouring rural areas, point out that 97 per cent of the rural respondents and 92 per cent urban, are not willing to marry again. In order to avoid prejudice against widow remarriage and to introduce it among all the castes, an attempt was made during the eighteenth century by Raja Rajaballabha of Deccan, and by the Chief of Kotab of Rajasthan, to get Shastric sanction in support of widow marriage by Pandits. In the first half of the nineteenth century, the social reformers of Bengal made continuous efforts in that direction and succeeded in abolishing *sati* system and legalizing widow remarriage.

Ishwar Chandra Vidyasagar conducted the first Hindu brahmin widow remarriage in Bengal after the passing of the Widow Remarriage Act on 26 July 1856, in spite of bitter opposition from the orthodox. He emancipated widows, lived for them and even died for them. Babu Sasipada Banurji who had been an advocate of the widow remarriage movement, solemnized the marriage of his widowed niece and rescued her from the hands of her orthodox relative. In the I860s, the widow marriage and rehabilitation movement made maximum progress in Bengal, followed by Bombay. One more reason for the negative attitude towards widow remarriage, as M.N. Srinivas observes is that due to Sanskritic civilization, the non-brahmins wish to rise in the social scale by imitating intolerable, irrational Brahmin customs and ceremonies. The simple tribes like the Soligas, the Korachas and the Dombas present the desire to climb the higher rungs. He further says that among the Devangas and the Nayinda, widow marriage prevailed originally, but now they prohibit it in imitation of the Brahmins. Among some castes, widow marriage is generally allowed, but is not popular among some groups. For example, among Sajjans, widow marriage is generally allowed but is not allowed among Sajjan Kumbaras. While allowing a widow to remarry the other non-brahamin castes except the lowest and primitive tribes look down upon the widow. They feel that widow marriage is not socially approved but it is inevitable as it is better to marry than to burn the widow.

Welfare of Widows

There are various legislations passed both before and after Independence to improve the condition of widows or at least to try to reduce the discriminations against them.

Before Independence:

- Bengal Sati Regulation XVII of 1829
- The Hindu Widow's Re-Marriage Act 1856
- Indian Succession Act 1925
- The Child Marriage Restraint

After Independence:

- Hindu Marriage Act 1955
- Hindu Succession Act 1956
- Hindu Adoption and Maintenance Act 1956

Besides, many resolutions were passed in different sessions by the Indian National Social Conference (INSC) at different stages and periods.

Role of Civil Societies

The government is not in a position to provide the infrastructural facilities to adjust and accommodate the widows by establishing widow homes for their survival. Therefore non-governmental organization have played an important role in taking initiative for their welfare. Sulabh International Social Service Organisation, the largest nationally and internationally recognized pan-India non-profit voluntary social organization, is engaged in promoting the human rights, environmental sanitation, health and hygiene, non-conventional sources of sanitation, waste management and social reforms movement through education, training and campaign. Sulabh has taken an initiative to improve the socio-economic condition of widows of Vrindavan and Varanasi. The founder of SISSO Padmbhushan Dr Bindeshwar Pathak, a social activist and a social reformer, has taken the initiative by establishing widow homes in both the places. The vocational training programmes in different vocations are been organized for providing training by creating production centres and giving financial assistance to each widow for maintenance. This is a unique experiment which has been made by Dr Bindheshwar Pathak which can be followed by other NGOs to solve this problem.

Sulabh Reform Movement

The Sulabh International Social Service Organisation is the only nationally and internationally acclaimed agency working in the sanitation sector. As the premier NGO, its contribution to the changes taking place in the sector has not only been path-breaking and revolutionary but deep-rooted. The professional and humane work culture of Sulabh provides scope for its social activists, engineers, scientists and motivators to undertake projects with commitment, honesty and accountability. It is also the strength behind the emergence of Sulabh as a leader and a centre of excellence.

The term 'social movement' is being used to denote a wide variety of collective attempts to bring about a change in certain social institutions or to create an entirely new order. Sometimes, the concept is used in distinction from religious or political movements and from movements among particular groups. For example, the women's movement or youth movement. As all these movements occur in society and tend to affect, directly or indirectly, the social order, it would be permissible to apply the term social movement to all of them. However, when the term first came into use, early in the nineteenth century, it had a more specialized meaning: it meant the movement of the new industrial working class, with its socialistic, communistic and anarchistic tendencies. A German scholar, Lorenz von Stein, was one of the first to recognize that the real political significance of socialism and communism lay not in their value as forms of social thought but in the fact that they gave expression and direction to the strivings of the industrial proletariat toward a new social order which would abolish economic exploitation and give the workers a chance to achieve full personality development.

On the continent of Europe, the identification of the social movement with the labour movement lasted until the second decade of this century. Today, this narrow definition of the concept is no longer possible in view of peasant's and fanner's movements, ethnic movements and of the independence movement in colonial countries. It is advisable, however, to distinguish between movements which, because of their limited goals, never attract more than small groups of people and those of which, aiming at comprehensive and fundamental changes in the social order, become true mass movements of historical significance. The latter will be referred to as social movements in the strict or 'classical' sense. The former are sometimes referred to as 'protest movements', but this term may also be used to designate mass movements which seek to redress grievances of certain group as Negro movement.

Social movements are a specific kind of concerted-action groups; they last longer and are more integrated than mobs, masses and crowds. A social movement may, however, comprise organized groups without having one over-all formal organization (for example, the labour movement, which comprises trade unions, political parties, consumer, cooperatives, and many other organizations). Group consciousness, that is, a sense of belonging and of solidarity among the members of a group, is essential for a social movement, although empirically it occurs in various degrees. This consciousness is generated through active participation and may assume various socio-psychological characteristics. By this criterion social movements are distinguished from 'social trends', which are often referred to as social movements and are the result of similar but uncoordinated actions of many individuals.

The classical concept of social movement implies the creation of an entirely new socio-economic and political order, especially. as concerns the institutions of property and the distribution of power. To justify these aims, all major social movements develop a more or less elaborate, more or less consistent set of ideas which its members must accept more or less uncritically. From these 'ideologies' or 'constitutive ideas' are derived 'action programmes' of a more changing nature. Social movements tend to spread beyond the boundaries of states or national societies and to extend over the entire area of civilization, or even beyond, so far as the social order that is their target reaches. In spite of their different and often antagonistic aims and ideologies, certain social movements show similarities in structure, tactics, and other formal aspects, while other movements, although similar in their ideologies, are significantly different in other respect. While the earlier studies of social movements have concentrated on the ideas, more recent researches has given equal attention to the structural and psychological aspects.

Movements aiming consciously at a radically different social order, a 'change from the roots', are possible only when the social order is seen not as a divine creation but as a work of men, subject to man's will. Movements of this kind are concomitant with the secularization of thought. Such movements have occurred in the eighteenth century in the West. In the Third World, such movements have occurred during the colonial era and the impact of socio-cultural changes. Earlier revolts and disturbances among the lower social strata typically aimed at improving their social position without attacking the social order in its foundations. These movements were, as a rule, defeated unless they adopted the organization, tactics and ideology of modern movements.

In the attempt to justify their aims, modern social movements typically resort to abstract principles concerning the nature of men, his distinction and his natural rights in combination with a critique of the existing economic, political and cultural institutions. The ideas of liberty and equality are common to all major social movements, sometimes in combination with the idea of national unity and independence. The motivations of individuals in joining a social movement may range from rational belief in the movements' aims (value-rational orientation) to pure opportunism. Quite often the decision to join is more emotional than rational, one can distinguish the following socio-psychological types of movements according to the prevailing motivation of their members:

- The value-rational 'spiritual community' of believers in the truth of the constitutive ideas and in the practical aims of movements
- The emotional-effectual 'following' of a charismatic leader
- The purposive-rational or utilitarian association for the pursuit of individual interests

Combinations of these types are frequent, and transitions from one type to another may occur during the life cycle of a movement. What started as a community of believers in a 'cause' may develop into a 'bandwagon' attracting socially or politically ambitions opportunists. In some revolutionary movements, the devotion to cause becomes paramount to the degree that personal friendship and love among members and all personal, intimate relations with outsiders are discouraged – a paradox in movements which aim at the establishment of a more human and more fraternal order of society. The nature of a movement may also change as a new generation grows into it.

The analysis of social movements has constituted an amorphous and diffuse field of social research and theory that is sometimes conceived as part of the general field of collective behaviour and sometimes as part of the study of voluntary associations were, however, social movement is defined as 'socially shared demands for change in some aspect of the social order'. This definition emphasizes the part played by social movements as a catalytic agent for social development.

At various times and under various conditions the legitimacy of a society's customary institutions or values may come under attack from different parts of the society. New arrangements are advocated; but the demand for change meets with resistance, and old habits and the arrangements of social relationship patterns are maintained. Thus, it comes about that group members face each other in some form of conflict. In this context, Sulabh Movement is not the unnoticed accretion of many unrecognized changes; rather, it has the character of an explicit and conscious indictment of whole of the social order, together with a conscious demand for change. It also has an ideological component – that is, a set of ideas which specify discontents, prescribe solutions, and justify change.

Sulabh movement is based on six value postulates – egalitarianism, altruism, non-violence, commitment, discipline and sacrifice. Its ultimate aim is to create a pollution free society, liberate the scavengers and improve the socio-economic conditions of weaker sections of society specially widows, scavengers who have been performing the dehumanizing practice for carrying the human excreta on head. The complex character of India's socio-economic transformation during the past five decades of planned and programmed development endeavours, following Independence, can only be understood through an unbiased and objective appreciation of the intertwined process of 'continuity and change' that indeed characterize the culture of contemporary Indian society. The continuance of some of the profoundly perplexing problems of the past, and the presence of tremendous progressive changes in the field of science and technology, as also in social and economic walks of life, explains the oriental duality and the dilemmas of Indian society. Whilst the country is legitimately proud of its culture and civilization, and rightly reverse its old traditions, beliefs and value systems, an overwhelming number of people are unfortunately confronted with problems of survival and sustenance in their daily existence. Amongst the long list of social, economic and political problems, the population and poverty related problems of environmental sanitation are also a major source of considerable concern. The lack of basic healthcare and sanitation infrastructure is one of the biggest challenges confronting the country even now. And, it is this problem which has engaged Sulabh's entire, attention and energy.

India is a country of more than 1000 million people. Famous for its ancient culture and civilization, this is the land of the river Ganga, the Taj Mahal, the Red Fort, the Churches of Goa and the Golden Temple. The country has made tremendous progress in different fields after its Independence in 1947. The country which used to import food has become self-sufficient in foodgrain production after the Green Revolution in the late 1960s. Major growth in economy and industry has made India one of the most industrialized nations of the world. The other revolution that has taken place is in the field of telecommunications. Now, even the remotest village of India has the facilities of telephones and the internet. Development in science and technology including atomic energy has become the strength of the nation.

Mahatma Gandhi in his own lifetime tried to bring the scavengers into the mainstream of society but his task remained unfulfilled. After Independence, the Government of India formed many high-level committees to improve the living condition of the scavengers but no tangible results emerged. It was in 1969, the Gandhi Centenary year that the nation stood up to take a vow to abolish scavenging. That was the most fitting tribute the country could pay to Mahatma Gandhi. That also marked the beginning of the Sulabh Sanitation Movement.

The Sulabh Sanitation Movement is a crusade to restore human rights and dignity to the downtrodden, especially the scavengers, and to provide basic sanitation for all. This movement was started by Dr Bindeshwar Pathak in the year 1970. Dr Pathak, apart from being a sociologist, is a humanist and a social reformer who cares for the people of the downtrodden community from the core of his heart. His drive, determination and missionary zeal for a happy society with improved living conditions has taken the shape of a nationwide movement. Dr Pathak developed his own approach to improve the social condition of scavengers, weaker section of society and widows of Vrindavan and Varanasi who were neglected and marginalized, Dr Pathak is keenly interested in three social issues, namely, environmental sanitation, liberation of scavengers and rehabilitation of widows. Dr Pathak visited Vrindavan on 11 August 2012 for the first time in pursuance of the directions of Supreme Court. He visited widows ashrams and examined their problems. He decided to provide the respectful life to the widows living in Vrindavan. He started to provide financial help for food on regular basis besides one-time financial help to them. He also provided mobile medical vans to the ashrams for providing health and medical care to widows. Dr Pathak decided to take care of each widow and declared that no one will sleep hungry, besides graceful funeral of the deceased widows. He also started to provide vocational and skill training to widows.

In the beginning, Sulab movement focused on the liberation of manual scavengers, as a class of persons united in their suffocating miseries, were traditionally ordained in Indian society to clean and carry human waste which majority of them have been doing till quite recently. Their appalling hardship, humiliation and savage exploitation have no parallel in human history. Living in the filthiest of surroundings under most trying circumstances, scavengers are hated even by those whose excreta they carry on their heads. Reduced to the depth of degradation as untouchables and forced to lead a sub-human existence, they are the worst victims of a cruel social order. Their story is the sordid story of the utmost violation of human rights. Their heart-rending plight stretching over centuries is a blot on Indian civilization. It is a black chapter of our history which most of us, and above all, scavengers themselves, would like to forget like a bad dream. Despite endeavours of the government and civil society in modern times to liberate scavengers from the suffocating situation, the long shadow of institutionalized discrimination, stigmatization and marginalization still refuses to fade out. If there is one man who can be singled out as the leader of a national crusade for restoration of human rights and dignity of millions of scavengers in recent years, it is Dr Bindeshwar Pathak a noted action-sociologist, renowned social activist, who conceived, nurtured and shaped the Sulabh Movement against overwhelming odds. He is a dreamer and a doer who has transformed the nation by providing the infrastructure and improve their socio-economic conditions and bring them in the mainstream of the nations.

He has antiquated the challenge to rehabilitates the widows who were marginalized by the family, community and society. He clearly realized that liberation and rehabilitation of widows was not an easy task. It was indeed very difficult for they mere worst victims of institutionalized discrimination over the centuries to break out of the vicious circle and join the mainstream of society in the real sense of the term. Hence, he devised a well thought-out and multi-pronged strategy to rehabilitate the widows by providing them alternative employment and integrating them into the mainstream of the society. His successful strategy for the liberation of widows through the Sulabh movement consists of a mixed package of technology, suitable rehabilitation with alternative employment and social reforms. This holistic approach is radically different from other social reform movements in that he combines technology with social idealism. His scientific and humane step-by-step approach to abolish old practices is inspired by a commitment to basic human rights and based on years of deep research and study of the problem.

The Sulabh approach to restore human dignity of widows has five distinct stages:

- Liberation
- Rehabilitation
- Vocational training
- Proper education of next generation
- Social elevation

Though Sulabh has now received global recognition as a sanitation movement, its key component is social reform – an imaginatively packaged programme for restoring human dignity.

Since sanitation is a matter of faith for Sulabh, its movement experiments with change and believes in doing and delivering results. Sulabh's thought process and its action programmes are in harmony with synergy – a life force-which is tangible and transparent. It is a holistic and not a piecemeal approach. Sulabh has blazed a new trail by integrating sanitation technologies with humanitarian ideology for the best results. Recognizing that mind matters the most Sulabh approach to social sector emphasises attitudinal changes in accepting modern and rational values for social transformation and integrating the widows in family, community and society.

Sulabh is prompting widows to form self-help group after training, which will ensure self-sustainable development. Sulabh has started a big movement for social awareness and is spreading message among urban and rural people regarding the conditions of widows and is helping them to bring changes in their attitude and style of life. Students, teachers, NGOs, retired people, etc. are involved on a mass scale to understand their problem and solve them. Sulabh uses poets, writers, street plays, newspapers, documentaries and feature films to inform and educate the public under this mass movement. Sulabh's successful journey can be aptly summed up in the Sulabh's adoption of multipronged and holistic strategy that has not only made a difference in the situation but has also created a distinct place for itself in the illustrious list of social movements in India.

The most remarkable thing about Sulabh Movement is that it does not take any grant, assistance or subsidy from any agency, national or international. It raises its own resources and is effectively functioning as self-sustaining social service organization. The professional and humane work culture of Sulabh provides scope for its social activists, engineers, scientists and motivators to undertake projects with commitment, honesty and accountability. Sulabh's social service volunteers are the real strength behind its emergence as a global leader in social sector. Sulabh has also taken care of widows of society who are given proper education enabling them to earn their livelihood with dignity. They are given ₹ 2,000 per month to enable them to take vocational education as per aptitude as organized by Sulabh International Social Service Organisation. Under the vocational training programme, widows are imparted training in various trades and occupations, namely, tailoring, typing, dress-designing, embroidery, beauty-care, shorthand, computer education and photography. Under Dr Pathak's dynamic and inspiring leadership, a committed team of sociologists, scientists, engineers, doctors, journalists and public-spirited persons has come forward to build a stupendous national network. Sulabh is well set to write a glorious chapter in the annals of independent India. A budding movement in 1970, Sulabh is now making waves in India from Kashmir to Kanyakumari and its methodology is appropriately poised for global application.

India has long history of social reforms. However, credit also goes to the British for introducing legal provisions and Acts for gender equality and social justice. The life of widows in many societies has been worse as widowhood is a curse. Widows have been neglected, exploited and restricted from

participation in socio-cultural ceremonies, wearing colour clothes and taking rich food. Initially, widows were provided proper care and support by their in-laws and parents at religious places. There are a number of buildings constructed by Zamindars in Varanasi and Mathura-Vrindavan for widows. However, with the passing of time, widows were neglected by their relatives and thus, their life became pitiful. Thus, modern reforms for improving the lives of widows at religious places are required. The role and contribution of Sulabh International Social Service Organisation has been remarkable for rehabilitation of widows in Vrindavan.

6

Conditions of Widows and Social Change

Widows in India face several problems in their life as widowhood has been considered a social problem. Early marriage has been practiced in India since time immemorial. This has also resulted in widowhood at an early age. Widowhood has been a social curse to women in India. A large segment of widows, even in the early age, were left at religious places to live there and perform cultural-religious functions such as praying, doing *bhajans* and *satsang* and thus pass time in a peaceful way. For the time being, family members provided necessary support and facilities for their better boarding and lodging. However, during the course of time, they were neglected and ignored by the family members. Thus, the life of widows in religious places became pathetic in absence of proper boarding and lodging facilities. A large number of widows are living in widow ashrams, temples, dharamshalas and other settlements in the religious places such as Kashi (Varanasi), Vrindavan and Ayodhya. Most widows depend on charity and meagre wages for performing *bhajans* and cooking *prasad* in temples. Their living conditions are highly unhygienic and pathetic as they lack proper accommodation, fooding and clothings. Being the old age of significant number of widows, their health conditions are also poor due to lack of health care and medical treatment. Government, no doubt, has set up widow homes for their rehabilitation. However, government support to the widows is grossly inadequate in religious places.

Profile of Widows

Age of respondent is shown in Table 6.1. Most of the widows were of higher age group i.e. 56 and above years. This was found more pronouncing in Vrindavan (86.7%) as compared to Varanasi (75.6%). About 10 per cent respondents were from the age group of 46–55 years, while about 5 per cent respondents were from the age group of 36–45 years. This was found more pronouncing in Varanasi (12.4%) as compared to Vrindavan (2.4%).

Table 6.1

Age of Respondents

Age Group	*Varanasi*	*%*	*Vrindavan*	*%*	*Total*	*%*
16–25	0	0	0	0	0	0
26–35	0	0	9	1.3	9	1.23
36–45	28	12.4	11	2.4	39	5.33
46–55	27	12.0	46	9.6	73	9.97
56 and above	170	75.6	441	86.7	611	83.47
Total	225	100.0	507	100.0	732	100.0

Source: Field Survey.

The caste system in India has been studied with three perspectives: Indo-logical, socio-anthropological and sociological. The Indologists have viewed caste from the scriptural point of view, socio-anthropologist from the cultural point of view, and sociologists from the stratification point of view. There are several theories for the study of the caste system in India. The sociological perspective views the caste system in terms of social stratification in a society, and as a phenomenon of social inequality (Ahuja, 2007: 229). Scholars like Leach, Dumont, Pocock, Bougle, Hocart, Hutton, Senart, Srinivas, Gould, etc. feel that the caste is a phenomenon peculiar to India only. However, Risley, Crook, etc. believe that a caste is a universal phenomenon. Ghurye (1961: 138–56) has analysed the elements of caste outside India. Leach (1960: 4) has also studied social stratification system of Muslims in Swat, north Pakistan. Dumont (1958) feels that caste is confined to India. Hocart (1950: 45) maintains that castes are merely families to whom various offices in the ritual are assigned by heredity. Senart (1930: 26) also feels that caste is peculiar to India since it is determined by ethnological, economic, geographical and psychological conditions which are essentially native. Hutton (1961: 46) also refers to its uniqueness due to its complex origin. Gould (1986: 33) is of the view that caste in its fullest sense is an exclusively Indian phenomenon. Nowadays, caste has acquired a new shape with the social change. The political mobilization of caste system has created social problems resulting in caste and class conflict. The social cohesion is being deteriorated with the change in caste system. No doubt education, inter-caste marriages, ban on untouchability, positive discrimination for the lower caste in job and education etc. have weakened the caste system; however, it has not totally withered away. With the introduction of decentralized governance and politicization of caste system, the politics of reservation is gaining momentum. The concept of sociology of religion was given by Durkheim. Durkheim argued that religious phenomenon emerged in any society when a separation is made between the spheres of the profane – the realm of every day utilitarian activities – and the sphere of the secret – the area that pertains to the numinous, the transcendental, the extraordinary. The religion is a great binding force. Thus, religion is not only a social creation but it is in fact society divinized (Coser, 2002: 137–38).

About half of the respondents were from General Caste while about 21 per cent respondents were from OBCs. The proportion of Scheduled Caste respondents was recorded higher in Varanasi (18.6%) as compared to Vrindavan (15.4%). About 6 per cent respondents were from minority communities. This was found more pronouncing in Varanasi (13%) as compared to Vrindavan (7.1%). It is to be noted that a large number of widows from Jain and Muslim communities are also living in these religious places (Table 6.2).

Table 6.2

Caste of Respondents

Caste	*Varanasi*	*%*	*Vrindavan*	*%*	*Total*	*%*
General	106	47.1	256	50.6	362	49.45
Scheduled Caste	42	18.6	79	15.4	121	16.53
Scheduled Tribes	0	0	31	6.4	31	4.23
OBC	48	21.3	106	20.5	154	21.04
Muslims/Christians/Jains	29	13.0	17	7.1	46	6.28
Others	0	0	18	3.5	18	2.46
Total	225	100.0	507	100.0	732	100.0

Source: Field Survey.

Age-wise caste of respondents is shown in Table 6.3. Majority of the respondents from General Caste were found belonging to the lower age group while majority of the respondents from Scheduled Caste were from the middle age group. About half of the respondents from the higher age group were from General Caste.

Table 6.3

Age-wise Caste of Respondents

Caste	*Varanasi*				*Vrindavan*			
	26–35 Years	*36–45 Years*	*46–55 Years*	*56 Years and Above*	*26–35 Years*	*36–45 Years*	*46–55 Years*	*56 Years and Above*
General	66.7	37.5	41.6	48.3	60.7	30.7	35.6	58.3
SC	33.3	52.5	20.9	20.0	30.3	45.3	26.9	15.0
ST	0.0	0.0	25.0	19.4	3.5	7.1	20.0	14.4
OBC	0.0	0.0	12.5	12.3	5.5	15.9	17.5	12.3
Total	100.0	100.0	100.0	100.0	100.0	100.0	100.0	100.0

Source: Field Survey.

Education is an important social variable. This has direct bearing on the social status of an individual both in the family and the society. Education in the context of domestic violence is also significant variable as it influences the awareness and sensitization towards the social and legal measures for preventing the domestic violence and also social rehabilitation.

Educational level of respondents is shown in Table 6.4. Educational level of widows has been reported to be very poor. About 70 per cent widows were found to be illiterate. This was found more pronouncing in Vrindavan (73.2%) as compared to Varanasi (63.5%). About 22 per cent respondents were found educated up to primary level while only 8 per cent respondents were found educated beyond primary level. The educational level among widows was found slightly higher in Varanasi as compared to Vrindavan.

Table 6.4

Educational Level of Respondents

Level of Education	*Varanasi*	*%*	*Vrindavan*	*%*	*Total*	*%*
Illiterate	143	63.5	370	73.2	513	70.08
Primary	51	22.7	111	21.9	162	22.13
Secondary	17	7.5	17	3.5	34	4.64
Higher Studies	14	6.2	9	1.4	23	3.14
Total	225	100.0	507	100.0	732	100.0

Source: Field Survey.

Caste-wise educational level of respondents is shown in Table 6.5. Illiteracy has been reported high among respondents from Scheduled Caste and OBC communities while level of education was slightly high among the respondents from General Caste.

Table 6.5

Caste-wise Educational Level of Respondents

Level of Education	*Varanasi*				*Vrindavan*			
	General	*SC*	*ST*	*OBC*	*General*	*SC*	*ST*	*OBC*
Illiterate	53.8	90.5	70.8	83.9	60.2	92.1	75.8	90.8
Primary	28.2	7.1	18.8	8.3	26.8	6.5	15.8	5.3
Secondary	14.1	2.4	8.3	3.9	10.9	1.4	6.3	2.9
Higher Studies	3.9	0.0	2.1	3.9	2.1	0.0	2.1	1.0
Total	100.0	100.0	100.0	100.0	100.0	100.0	100.0	100.0

Source: Field Survey.

Age-wise educational level of respondents is shown in Table 6.6. Illiteracy has been reported high among respondents from higher age group as compared to respondents from lower age group.

It is very difficult to compare rural and urban society. Gist and Halbert are of the view that rural and urban is more of a theoretical concept than a division based upon the facts of community life. The rural and urban societies may be differentiated in terms of social organizations – family, marriage, conditions of women, neighbourhood, inequality of classes, social cohesion, etc.; differences in social restrictions; differences in social relationships; differences in social interactions; differences in social view point and differences in social mobility and stability (Sharma, 2005: 17–19).

Transportation and communication result in successful rural-urban contracts. It reduces the hold of religion and folk believes upon rural people and introduces some aspects of scientific attitude into the rural mentality. There may be several factors including economic, social, better living standards, better housing facilities, etc. that promote the rural-urban migration. However, migration from rural to urban areas creates problems to the urban dwellers since the poor cannot afford good living environment and are forced to live in squatters and slums where the environmental conditions are reported to be worse.

Table 6.6

Age-wise Educational Level of Respondents

Level of Education	*Varanasi*				*Vrindavan*			
	26–35 Years	*36–45 Years*	*46–55 Years*	*56 Years and Above*	*26–35 Years*	*36–45 Years*	*46–55 Years*	*56 Years and Above*
Illiterate	25.0	40.0	70.8	68.9	20.0	43.0	70.8	70.9
Primary	41.7	13.2	16.7	23.5	51.7	10.3	18.7	21.5
Secondary	33.3	46.7	12.5	4.2	25.3	41.7	10.5	5.2
Higher Studies	0.0	0.0	0.0	3.4	3.0	5.0	0.0	2.4
Total	100.0	100.0	100.0	100.0	100.0	100.0	100.0	100.0

Source: Field Survey.

It is said that the Marxian class and class conflict theory has been reputed by certain unforeseen social changes that have taken place since Marx like separation of ownership and control, differentiation in the working class, rise of the so-called middle class, etc. in modern industrial society (Dahrendorf, 1959). Many sociologists conceptualize class chiefly in terms of occupation and income (Packard, 1964). There is another criterion to define social class. Cooley holds that the relation between the class of employer and the class of manual labour is a primarily a question of individual point of view (Cooley, 1902: 98). Richard Centers puts it, 'social class is a psychological phenomena in the fullest sense of the term' (Centers, 1949: 27). Jordan, while analysing the Marxist theory, defines the term as a distributive sense that it ceases to be a real and independent entity (Jordan, 1971: 23).

Table 6.7

Place of Present Stay of Respondents

Place of Stay	*Varanasi*	*%*	*Vrindavan*	*%*	*Total*	*%*
Widow Home	99	44.0	487	96.4	586	80.05
Independently	96	42.7	7	1.2	103	14.07
With Relatives	30	13.3	13	2.4	43	5.87
Others	0	0	0	0	0	0
Total	225	100.0	507	100.0	732	100.0

Source: Field Survey.

Most of the widows were found living in widow homes. This was found more pronouncing in Vrindavan (96.4%). About 14 per cent respondents were found living independently. This was reported high in Varanasi (42.7%) as compared to Vrindavan (1.2%). About 6 per cent respondents were found living with their relatives. This was reported high in Varanasi (13.3%) (Table 6.7).

Caste-wise place of domicile of respondents is shown in Table 6.8. There is no correlation between caste and place of domicile. More than half of the respondents from General Caste were found living in widow homes as compared to less than one-fourth respondents from OBC communities living in widow homes. About 62 per cent respondents from OBC communities in both the districts were found living independently.

Table 6.8

Caste-wise Place of Domicile of Respondents

Place of Domicile	*Varanasi*				*Vrindavan*			
	General	*SC*	*ST*	*OBC*	*General*	*SC*	*ST*	*OBC*
Widow Home	51.9	47.7	37.5	23.1	51.9	47.7	37.5	23.1
Independently	39.1	35.7	47.4	61.5	39.1	35.7	47.4	61.5
With Relatives	9.0	16.6	15.1	15.4	9.0	65.6	15.1	15.4
Others	0.0	0.0	0.0	0.0	0.0	0.0	0.0	0.0
Total	100.0	100.0	100.0	100.0	100.0	100.0	100.0	100.0

Source: Field Survey.

Age-wise place of domicile of respondents is shown in Table 6.9. Majority of the respondents from lower age group were found living independently while more than half of the respondents from higher age group were found living in widow homes. About one-fourth respondents from the age group of 46–55 years were found living with their relatives.

Table 6.9

Age-wise Place of Domicile of Respondents

Place of Domicile	*Varanasi*				*Vrindavan*			
	26–35 Years	*36–45 Years*	*46–55 Years*	*56 Years and Above*	*26–35 Years*	*36–45 Years*	*46–55 Years*	*56 Years and Above*
Widow Home	16.7	18.8	12.5	53.5	15.7	14.8	10.5	55.5
Independently	75.0	62.4	62.5	36.4	79.0	65.4	66.5	33.4
With Relatives	8.3	18.8	25.0	10.1	13.3	19.8	23.0	11.1
Others	0.0	0.0	0.0	0.0	0.0	0.0	0.0	0.0
Total	100.0	100.0	100.0	100.0	100.0	100.0	100.0	100.0

Source: Field Survey.

Education-wise place of domicile of respondents is shown in Table 6.10. Majority of the respondents from low education level were found living independently while a significant proportion of respondents from higher education level were found living in widow homes.

Table 6.10

Education-wise Place of Domicile of Respondents

Place of Domicile	*Varanasi*				*Vrindavan*			
	Illiterate	*Primary*	*Middle*	*Higher Studies*	*Illiterate*	*Primary*	*Middle*	*Higher Studies*
Widow Home	16.7	18.8	12.5	53.5	10.3	14.5	10.5	40.5
Independently	75.0	62.5	62.5	36.5	80.0	70.8	69.5	40.5
With Relatives	8.3	18.7	25.0	10.0	9.7	14.7	20.0	10.0
Others	0.0	0.0	0.0	0.0	0.0	0.0	0.0	0.0
Total	100.0	100.0	100.0	100.0	100.0	100.0	100.0	100.0

Source: Field Survey.

Duration of stay is shown in Table 6.11. About two-fifth respondents were found living in Varanasi and Vrindavan for more than 10 years. About 58 per cent respondents in Varanasi were found living in the city from more than 10 years while about one-third respondents in Vrindavan were found living in the city for more than 10 years. More than one-fourth respondents were found living in the city for 5 years. This was reported higher in Vrindavan (33.7%) as compared to Varanasi (12.4%). About 18 per cent respondents further reported that they are living in the city for 5 to 10 years. This was found more pronouncing in Vrindavan (22.7%) as compared to Varanasi (8.4%).

Table 6.11

Duration of Stay

Duration of Living	*Varanasi*	*%*	*Vrindavan*	*%*	*Total*	*%*
Less Than One Month	28	12.4	12	2.5	40	5.46
One Month to One Year	19	8.4	37	7.3	56	7.65
One Year to Five Years	28	12.4	171	33.7	199	27.19
Five Years to Ten Years	19	8.4	116	22.7	135	18.44
Ten Years and Above	131	58.4	171	33.8	302	41.26
Total	225	100.0	507	100.0	732	100.0

Source: Field Survey.

Caste-wise duration of stay of respondents is shown in Table 6.12. Majority of the respondents from General communities reported that they are living in the city for more than 10 years. However, respondents from Scheduled Caste and OBC were found living in the city for fewer periods.

Table 6.12
Caste-wise Duration of Stay of Respondents

Duration	Varanasi				Vrindavan			
	General	SC	ST	OBC	General	SC	ST	OBC
Less Than One Month	11.4	14.3	14.6	11.5	12.4	10.3	10.6	10.5
Less Than One Year	5.6	9.5	8.4	7.8	6.6	7.5	8.4	6.8
One to Five Years	7.5	28.5	10.4	11.5	8.5	25.5	10.4	10.5
Five to Ten Years	4.7	7.1	8.3	26.9	6.7	6.1	8.2	21.9
Ten Years and Above	70.8	40.6	58.3	42.3	65.8	50.6	62.3	50.3
Total	100.0	100.0	100.0	100.0	100.0	100.0	100.0	100.0

Source: Field Survey.

Age-wise duration of stay of respondents is shown in Table 6.13. Respondents from higher age group were found living in the city for more than 10 years while respondents from lower age group are living in the city for fewer periods.

Table 6.13
Age-wise Duration of Stay of Respondents

Duration	Varanasi				Vrindavan			
	26–35 Years	36–45 Years	46–55 Years	56 Years and Above	26–35 Years	36–45 Years	46–55 Years	56 Years and Above
Less Than One Month	8.3	37.5	8.3	11.2	8.3	30.5	9.3	10.2
Less Than One Year	16.7	6.2	0.0	7.7	12.7	8.2	0.0	7.7
One to Five Years	16.7	6.2	12.5	12.9	13.7	9.3	14.5	9.9
Five to Ten Years	25.0	6.3	4.2	8.2	20.0	8.2	6.2	8.2
Ten Years and Above	33.3	43.7	75.0	60.0	43.3	43.8	70.0	64.0
Total	100.0	100.0	100.0	100.0	100.0	100.0	100.0	100.0

Source: Field Survey.

Table 6.14
Education-wise Duration of Stay of Respondents

Duration	Varanasi				Vrindavan			
	Illiterate	Primary	Middle	Higher Studies	Illiterate	Primary	Middle	Higher Studies
Less Than One Month	8.3	37.5	8.4	11.2	7.7	30.2	10.4	10.2
Less Than One Year	16.7	6.2	0.0	7.6	14.3	6.5	0.0	6.6
One to Five Years	16.7	6.3	12.5	12.9	15.3	6.3	15.5	10.9
Five to Ten Years	25.0	6.2	4.1	8.3	20.0	6.2	4.1	7.3
Ten Years and Above	33.3	43.8	75.0	60.0	40.7	50.8	70.0	65.0
Total	100.0	100.0	100.0	100.0	100.0	100.0	100.0	100.0

Source: Field Survey.

Education-wise duration of stay of respondents is shown in Table 6.14. Respondents with higher education were found living from a longer period as compared to the respondents with low education level living in the city from a fewer period.

Fulfillment of financial needs is shown in Table 6.15. About two-third respondents reported that they depend on charity for fulfillment of financial needs. This was found more pronouncing in Vrindavan (72.3%) as compared to Varanasi (49%). About 19 per cent respondents reported that they depend on menial work for fulfillment of their financial needs. This was found more pronouncing in Varanasi (26.7%) as compared to Vrindavan (15.2%). About 2 per cent respondents admitted that they depend on begging for fulfillment of their financial needs.

Table 6.15

Fulfillment of Financial Needs

Means of Finances	*Varanasi*	*%*	*Vrindavan*	*%*	*Total*	*%*
Menial Work	58	25.7	78	15.2	136	18.58
Begging	6	2.6	12	2.3	18	2.46
Charity	110	49.0	366	72.3	476	65.03
Other Source	49	21.8	53	10.2	102	13.93
Total	225	100.0	507	100.0	732	100.0

Source: Field Survey.

Level of education of the deceased husband is shown in Table 6.16. Educational levels of husbands of widows were reported to be poor. About two-fifth respondents reported that their husbands were educated up to primary level while about 29 per cent respondents further reported that their husbands were illiterate. The proportion of respondents reporting that their husbands were illiterates was recorded high in Vrindavan (35.9%). About 13 per cent respondents reported that their husbands were educated up to secondary level. Thus, about 8 per cent respondents admitted that their husbands were graduates and above. This was found more pronouncing in Varanasi (12%).

Table 6.16

Level of Education of Deceased Husband

Level of Education	*Varanasi*	*%*	*Vrindavan*	*%*	*Total*	*%*
Primary	87	38.0	223	44.9	310	42.35
Secondary	33	15.0	65	12.9	98	13.39
Higher Studies	25	12.0	30	5.1	55	7.51
Vocational Education	51	23.0	9	1.2	60	8.20
Illiterate	29	12.0	180	35.9	209	28.55
Others	0	0	0	0	0	0
Total	225	100.0	507	100.0	732	100.0

Source: Field Survey.

Occupation of respondents is important social variable as it influences the social status of respondents in the family and society. It has also direct bearing on the income of an individual because most of the occupations enable individuals to earn money.

Main occupation of the deceased husband is shown in Table 6.17. The respondents were asked regarding the main occupation of their deceased husband. About 38 per cent respondents reported that their deceased husbands were labour. This was found more pronouncing in Varanasi (39.6%). About one-fourth respondents did not report any occupation of their deceased husbands as they were most probably landlords and zamindars. About 9 per cent respondents reported that their deceased husbands were in private job. This was found more pronouncing in Varanasi. Only 4 per cent respondents revealed that their deceased husbands were in government job. This was found more pronouncing in Vrindavan.

Table 6.17

Main Occupation of Deceased Husband

Main Occupation	*Varanasi*	*%*	*Vrindavan*	*%*	*Total*	*%*
General Store	10	4.5	16	3.5	26	3.55
Petty or Large Business	22	9.8	72	14.6	94	12.84
Labour	89	39.6	186	36.7	275	37.57
Government Job	6	2.6	24	4.7	30	4.10
Private Job	26	11.5	42	8.3	68	9.29
Agriculture	0	0	36	7.1	36	4.92
Others	62	27.6	116	22.6	178	24.32
None	10	4.4	15	2.5	25	3.42
Total	225	100.0	507	100.0	732	100.0

Source: Field Survey.

Monthly income of the deceased husbands is shown in Table 6.18. Most of the respondents reported that monthly income of their deceased husbands was less than ₹ 5,000. This was found more pronouncing in Vrindavan (84.6%) as compared to Varanasi (81.3%). About 13 per cent respondents reported that the monthly income of their deceased husband was in between ₹ 5,000 to ₹ 10,000.

Table 6.18

Monthly Income of Deceased Husband

Monthly Income	*Varanasi*	*%*	*Vrindavan*	*%*	*Total*	*%*
Less Than ₹ 5,000	183	81.3	426	84.6	609	83.20
₹ 5,000 to ₹ 10,000	29	12.9	63	12.8	92	12.57
₹ 10,000 to ₹ 15,000	11	4.9	5	0.9	16	2.19
₹ 15,000 and above	4	1.8	9	1.7	13	1.77
Total	225	100.0	507	100.0	732	100.0

Source: Field Survey.

Family Background

Family is basic and universal social structure of the human society. It fulfils needs and performs functions which are indispensable for the community, integration and change in the social system. The forms and functions of family have undergone adoptive changes with changes in the technological and economic superstructure of the society (Singh, 2006: 174). One way to characterize this change is to associate conjugal or nuclear forms of families with relatively modernized or industrial society and extended or joint types of families with traditional agrarian and pre-industrial societies. The transition from extended family-based society to nuclear family-based society, is thus, an example of the structural change. Changes in the structure and functions of the joint families in India are, thus, following a reconciliatory pattern, a pattern common in the structural changes in the Indian society.

According to Cooley, the sociologist, and Freud, the psychoanalyst, the most important element of the society is the family. However, Marxist social analyst treat class as a basic personality shaping group force, stating that the family is but a part of the super structure and is therefore itself shaped by the economic system (Marx and Engels,1875). Thus, the family cannot be viewed in isolation from a society's economic framework, in other words family is a dependent variable (Worsley et al., 1970: 141). The family has lost many of its earlier functions in modern industrial urban society. The family plays a vital role in one's socialization (Lasswell and Kaplan, 1950: 145). Robertlane suggests three ways in which family may play its important role: (1) overt and covert indoctrination, (2) putting the child in a particular social context, and molding the child's personality (Lane, 1959: 502–11).

More than half of the respondents reported that they belong to nuclear families. This was found more pronouncing in Varanasi (68%) as compared to Vrindavan (43.3%), More than one-third respondents were from joint families. About two-fifth respondents in Vrindavan were from joint families (Table 6.19).

Table 6.19
Type of Family of Respondents

Type of Family	*Varanasi*	*%*	*Vrindavan*	*%*	*Total*	*%*
Joint Family	35	15.6	226	44.9	261	35.66
Nuclear Family	153	68.0	223	43.3	376	51.37
Mixed Family	16	7.1	18	3.6	34	4.64
None	21	9.3	40	7.9	61	8.33
Total	225	100.0	507	100.0	732	100.0

Source: Field Survey.

Caste-wise type of family of respondents is shown in Table 6.20. A higher proportion of respondents from Scheduled Caste was found living in joint families. Similarly, a high proportion of respondents from Scheduled Caste was also found living in nuclear families. Thus, there is no correlation between caste and type of family.

Table 6.20
Caste-wise Type of Family of Respondents

Type of Family	Varanasi				Vrindavan			
	General	SC	ST	OBC	General	SC	ST	OBC
Joint Family	14.1	16.6	14.6	11.5	19.1	21.6	16.6	11.5
Nuclear Family	75.5	80.8	72.9	76.9	70.5	75.9	70.9	76.9
Mixed Family	8.5	2.5	8.4	11.6	8.5	2.5	8.4	11.6
None	1.9	0.0	4.1	0.0	1.9	0.0	4.1	0.0
Total	100.0	100.0	100.0	100.0	100.0	100.0	100.0	100.0

Source: Field Survey.

Age-wise type of family of respondents is shown in Table 6.21. A high proportion of respondents from higher age group were found living in nuclear families while respondents from lower age group were found living mainly in joint families.

Table 6.21
Age-wise Type of Family of Respondents

Type of Family	Varanasi				Vrindavan			
	26–35 Years	36–45 Years	46–55 Years	56 Years and Above	26–35 Years	36–45 Years	46–55 Years	56 Years and Above
Joint Family	33.3	12.5	29.2	11.2	29.3	10.5	25.2	10.2
Nuclear Family	66.7	62.5	66.7	79.4	70.7	65.5	70.7	80.4
Mixed Family	0.0	18.7	4.1	7.7	0.0	15.7	4.1	5.7
None	0.0	6.3	0.0	1.7	0.0	8.3	0.0	3.7
Total	100.0	100.0	100.0	100.0	100.0	100.0	100.0	100.0

Source: Field Survey.

Table 6.22
Education-wise Type of Family of Respondents

Type of Family	Varanasi				Vrindavan			
	Illiterate	Primary	Middle	Higher Studies	Illiterate	Primary	Middle	Higher Studies
Joint Family	33.4	12.5	29.2	11.2	30.0	15.0	30.0	11.0
Nuclear Family	66.6	62.5	66.6	79.4	70.0	60.0	65.0	81.0
Mixed Family	0.0	18.7	4.2	7.6	0.0	18.0	5.0	7.0
None	0.0	6.3	0.0	1.8	0.0	6.0	0.0	1.0
Total	100.0	100.0	100.0	100.0	100.0	100.0	100.0	100.0

Source: Field Survey.

Education-wise type of family of respondents is shown in Table 6.22. The high proportion of respondents from higher education level were found living in nuclear families while a significant proportion of respondents from low education level were found living in nuclear families.

Socio-economic class of family is shown in Table 6.23. Majority of the respondents were from lower class (70.22%). This was found more pronouncing in Vrindavan (74.1%) as compared to Varanasi (62.2%). Slightly less than one-fourth respondents were from middle class. This was found more pronouncing in Varanasi (32.9%). Thus, only 1 per cent respondents were from higher class.

Table 6.23

Socio-Economic Class of Family

Class of Family	*Varanasi*	*%*	*Vrindavan*	*%*	*Total*	*%*
Higher Class	4	1.8	4	0.3	8	1.09
Middle Class	74	32.9	101	20.1	175	23.63
Lower Class	140	62.2	374	74.1	514	70.22
None	7	3.1	28	5.5	35	4.78
Total	225	100.0	507	100.0	732	100.0

Source: Field Survey.

Head of the family is shown in Table 6.24. About two-fifth respondents reported that they were themselves head of the family. Similarly, about 43 per cent respondents reported that their sons were the head of the family. This was found more pronouncing in Varanasi (67.1%).

Table 6.24

Head of the Family

Head	*Varanasi*	*%*	*Vrindavan*	*%*	*Total*	*%*
Self	60	26.7	265	52.9	325	44.40
Son	151	67.1	161	31.7	312	42.62
None	14	6.2	81	15.9	95	12.98
Total	225	100.0	507	100.0	732	100.0

Source: Field Survey.

Occupation of head of the family is shown in Table 6.25. Slightly less than one-third respondents reported that head of their family was unemployed and engaged in house work. This was found more pronouncing in Vrindavan (33.2%) as compared to Varanasi (26.7%). Slightly less than one-fourth respondents reported that the main occupation of the head of their family was labour. This was found more pronouncing in Varanasi. About 17 per cent respondents reported agriculture as main occupation of their family while about 16 per cent respondents reported that the heads of their family were in private job. This was found more pronouncing in Varanasi (28.9%).

Table 6.25
Occupation of Head of the Family

Occupation of Head of the Family	*Varanasi*	*%*	*Vrindavan*	*%*	*Total*	*%*
Petty or Large Business	15	6.7	78	15.3	93	12.70
Labour	60	26.7	119	23.4	179	24.45
Private Job	65	28.9	50	9.6	115	15.71
Government Job	0	0	0	0	0	0
Agriculture	25	11.0	96	18.5	121	16.53
Unemployed/House Work	60	26.7	164	33.2	224	30.60
Total	225	100.0	507	100.0	732	100.0

Source: Field Survey.

Relations with head of the family are shown in Table 6.26. About half of the respondents reported that their relations with head of their family were normal. This was found more pronouncing in Varanasi (69.8%) as compared to Vrindavan (39.6%). About 22 per cent respondents further reported that their relations with head of the family were formal. This was found more pronouncing in Vrindavan (26.4%). About 15 per cent respondents revealed that their relations with their head of the family were strained. This was found more pronouncing in Vrindavan (18.7%). Thus, about 15 per cent respondents reported that their relations with head of their families were harmonious.

Table 6.26
Relations with Head of the Family

Relation	*Varanasi*	*%*	*Vrindavan*	*%*	*Total*	*%*
Harmonious	29	12.8	78	15.3	107	14.62
Normal	157	69.8	201	39.6	358	48.91
Formal	26	11.6	135	26.4	161	21.99
Strained	13	5.8	93	18.7	106	14.48
Total	225	100.0	507	100.0	732	100.0

Source: Field Survey.

Table 6.27
Caste-wise Relations With Head of Family

Relation	*Varanasi*				*Vrindavan*			
	General	*SC*	*ST*	*OBC*	*General*	*SC*	*ST*	*OBC*
Harmonious	10.4	10.4	16.7	23.1	12.4	12.4	4.7	25.1
Normal	39.6	32.6	4.3	23.1	47.6	44.6	16.3	26.1
Formal	16.1	24.2	39.6	7.9	14.1	22.2	48.6	7.9
Strained	33.9	32.8	39.4	45.9	25.9	20.8	30.4	40.9
Total	100.0	100.0	100.0	100.0	100.0	100.0	100.0	100.0

Source: Field Survey.

Caste-wise relations with head of family are shown in Table 6.27. A higher proportion of respondents from General Caste reported that they have normal relations with head of family while a high proportion of respondents from OBC communities reported that they have strained relations with head of family.

Age-wise relations with head of family are shown in Table 6.28. The proportion of strained relationship with head of families was recorded high among the respondents from lower age group as compared to the respondents from the higher age group. About two-third respondents from higher age group reported that they have harmonious and normal relations with head of family.

Table 6.28

Age-wise Relations With Head of Family

Relation	*Varanasi*				*Vrindavan*			
	26–35 Years	*36–45 Years*	*46–55 Years*	*56 Years and Above*	*26–35 Years*	*36–45 Years*	*46–55 Years*	*56 Years and Above*
Harmonious	33.3	30.3	33.3	31.2	44.3	35.3	38.3	35.2
Normal	16.7	26.0	20.7	31.8	11.7	29.0	22.7	35.8
Formal	8.3	12.5	21.9	13.6	8.3	10.5	19.9	13.6
Strained	41.7	31.2	25.1	33.4	35.7	25.3	19.1	25.4
Total	100.0	100.0	100.0	100.0	100.0	100.0	100.0	100.0

Source: Field Survey.

Education-wise relations with head of family are shown in Table 6.29. Education has direct bearing with the relations with head of the family. A higher proportion of respondents from lower age group reported that they have strained relations with head of the family while about two-fifth respondents from higher education level had harmonious relations with head of the family.

Table 6.29

Education-wise Relations With Head of Family

Relation	*Varanasi*				*Vrindavan*			
	Illiterate	*Primary*	*Middle*	*Higher Studies*	*Illiterate*	*Primary*	*Middle*	*Higher Studies*
Harmonious	33.4	28.8	33.3	39.2	30.4	30.0	30.0	40.0
Normal	16.6	25.0	20.8	30.8	15.6	25.0	20.0	30.0
Formal	8.3	23.5	40.2	14.5	8.3	25.0	40.0	14.0
Strained	41.7	22.7	5.7	15.6	45.7	20.0	10.0	16.0
Total	100.0	100.0	100.0	100.0	100.0	100.0	100.0	100.0

Source: Field Survey.

Number of dependent members is shown in Table 6.30. About half of the respondents revealed that they do not have any dependent member. This was found more pronouncing in Varanasi (76.5%) as compared to Vrindavan (36.7%). About one-fourth respondents reported that they have one dependent member. This was found more pronouncing in Vrindavan (34.9%). About 14 per cent respondents reported that they have two dependent members. This was also found higher in Vrindavan (16.1%).

Table 6.30

Number of Dependent Members

Dependent Members	*Varanasi*	*%*	*Vrindavan*	*%*	*Total*	*%*
One	13	5.9	176	34.9	189	25.82
Two	19	8.5	84	16.1	103	14.07
Three	10	4.4	43	8.5	53	7.24
Four	8	3.7	21	4.2	29	3.96
None	172	76.5	186	36.7	358	48.91
Total	225	100.0	507	100.0	732	100.0

Source: Field Survey.

Number of non-dependent members is shown in Table 6.31. More than half of the respondents reported that they do not have any non-dependent member. This was found significantly higher in Vrindavan (65.4%) as compared to Varanasi (23.6%). About 19 per cent respondents reported one non-dependent member while 19 per cent respondents further reported that they have two non-dependent members. About 10 per cent respondents said that they have three non-dependent members. This was found more pronouncing in Varanasi (23.1%).

Table 6.31

Number of Non-Dependent Members

Dependent Members	*Varanasi*	*%*	*Vrindavan*	*%*	*Total*	*%*
One	46	20.4	93	18.3	139	18.99
Two	74	32.9	64	12.6	138	18.85
Three	52	23.1	19	3.6	71	9.70
Four	0	0	0	0	0	0
None	53	23.6	331	65.4	384	52.46
Total	225	100.0	507	100.0	732	100.0

Source: Field Survey.

Satisfaction with family conditions is shown in Table 6.32. Slightly less than one-fourth respondents were found fully satisfied with their family conditions. This was found more pronouncing in Vrindavan (48.7%). About 48 per cent respondents in Vrindavan were found partially satisfied with their family conditions. However, about 56 per cent respondents in Varanasi were found dissatisfied with their family conditions.

Table 6.32

Satisfaction with Family Conditions

Satisfaction	*Varanasi*	*%*	*Vrindavan*	*%*	*Total*	*%*
Fully	27	12.0	146	28.7	173	23.63
Partial	72	32.0	242	47.7	314	42.90
No	126	56.0	119	23.6	245	33.47
Total	225	100.0	507	100.0	732	100.0

Source: Field Survey.

Nature of behaviour of parents and other family members towards widows is shown in Table 6.33. About 39 per cent respondents reported that behaviour of parents and other family members towards them have been normal. This was found more pronouncing in Vrindavan (44.5%). About 27 per cent respondents reported that behaviour of their parents and other family members towards them has been formal. However, about 21 per cent respondents revealed that the behaviour of their parents and other family members towards them has been strained. This was found more pronouncing in Varanasi (40.4%).

Table 6.33

Nature of Behaviour of Parents and Other Family Members towards Respondents

Nature of Behaviour	*Varanasi*	*%*	*Vrindavan*	*%*	*Total*	*%*
Harmonious	24	10.7	74	14.5	98	13.39
Normal	56	24.9	226	44.5	282	38.52
Formal	54	24.0	146	28.7	200	27.32
Strained	91	40.4	61	12.3	152	20.77
Total	225	100.0	507	100.0	732	100.0

Source: Field Survey.

Receiving of support from family is shown in Table 6.34. About three-fourth respondents revealed that they never received support from their family. This was found more pronouncing in Varanasi (78.7%). About 20 per cent respondents reported that they sometime received support from their families. This was found more pronouncing in Vrindavan (22.6%). Thus, only 6 per cent respondents said that they always received support from their families.

Table 6.34

Receiving of Support from Family

Support	*Varanasi*	*%*	*Vrindavan*	*%*	*Total*	*%*
Always	11	4.9	36	7.1	47	6.42
Sometimes	37	16.4	113	22.6	150	20.49
Never	177	78.7	358	70.3	535	73.09
Total	225	100.0	507	100.0	732	100.0

Source: Field Survey.

Caste-wise family support to respondents is shown in Table 6.35. Family support has been found higher in case of respondents from Scheduled Tribes and Scheduled Caste while majority of the respondents from General Caste and OBCs admitted that they are not getting any support from their families.

Table 6.35

Caste-wise Family Support to Respondents

Support	*Varanasi*				*Vrindavan*			
	General	*SC*	*ST*	*OBC*	*General*	*SC*	*ST*	*OBC*
Full	12.9	14.8	16.6	3.8	10.9	8.8	9.6	3.9
Partial	16.9	21.6	16.7	26.9	14.9	20.6	9.7	25.9
Nothing	70.2	64.6	66.7	69.2	75.2	70.6	70.7	70.2
Total	100.0	100.0	100.0	100.0	100.0	100.0	100.0	100.0

Source: Field Survey.

Age-wise family support to respondents is shown in Table 6.36. A higher proportion of respondents from higher age group admitted that they are receiving full support from their families while majority of the respondents from middle age group reported that they are not getting any support from their families.

Table 6.36

Age-wise Family Support to Respondents

Support	*Varanasi*				*Vrindavan*			
	26–35 Years	*36–45 Years*	*46–55 Years*	*56 Years and Above*	*26–35 Years*	*36–45 Years*	*46–55 Years*	*56 Years and Above*
Full	8.4	6.3	12.5	13.2	7.4	5.3	11.5	17.2
Partial	25.0	37.5	25.0	14.8	23.0	32.5	18.0	14.8
Nothing	66.6	56.2	62.5	72.0	69.6	72.2	70.5	66.0
Total	100.0	100.0	100.0	100.0	100.0	100.0	100.0	100.0

Source: Field Survey.

Table 6.37

Education-wise Family Support to Respondents

Support	*Varanasi*				*Vrindavan*			
	Illiterate	*Primary*	*Middle*	*Higher Studies*	*Illiterate*	*Primary*	*Middle*	*Higher Studies*
Full	8.3	6.3	12.5	12.6	5.0	5.0	10.0	13.0
Partial	25.0	37.5	25.0	14.7	26.0	35.0	25.0	15.0
Nothing	66.7	56.2	62.5	72.7	70.0	60.0	65.0	72.0
Total	100.0	100.0	100.0	100.0	100.0	100.0	100.0	100.0

Source: Field Survey.

Education-wise family support to respondents is shown in Table 6.37. A higher proportion of respondents from higher education level admitted that they are not getting any support from their families. However, a higher proportion of respondents from lower education level are receiving family support.

Receiving of financial support from families is shown in Table 6.38. About 71 per cent respondents reported that they did not receive any financial support from their families. This was found more pronouncing in Varanasi (80%). About 18 per cent respondents reported that they get partial financial support from their families, while about 11 per cent respondents said that they get full financial support from their families. The respondents getting full financial support from their families was recorded high in Vrindavan (14.7%) as compared to Varanasi (3.5%).

Table 6.38

Do You Get Financial Support from Your Family

Financial Support	*Varanasi*	*%*	*Vrindavan*	*%*	*Total*	*%*
Full	8	3.5	75	14.7	83	11.34
Partial	37	16.5	92	18.1	129	17.62
Nothing	180	80.0	340	67.2	520	71.04
Total	225	100.0	507	100.0	732	100.0

Source: Field Survey.

Social Conditions

The respondents were asked that whether their deceased husbands left any property for them. Most of the respondents reported that their deceased husbands did not leave any property for them. This was found more pronouncing in Vrindavan (85.4%) as compared to Varanasi (76.5%). Thus, about 17 per cent respondents revealed that their deceased husbands left property for them. The property has been in form of house only (Table 6.39).

Table 6.39

Did Your Deceased Husband Left Property

	Varanasi	*%*	*Vrindavan*	*%*	*Total*	*%*
Yes	53	23.5	74	14.6	127	17.35
No	172	76.5	433	85.4	605	82.65
Total	225	100.0	507	100.0	732	100.0
If Yes						
House	53	23.5	74	100.0	127	100.0
Agriculture Land						
Cash						
Others						
Total	53	100.0	74	100.0	127	100.0

Source: Field Survey.

The respondents were asked about their issues. About 28 per cent respondents revealed that they do not have any issue. This was found more pronouncing in Varanasi (33.8%). About 57 per cent respondents reported that they have sons. This was reported high in Vrindavan (63.5%) as compared to Varanasi (43.5%). About 15 per cent respondents have daughters (Table 6.40).

Table 6.40
How Many Children You Have

Number of Children	*Varanasi*	*%*	*Vrindavan*	*%*	*Total*	*%*
Son	98	43.5	322	63.5	420	57.38
Daughters	51	22.7	57	11.2	108	14.75
None	76	33.8	128	25.3	204	27.87
Total	225	100.0	507	100.0	732	100.0

Source: Field Survey.

The respondents were asked about the nature of work in which their children are engaged. About 27 per cent respondents reported that their children are engaged in agriculture. This was found more pronouncing in Vrindavan (31.9%) as compared to Varanasi (15.5%). About 22 per cent respondents reported that their children are labourers. This was found more pronouncing in Vrindavan (26.6%). About 36 per cent respondents revealed that their children are unemployed, engaged in house work or doing nothing for their earnings. This was found more pronouncing in Varanasi (Table 6.41).

Table 6.41
Type of Work in Which Children are Engaged

Type of Work	*Varanasi*	*%*	*Vrindavan*	*%*	*Total*	*%*
Agriculture	35	15.5	162	31.9	197	26.91
Trade	3	1.3	70	13.2	73	9.97
Petty or Large Business	8	3.6	26	5.3	34	5.05
Labour	28	12.4	135	26.6	163	22.27
Artisan	0	0	0	0	0	0
Job	0	0	0	0	0	0
Student	0	0	0	0	0	0
Unemployed/House Work	96	42.7	26	5.1	122	16.67
Nothing	55	24.4	88	17.9	143	19.54
Total	225	100.0	507	100.0	732	100.0

Source: Field Survey.

Caring of children is shown in Table 6.42. Majority of the respondents reported that they are themselves caring for their children. This was found more pronouncing in Vrindavan (78.5%). About 13 per cent respondents reported that their other relatives are taking care of their children. This was reported significantly higher in Vrindavan (15.3%). About 18 per cent respondents said that others are taking care of their children.

Table 6.42
Caring of Children

Caring	*Varanasi*	*%*	*Vrindavan*	*%*	*Total*	*%*
Self	101	44.9	398	78.5	499	68.17
Grand Parents	0	0	0	0	0	0
Other Relatives	20	4.5	78	15.3	98	13.39
Others	104	46.2	31	6.2	135	18.44
Total	225	100.0	507	100.0	732	100.0

Source: Field Survey.

The respondents were asked that whether their children are consulting with them. About 55 per cent respondents revealed that their children never consult them. This was found more pronouncing in Varanasi (66.7%). Slightly less than one-third respondents reported that sometimes their children consult them. This was found more pronouncing in Vrindavan (34.4%). Only 14 per cent respondents said that their children often consult with them. This was found more pronouncing in Vrindavan (15.3%) (Table 6.43).

Table 6.43
Whether Your Children Consult With You

Consult	*Varanasi*	*%*	*Vrindavan*	*%*	*Total*	*%*
Never	150	66.7	252	49.3	402	54.92
Sometimes	53	23.5	175	34.4	228	31.15
Often	22	9.8	80	15.3	102	13.93
Occasionally	0	0	0	0	0	0
Total	225	100.0	507	100.0	732	100.0

Source: Field Survey.

The respondents were asked that how they take important life decisions. Most of the respondents reported that they themselves take important life decisions (84.15%). About 10 per cent respondents reported that they consult with their friends for taking important life decisions. This was found more pronouncing in Varanasi (15.6%). Only 6 per cent respondents revealed that they are consulting with their relatives for taking important life decisions (Table 6.44).

Table 6.44
How Do You Take Important Life Decisions

Decisions	*Varanasi*	*%*	*Vrindavan*	*%*	*Total*	*%*
Consulting With Relatives	7	3.1	37	7.2	44	6.07
Consulting With Friends	35	15.6	37	7.2	72	9.84
Self	183	81.3	433	85.6	616	84.15
Other	0	0	0	0	0	0
Total	225	100.0	507	100.0	732	100.0

Source: Field Survey.

Type of belief in social values is shown in Table 6.45. About two-third respondents reported that they believe in traditional social values. This was found more pronouncing in Varanasi (78.2%) while about one-third respondents reported that they believe in adaptable social values. This was found more pronouncing in Vrindavan (39.1%).

Table 6.45

Type of Believe in Social Values

Social Values	*Varanasi*	*%*	*Vrindavan*	*%*	*Total*	*%*
Traditional	176	78.2	309	60.9	485	66.26
Modern	0	0	0	0	0	0
Adaptable	49	21.8	198	39.1	247	33.74
Logical	0	0	0	0	0	0
Total	225	100.0	507	100.0	732	100.0

Source: Field Survey.

Getting respect from society is shown in Table 6.46. Most of the respondents reported that they get respect from society. However, 2 per cent respondents revealed that they do not get respect from society. This was found more pronouncing in Varanasi (4.9%).

Table 6.46

Do You Get Respect from Society

Respect	*Varanasi*	*%*	*Vrindavan*	*%*	*Total*	*%*
Yes	214	95.1	501	98.8	715	97.68
No	11	4.9	6	1.2	17	2.32
Total	225	100.0	507	100.0	732	100.0

Source: Field Survey.

Table 6.47

Behaviour of Colleague/Classmate and Relatives towards Respondents

Behaviour	*Varanasi*	*%*	*Vrindavan*	*%*	*Total*	*%*
Harmonious	46	20.4	217	42.8	263	35.93
Normal	96	42.7	126	24.8	222	30.33
Formal	38	16.9	94	39.2	132	18.03
Strained	45	20.0	70	13.2	115	15.71
Total	225	100.0	507	100.0	732	100.0

Source: Field Survey.

About 36 per cent respondents reported that the behaviour of their colleagues and relatives towards them is harmonious. This was found more pronouncing in Vrindavan (42.8%). About 30 per cent respondents said that the behaviour of their colleagues and relatives towards them is normal. This was found more pronouncing in Varanasi (42.7%). About 18 per cent respondents further reported that the behaviour of their colleagues and relatives is formal towards them. Thus, about 16 per cent respondents revealed that the behaviour of their colleagues and relatives towards them is strained. This was found more pronouncing in Varanasi (20%) (Table 6.47).

Satisfaction with conditions is shown in Table 6.48. Majority of the respondents were found satisfied with their conditions (58.44%). About 21 per cent respondents reported that somewhat they are satisfied with their conditions. This was reported significantly higher in Varanasi (47.1%). About 22 per cent respondents in Varanasi were found dissatisfied with their conditions.

Table 6.48

Are You Satisfied With Your Condition

Satisfaction	*Varanasi*	*%*	*Vrindavan*	*%*	*Total*	*%*
Yes	70	31.1	431	85.4	501	68.44
Somewhat	106	47.1	46	9.4	152	20.77
No	49	21.8	30	5.2	79	10.79
Total	225	100.0	507	100.0	732	100.0

Source: Field Survey.

The respondents were asked that whether they are feeling insecure and alone. Most of the respondents reported that they are not feeling insecure and alone (91.94%). However, about 11 per cent respondents in Varanasi revealed that they are feeling insecure and alone (Table 6.49).

Table 6.49

Are You Feel Insecure and Alone

Feeling	*Varanasi*	*%*	*Vrindavan*	*%*	*Total*	*%*
Yes	24	10.7	35	6.1	59	8.06
No	201	89.3	472	93.9	673	91.94
Total	225	100.0	507	100.0	732	100.0

Source: Field Survey.

Table 6.50

Who Selected Your Deceased Husband

	Varanasi	*%*	*Vrindavan*	*%*	*Total*	*%*
Father/Brother	215	95.6	486	95.8	701	95.77
Maternal Uncle	10	35.1	21	4.14	31	4.23
Paternal Uncle	0	0	0	0	0	0
Some Other Relative	0	0	0	0	0	0
Total	225	100.0	507	100.0	732	100.0

Source: Field Survey.

The respondents were asked regarding the selection of their deceased husbands. Most of the respondents reported that their fathers/brothers selected their deceased husbands. However, about 4 per cent respondents revealed that their husbands were selected by their maternal uncle (Table 6.50).

Marriage is conceived differently by social scientists in different fields. While the popular concept of marriage is a union between man and woman, but it is accomplished through different rituals and ceremonies in order to promote cordial relations for a life time. Sociologist likes Blood, Lantz and Snyder, Bowman, Baber, Burgess, etc. view it as a system of roles and as involving primary relationships. A sociologist, while studying marriage, analyses not only the primary relationship involved in marriage but also how marriage involves performing new and varied roles and whether the persons involved are capable of performing those new roles or not, and how the inadequacy of performing these roles leads to family disorganization. What is important in marriage is how the role enactment of one partner corresponds to the role expectations of the other (Blood, 1960: 189).

According to Koos (1953: 44), marriage is a dividing line between the family of orientation and family of procreation in terms of the nature of roles one performs in the two families. According to Bowman (1960), the basic objects of the marriage are sex gratification, desire for home and children, companionship, social position and prestige, and economic security and protection. Today, as traditional society is changing into modern one, marriage has become a social necessity rather than a social ceremony. It is believed that spouse may significantly contribute in the development and maintenance of a house that is essential for performing human activities. Thus, the traditional concept of Hindu marriage as a sacrament to perform *dharma* is gradually changing. Nowadays, the new considerations are influencing the nature and rituals of Hindu marriage system. Couples are preferring marriages that fulfil the emerging needs of individual family. Thus, personal interest, economic earnings, mutual adjustment and compromising lifestyle is replacing the traditional criterion of Hindu marriage. Similarly, the nature and motives of Muslim marriage is also gradually changing with the change of time and technology. Thus, the basic concept of marriage in Muslim society as a contract is changing with the change of time. Perhaps, it is the growing influence of western culture and values of other religions. Earlier, the marriages were based on social value system rather than mutual understanding, personal relationship, personal interest and compromising living patterns. It is a growing tendency of later marriage due to economic reasons. It has also affected the social values, biological considerations and motives for the marriage.

Age at marriage is an important demographic variable as it influences the social status and the health of an individual. It has been observed that in the Indian perspective, majority of the women do not enjoy the reproductive rights and entitlements and a large number of girls are being married before attaining the mature age. They are also forced to bear the pregnancy and child birth which has negative consequences on their health. Due to early marriage of girls, they are unable to continue their education and, thus, they are being deprived of socio-economic opportunities for their career advancement.

Age at marriage is shown in Table 6.51. Majority of the respondents revealed that they were married before attaining the age of 15 years (74.18%). This was reported higher in Vrindavan (77.7%). About one-fourth respondents further reported that they were married in the age bracket of 16–25 years. This was found more pronouncing in Varanasi (35.1%).

Table 6.51

Age at Marriage of Respondents

Age	*Varanasi*	*%*	*Vrindavan*	*%*	*Total*	*%*
Less Than 15 Years	146	64.9	397	77.7	543	74.18
16 to 25 Years	79	35.1	110	22.3	189	25.82
26 to 35 Years	0	0	0	0	0	0
36 to 45 Years	0	0	0	0	0	0
Total	225	100.0	507	100.0	732	100.0

Source: Field Survey.

Age at marriage of their deceased husbands is shown in Table 6.52. About two-third respondents reported that at the time of their marriage, the age of their deceased husbands was between 16–25 years. However, about 18 per cent respondents revealed that they were less than 15 years at the time of marriage. This was found more pronouncing in Vrindavan (19.5%). About 4 per cent respondents reported that the age of their deceased husbands at the time of their marriage was in between 36 to 45 years. Thus, about 12 per cent respondents reported that the age of their deceased husbands at the time of their marriage was between 26 to 35 years.

Table 6.52

Age at Marriage of Deceased Husband of Respondents

Age	*Varanasi*	*%*	*Vrindavan*	*%*	*Total*	*%*
Less Than 15 Years	30	13.4	99	19.5	129	17.62
16 to 25 Years	153	68.0	335	67.1	488	66.67
26 to 35 Years	32	14.2	54	10.2	86	11.75
36 to 45 Years	10	4.4	19	3.2	29	3.96
Total	225	100.0	507	100.0	732	100.0

Source: Field Survey.

The respondents were further asked that whether they were satisfied with their martial life. Most of the respondents were found satisfied with their martial life (89.34%). However, about 11 per cent respondents were found dissatisfied with their marital life. This was reported slightly high in Varanasi (13.3%) (Table 6.53).

Table 6.53

Whether You Were Satisfied With Your Marital Life

Satisfaction	*Varanasi*	*%*	*Vrindavan*	*%*	*Total*	*%*
Yes	195	86.7	459	90.5	654	89.34
No	30	13.3	48	9.5	78	10.66
Total	225	100.0	507	100.0	732	100.0

Source: Field Survey.

Age of respondents at the time of death of their husbands is shown in Table 6.54. About 62 per cent respondents reported that they were above 45 years at the time of death of their husbands. This was found more pronouncing in Varanasi (67.5%). About 21 per cent respondents reported that they were in the age group of 36–45 years at the time of death of their husbands. About 7 per cent respondents revealed that they were less than 25 years at the time of death of their husbands. This was found more pronouncing in Vrindavan. About 10 per cent respondents were in the age group of 26–35 years at the time of death of their husbands.

Table 6.54

Age of Respondents at the Time of Death of Husband

Age	*Varanasi*	*%*	*Vrindavan*	*%*	*Total*	*%*
Less Than 15 Years	0	0	13	2.5	13	1.78
16 to 25 Years	6	2.7	34	6.8	40	5.46
26 to 35 Years	9	4.0	62	12.3	71	9.70
36 to 45 Years	58	25.8	99	20.6	157	21.45
45 Years and Above	152	67.5	299	58.8	451	61.61
Total	225	100.0	507	100.0	732	100.0

Source: Field Survey.

Table 6.55

Caste-wise Age of Respondents at the Time of Demise of Spouse

Age	*Varanasi*				*Vrindavan*			
	General	*SC*	*ST*	*OBC*	*General*	*SC*	*ST*	*OBC*
Less Than 15 Years	4.8	4.8	6.1	7.8	4.8	7.8	5.1	6.8
16–25 Years	3.8	2.4	4.2	3.8	3.8	2.4	5.2	4.8
26–35 Years	29.2	23.8	18.8	26.9	30.2	20.8	18.2	26.9
36–45 Years	27.5	28.5	27.1	23.1	30.5	23.5	20.1	21.1
45 Years and Above	34.7	40.5	43.8	38.4	30.7	45.5	50.8	40.4
Total	100.0	100.0	100.0	100.0	100.0	100.0	100.0	100.0

Source: Field Survey.

Caste-wise age of respondents at the time of demise of spouse is shown in Table 6.55. A significant proportion of respondents from lower communities reported that they were widows in the early age i.e. less than 15 years. However, a higher proportion of respondents from the Scheduled Tribes reported that they became widows in the higher age.

The age of respondents at the time of demise of spouse is shown in Table 6.56. Majority of the respondents from the higher age group reported that they became widows during the age of 46–55 years and 26–35 years. A significant proportion of respondents from higher age group became widows at a lower age.

Table 6.56

Age-wise Age of Respondents at the Time of Demise of Spouse

Age of Respondents/ Time of Demise	*Varanasi*				*Vrindavan*			
	26–35 Years	*36–45 Years*	*46–55 Years*	*56 Years and Above*	*26–35 Years*	*36–45 Years*	*46–55 Years*	*56 Years and Above*
Less Than 15 Years	0.0	0.0	0.0	2.9	0.0	0.0	0.0	1.0
16–25 Years	0.0	6.2	0.0	2.3	3.0	5.2	0.0	2.0
26–35 Years	8.3	6.3	8.4	29.5	6.3	5.3	5.4	26.5
36–45 Years	33.3	37.5	20.8	27.1	30.3	35.5	18.8	25.3
45 Years and Above	58.4	50.0	70.8	38.2	60.4	54.0	75.8	45.2
Total	100.0	100.0	100.0	100.0	100.0	100.0	100.0	100.0

Source: Field Survey.

Education-wise age of respondents at the time of demise of spouse is shown in Table 6.57. Majority of the respondents from middle and low education level became widows in the higher age; however, a significant proportion of respondents from higher education level became widow in the age group of 26–35 years.

Table 6.57

Education-wise Age of Respondents at the Time of Demise of Spouse

Age of Respondents/ Time of Demise	*Varanasi*				*Vrindavan*			
	Illite-rate	*Prim-ary*	*Middle*	*Higher Studies*	*Illite- rate*	*Prim-ary*	*Middle*	*Higher Studies*
Less Than 15 Years	0.0	0.0	0.0	2.9	0.0	0.0	0.0	2.0
16–25 Years	0.0	6.2	0.0	2.3	0.0	6.0	0.0	2.0
26–35 Years	8.3	6.3	8.4	29.4	7.0	6.0	8.0	30.0
36–45 Years	33.3	37.5	20.8	27.1	33.0	38.0	20.0	26.0
45 Years and Above	58.4	50.0	70.8	38.3	60.0	50.0	72.0	40.0
Total	100.0	100.0	100.0	100.0	100.0	100.0	100.0	100.0

Source: Field Survey.

Causes of death of husbands are shown in Table 6.58. Majority of the respondents reported that the main cause of death of their husband was a prolonging disease (72.13%). This was found more pronouncing in Varanasi (82.2%) as compared to Vrindavan (67.7%). About 13 per cent respondents reported that the main cause of death of their husbands was heart disease. This was reported slightly high in Vrindavan (14.2%). Other main reasons for death of husbands were cholera and typhoid.

Table 6.58

Causes of Death of Husband

Causes	*Varanasi*	*%*	*Vrindavan*	*%*	*Total*	*%*
Heart Disease	24	10.7	71	14.2	95	12.98
Cholera	5	2.2	26	5.6	31	4.23
Asthma	0	0	0	0	0	0
Typhoid	2	0.9	27	5.2	29	3.96
Prolonged Disease	185	82.2	343	67.7	528	72.13
Sudden Death	0	0	0	0	0	0
Old Age	0	0	0	0	0	0
None	9	4.0	40	7.3	49	6.69
Total	225	100.0	507	100.0	732	100.0

Source: Field Survey.

The respondents were asked that whether treatment of the disease of their deceased husbands was provided. Majority of the respondents reported that treatment of the disease of their deceased husbands was provided. This was found more pronouncing in Varanasi. However, about one-third respondents reported that treatment was not provided to their deceased husbands. This was found more pronouncing in Vrindavan (37.3%). The main reasons for non-treatment were financial constraints, carelessness of doctors and lack of sufficient time (Table 6.59).

Table 6.59

Whether Treatment of the Disease of Your Husband was Provided

Treatment	*Varanasi*	*%*	*Vrindavan*	*%*	*Total*	*%*
Yes	181	89.4	318	62.7	499	68.17
No	44	19.6	189	37.3	233	31.83
Total	225	100.0	507	100.0	732	100.0
If No, Reason for Non Treatment						
Did Not Get Time	10	22.0	27	15.2	37	15.88
No Facility for Treatment	8	18.0	26	13.7	34	14.59
Financial Constraint	22	50.0	112	59.0	134	57.51
Family Tension	0	0	0	0	0	0
Carelessness of Doctor	4	4.0	24	12.1	28	12.02
Others	0	0	0	0	0	0
Total	44	100.0	189	100.0	233	100.0

Source: Field Survey.

Environment of Widow Home

The respondents were asked about the source of information about widow home. About 23 per cent respondents reported that they got information about widow homes from their neighbours, while 21 per cent respondents got information about widow homes from their relatives. Only 7 per cent respondents got information about widow homes from NGOs. This was found more pronouncing in Varanasi (14.7%). About two-fifth respondents reported that they get information about widow homes from others (Table 6.60).

Table 6.60

How Did You Know About the Widow Home

	Varanasi	%	*Vrindavan*	%	*Total*	%
From Newspaper	9	4.0	39	7.6	48	4.56
From Relatives	60	26.7	92	18.4	152	20.77
From Neighbours	55	24.4	110	21.6	165	22.54
From NGOs	33	14.7	21	4.1	54	7.38
From Others	68	30.2	245	48.3	313	42.76
Total	225	100.0	507	100.0	732	100.0

Source: Field Survey.

The respondents were asked about how people perceive widows. Most of the respondents reported that people look at the widows with sympathy. This was found more pronouncing in Varanasi (93.8%) as compared to Vrindavan (82.4%). About 14 per cent respondents revealed that people are having physical relationship with widows. This was found more pronouncing in Vrindavan (17.6%). It is to be noted that in Vrindavan and Varanasi, widows are being sexually assaulted and exploited by local people including rickshaw pullers, auto and taxi drivers, shop owners and religious leaders (Table 6.61).

Table 6.61

How Do People Perceive Widows

	Varanasi	%	*Vrindavan*	%	*Total*	%
With Sympathy	211	93.8	418	82.4	629	85.93
To Have Physical Relationship	14	6.2	89	17.6	103	14.07
Nothing Like This	0	0	0	0	0	0
It All Depends on Self	0	0	0	0	0	0
Others	0	0	0	0	0	0
Total	225	100.0	507	100.0	732	100.0

Source: Field Survey.

Reasons for coming to widow homes are shown in Table 6.62. About 48 per cent respondents reported that they themselves came to widow homes. This was found more pronouncing in Varanasi (58.3%). About 23 per cent respondents reported that they are in a widow home due to their family members. This was found more pronouncing in Vrindavan (27.2%). About 20 per cent respondents revealed that they are in a widow home due to the pressure of neighbours and society. This was found more pronouncing in Vrindavan (28.2%).

Table 6.62
Reasons for Coming to Widow Home

Reasons	*Varanasi*	*%*	*Vrindavan*	*%*	*Total*	*%*
Due to Family Members	32	14.2	136	27.2	168	22.95
Due to Pressure of Neighbours and Society	3	1.3	141	28.2	144	19.67
Self	131	58.3	217	42.2	348	47.54
Others	59	26.2	13	2.4	72	9.84
Total	225	100.0	507	100.0	732	100.0

Source: Field Survey.

Caste-wise reasons for coming to Widow homes are shown in Table 6.63. A higher proportion of respondents from OBC communities reported that due to the pressure of neighbours and societies and family members, they shifted to widow homes. However, a large proportion of respondents from General Caste admitted that they came to widow homes by themselves, out of choice.

Table 6.63
Caste-wise Reasons for Coming to Widow Home

Reasons	*Varanasi*				*Vrindavan*			
	General	*SC*	*ST*	*OBC*	*General*	*SC*	*ST*	*OBC*
Due to Family Members	5.3	7.1	9.3	16.4	3.3	4.1	9.3	18.4
Due to Pressure of Neighbours and Society	16.3	26.2	20.7	29.8	11.3	20.2	20.7	20.8
Self	78.4	66.7	70.0	53.8	85.4	75.7	70.0	60.8
Others	0.0	0.0	0.0	0.0	0.0	0.0	0.0	0.0
Total	100.0	100.0	100.0	100.0	100.0	100.0	100.0	100.0

Source: Field Survey.

Table 6.64
Age-wise Reasons for Coming to Widow Home

Reasons	*Varanasi*				*Vrindavan*			
	26–35 Years	*36–45 Years*	*46–55 Years*	*56 Years and Above*	*26–35 Years*	*36–45 Years*	*46–55 Years*	*56 Years and Above*
Due to Family Members	16.7	18.8	16.7	14.2	10.7	15.8	14.7	10.2
Due to Pressure of Neighbours and Society	0.0	0.0	0.0	2.9	0.0	0.0	0.0	2.9
Self	58.3	62.5	66.7	60.0	60.3	68.5	70.7	66.0
Others	25.0	18.7	16.6	22.9	29.0	15.7	14.6	20.9
Total	100.0	100.0	100.0	100.0	100.0	100.0	100.0	100.0

Source: Field Survey.

Age-wise reasons for coming to widow homes are shown in Table 6.64. A higher age group of respondents from higher and middle age group reported that they came to widow homes by themselves. However, a significant proportion of respondents from lower age group came to widow homes due to family members.

Education-wise reasons for coming to widow homes are shown in Table 6.65. There is no correlation between education and reasons for coming to widow homes. However, about two-third respondents from middle level education and primary level education reported that they came to widow homes by themselves as against about 60 per cent illiterate respondents who came to widow homes.

Table 6.65

Education-wise Reasons for Coming to Widow Home

Reasons	*Varanasi*				*Vrindavan*			
	Illiterate	*Primary*	*Middle*	*Higher Studies*	*Illiterate*	*Primary*	*Middle*	*Higher Studies*
Due to Family Members	16.7	18.8	16.7	15.1	15.0	17.0	17.0	16.0
Due to Pressure of Neighbours and Society	25.0	18.7	16.6	24.9	25.0	18.0	18.0	24.0
Self	58.3	62.5	66.7	60.0	60.0	65.0	65.0	60.0
Others	0.0	0.0	0.0	0.0	0.0	0.0		
Total	100.0	100.0	100.0	100.0	100.0	100.0	100.0	100.0

Source: Field Survey.

Table 6.66

Environment in Widow Home

Environment	*Varanasi*	*%*	*Vrindavan*	*%*	*Total*	*%*
Harmonious	119	52.9	179	35.4	298	40.71
Normal	78	34.7	313	61.7	391	53.42
Stressful	28	12.4	15	2.9	43	5.87
Total	225	100.0	507	100.0	732	100.0
If Stressful, Do You Scared						
Yes	28	100.0	15	2.9	43	100.0
No	0	0	0	0	0	0
Others	0	0	0	0	0	0
Total	28	100.0	15	100.0	43	100.0

Source: Field Survey.

Environment in widow homes is shown in Table 6.66. More than half of the respondents reported that the environment in widow homes is normal. This was found more pronouncing in Vrindavan (61.7%). About two-fifth respondents reported that the environment in widow homes is harmonious. This was reported significantly higher in Varanasi (52.9%) as compared to Vrindavan (35.4%). About 12 per cent respondents in Varanasi reported that the environment in widow homes is stressful while this was reported by only 2.9 per cent in Vrindavan.

Facilities in widow homes are shown in Table 6.67. Most of the respondents reported that proper facilities in widow homes are available. However, the proportion of respondents complained about the lack of proper facilities of drinking water, bathroom and toilets, mess, entertainment and security. The facilities in terms of drinking water, mess, bathrooms and toilets in widow homes were reported poor in Vrindavan as compared to Varanasi.

Table 6.67

Facilities in Widow Home

Facility	*Varanasi*	*%*	*Vrindavan*	*%*	*Total*	*%*
Proper Accommodation	194	86.2	499	98.4	693	94.67
Proper Drinking Water	211	93.8	334	65.8	545	74.45
Regular Electricity	212	94.2	498	98.2	710	96.99
Proper Facility of Bathroom and Toilet	208	92.4	377	74.3	585	79.92
Proper Cleanliness	209	92.9	494	97.4	703	96.04
Mess Facility	211	93.8	375	73.9	586	80.05
Entertainment and Security Arrangements	152	67.6	489	96.4	641	87.57
Others	0	0	0	0	0	0

Source: Field Survey.

Awareness about government welfare programmes is shown in Table 6.68. About 35 per cent respondents were found aware about government welfare programmes. This was found more pronouncing in Vrindavan (43.6%). About 35 per cent respondents were found unaware about the government welfare programmes. This was found more pronouncing in Varanasi (46.7%). About 30 per cent respondents were partially aware about government welfare programmes. This was recorded high in Varanasi (36.9%).

Table 6.68

Awareness about Government Welfare Programmes

Awareness	*Varanasi*	*%*	*Vrindavan*	*%*	*Total*	*%*
Yes	37	16.4	219	43.6	256	34.97
Partial	83	36.9	137	27.1	220	30.05
No	105	46.7	149	29.3	254	34.70
Total	225	100.0	507	100.0	732	100.0

Source: Field Survey.

Caste-wise awareness about government welfare schemes is shown in Table 6.69. There is no correlation between caste and awareness of government welfare schemes. However, most of the respondents from SC and ST communities were found unaware about the government welfare schemes.

Table 6.69

Caste-wise Awareness About Government Welfare Scheme

Awareness	Varanasi				Vrindavan			
	General	SC	ST	OBC	General	SC	ST	OBC
Yes	3.7	4.8	4.2	3.8	2.7	3.8	4.2	2.8
Partial	19.8	11.9	16.7	23.1	16.8	10.9	15.7	22.1
No	76.5	83.3	79.1	73.1	80.5	85.3	80.1	75.1
Total	100.0	100.0	100.0	100.0	100.0	100.0	100.0	100.0

Source: Field Survey.

Age-wise awareness about government welfare schemes is shown in Table 6.70. A higher proportion of respondents from lower age group were found aware about the government welfare schemes; however, majority of the respondents from higher age group were found unaware about the government welfare schemes.

Table 6.70

Age-wise Awareness About Government Welfare Scheme

Awareness	Varanasi				Vrindavan			
	26–35 Years	36–45 Years	46–55 Years	56 Years and Above	26–35 Years	36–45 Years	46–55 Years	56 Years and Above
Yes	16.7	12.5	8.4	11.2	15.7	9.5	8.4	9.2
Partial	25.0	31.2	20.8	35.2	20.0	30.2	20.8	30.2
No	58.3	56.3	70.8	53.6	64.3	60.3	70.8	60.6
Total	100.0	100.0	100.0	100.0	100.0	100.0	100.0	100.0

Source: Field Survey.

Table 6.71

Education-wise Awareness About Government Welfare Schemes

Awareness	Varanasi				Vrindavan			
	Illiterate	Primary	Middle	Higher Studies	Illiterate	Primary	Middle	Higher Studies
Yes	16.7	12.5	8.4	11.2	15.0	15.0	10.0	20.0
Partial	25.0	31.2	20.8	35.3	25.0	20.0	20.0	40.0
No	58.3	56.3	70.8	53.5	50.0	65.0	70.0	40.0
Total	100.0	100.0	100.0	100.0	100.0	100.0	100.0	100.0

Source: Field Survey.

Education-wise awareness about government welfare schemes is shown in Table 6.71. There has been positive correlation between education and awareness about government welfare schemes. A high proportion of respondents from higher education level were found partially and fully aware as compared to respondents from low education level.

The respondents were further asked whether they were getting government support. About one-third respondents reported that they were getting government support. This was reported significantly high in Vrindavan (45.7%). Thus, most of the respondents in Varanasi are not getting any government support (Table 6.72).

Table 6.72
Do You Get Government Support

Support	*Varanasi*	*%*	*Vrindavan*	*%*	*Total*	*%*
Yes	20	8.9	232	45.7	252	34.43
No	205	91.1	275	54.3	480	65.57
Total	225	100.0	507	100.0	732	100.0

Source: Field Survey.

Economic Conditions

The respondents were asked that in which age their deceased husbands faced financial problems. About two-third respondents reported that their deceased husbands faced financial problems in the age group of less than 40 years. About 17 per cent respondents further reported that their deceased husbands faced financial problems in the age group of 41–49 years. About 17 per cent respondents said that their deceased husbands faced financial problems in the age group of above 50 years (Table 6.73).

Table 6.73
In Which Age Your Deceased Husband Faced Financial Problem

Age	*Varanasi*	*%*	*Vrindavan*	*%*	*Total*	*%*
Less Than 40 Years	149	66.2	336	67.2	485	66.26
41–49	52	23.1	73	14.3	125	17.08
50–59	9	4.0	53	10.4	62	8.47
60 years and above	15	6.7	45	8.1	60	8.20
Total	225	100.0	507	100.0	732	100.0

Source: Field Survey.

The respondents were further asked whether they face financial problems after death of their husbands. More than three-fourth respondents admitted that they face financial problems after the death of their husbands. This was found more pronouncing in Varanasi (94.7%) as compared to Vrindavan (68.1%). Those who face financial problems after the death of their husbands further reported that they manage from widow homes (41.76%) and doing labour (28.67%) while about 30 per cent respondents did anything to manage the problem (Table 6.74).

Table 6.74
Did You Faced Financial Problems after Death of Your Husband

Problems	*Varanasi*	*%*	*Vrindavan*	*%*	*Total*	*%*
Yes	213	94.7	345	68.1	558	76.23
No	12	5.3	162	31.9	174	23.77
Total	225	100.0	507	100.0	732	100.0
If Yes, What You Did						
Managed from Widow Home	152	71.4	81	23.5	233	41.76
Labour	12	5.2	148	42.9	160	28.67
Petty Business	0	0	0	0	0	0
None	49	23.4	116	33.6	165	29.57
Total	213	100.0	345	100.0	558	100.0

Source: Field Survey.

In order to resolve the financial problems, the widows initiated work (63.81%), mobilize credit/borrowings and sold out their house. A significant number of respondents further reported that their children started working in order to resolve the economic problems. The proportion of respondents reporting that their children started working in order to resolve economic problems was recorded high in Varanasi (39.9%) as compared to Vrindavan (6.9%) (Table 6.75).

Table 6.75
What Work You Did for Resolving Economic Problems

	Varanasi	*%*	*Vrindavan*	*%*	*Total*	*%*
Selling of House	6	2.8	26	7.5	32	5.73
Borrowing/Loan	6	2.8	70	20.3	76	13.6
Initiating Work	121	56.8	196	56.8	317	56.81
Children Started Working	7	3.2	24	6.9	31	5.56
Other	85	4.0	191	55.4	276	49.46
Total	213	100.0	345	100.0	558	100.0

Source: Field Survey.

Table 6.76
What You Did to Resolve Your Problems

	Varanasi	*%*	*Vrindavan*	*%*	*Total*	*%*
Loan from Bank	8	3.6	20	3.9	28	3.83
Loan from Moneylender	19	8.4	41	8.1	60	8.20
Loan from Friend	69	30.7	155	30.6	224	30.60
None	129	57.3	291	57.4	420	57.38
Total	225	100.0	507	100.0	732	100.0

Source: Field Survey.

The respondents were further asked what they did to resolve their problems. About 57 per cent respondents revealed that they did nothing while slightly less than one-third respondents reported that they borrowed from their friends. About 12 per cent respondents further reported that they borrowed money from banks and moneylenders (Table 6.76).

About half of the respondents reported that they are getting widow pension. This was found more pronouncing in Vrindavan (63.9%) as compared to Varanasi (16.4%). Thus, most of the respondents in Varanasi reported that they are not getting widow pension. It is to be noted that amount of widow pension is meagre for maintenance (Table 6.77).

Table 6.77

Do You Get Widow Pension

	Varanasi	*%*	*Vrindavan*	*%*	*Total*	*%*
Yes	37	16.4	324	63.9	361	49.32
No	188	83.6	183	36.1	371	50.68
Total	225	100.0	507	100.0	732	100.0

Source: Field Survey.

The respondents were asked whether they got respect from their family members before being widows. About 58 per cent respondents reported that they sometimes received respect from their family members before becoming widows. This was found more pronouncing in Vrindavan (62.9%). About one-fourth respondents reported that they never received respect from their family members before being widows. About 18 per cent respondents further reported that they received respect often from their family members before becoming widows. This was found more pronouncing in Varanasi (27.5%) (Table 6.78).

Table 6.78

Did You Get Respect from Family Members before Being Widow

Respect	*Varanasi*	*%*	*Vrindavan*	*%*	*Total*	*%*
Never	54	24.0	122	24.1	176	24.04
Sometimes	109	48.44	316	62.9	425	58.06
Often	62	27.56	69	13.0	131	17.90
Total	225	100.0	507	100.0	732	100.0

Source: Field Survey.

The respondents were asked that how their family members treated them after being widow. About two-fifth respondents revealed that their family members did not bother them after they became a widow. This was found more pronouncing in Varanasi (68%) as compared to Vrindavan (31%). About 30 per cent respondents reported that their family members were harmonious towards them after they became widows. This was found more pronouncing in Vrindavan (36.8%). More than one-fourth respondents said that their family members treated them stressfully after they became widows. This was found more pronouncing in Vrindavan (32.2%) (Table 6.79).

Table 6.79

How Did Your Family Members Treat You After Becoming Widows

	Varanasi	*%*	*Vrindavan*	*%*	*Total*	*%*
Harmonious	35	15.6	187	36.8	222	30.33
Stressful	37	16.4	164	32.2	201	27.46
They Do Not Bother	153	68.0	156	31.0	309	42.21
Total	225	100.0	507	100.0	732	100.0

Source: Field Survey.

About 45 per cent respondents reported that they never visit their family. This was found more pronouncing in Varanasi (66.2%). About one-fourth respondents reported that they are visiting their family once in a year. This was found more pronouncing in Vrindavan (34.1%). About 16 per cent respondents further reported that they are visiting their family one time in 5 years while about 13 per cent respondents are visiting their family on festivals (Table 6.80).

Table 6.80

Do You Visit Your Family

	Varanasi	*%*	*Vrindavan*	*%*	*Total*	*%*
Once in a Year	23	10.2	167	34.1	190	25.96
On Festivals	22	9.8	75	14.7	97	13.25
One-Five Years	31	13.8	84	16.1	115	15.71
Never	149	66.2	181	35.1	330	45.08
Total	225	100.0	507	100.0	732	100.0

Source: Field Survey.

Caste-wise visit to family members is shown in Table 6.81. A high proportion of respondents from General Caste in Varanasi admitted that they never visit their family members. However, a large proportion of respondents from Scheduled Tribes and Scheduled Castes in Vrindavan reported that they never visit their family members. A significant proportion of respondents from Scheduled Caste and Scheduled Tribes in both the districts reported that they visit their family members on festivals.

Table 6.81

Caste-wise Visit to Family Members

Visit	*Varanasi*				*Vrindavan*			
	General	*SC*	*ST*	*OBC*	*General*	*SC*	*ST*	*OBC*
Once in a Year	4.7	2.4	2.1	11.7	6.7	1.4	2.1	10.7
On Festivals	11.3	21.4	18.7	11.5	15.3	20.4	15.7	9.5
1–5 Years	7.6	4.8	2.1	11.5	6.6	2.8	2.1	9.5
Never	76.4	71.4	27.1	65.3	70.4	75.4	80.1	70.3
Total	100.0	100.0	100.0	100.0	100.0	100.0	100.0	100.0

Source: Field Survey.

Age-wise visit to family members is shown in Table 6.82. A higher proportion of respondents from higher age group reported that they never visit their family members; however, a significant proportion of respondents from lower age group reported that they are visiting their family members on festivals.

Table 6.82
Age-wise Visit to Family Members

Visit	*Varanasi*				*Vrindavan*			
	26–35 Years	*36–45 Years*	*46–55 Years*	*56 Years and Above*	*26–35 Years*	*36–45 Years*	*46–55 Years*	*56 Years and Above*
Once in a Year	8.3	6.2	4.1	5.3	7.3	8.2	5.1	5.3
On Festivals	16.7	25.0	12.5	17.0	14.7	25.0	15.5	15.0
1–5 Years	8.3	6.3	4.2	10.7	7.3	6.3	4.2	9.7
Never	66.7	62.5	79.2	67.0	70.4	60.5	75.2	70.0
Total	100.0	100.0	100.0	100.0	100.0	100.0	100.0	100.0

Source: Field Survey.

Education-wise visit to family members is shown in Table 6.83. There is no correlation between education and visit to family members. A higher proportion of respondents from middle and higher education level reported that they never visit their family members; however, about two-third illiterate respondents in Varanasi and 70 per cent illiterate respondents in Vrindavan reported that they never visit their family members.

Table 6.83
Education-wise Visit to Family Members

Visit	*Varanasi*				*Vrindavan*			
	Illiterate	*Primary*	*Middle*	*Higher Studies*	*Illiterate*	*Primary*	*Middle*	*Higher Studies*
Once in a Year	8.3	6.2	4.2	5.3	7.0	5.0	5.0	6.0
On Festivals	16.7	25.0	12.5	18.1	15.0	25.0	10.0	18.0
1–5 Years	8.3	12.5	4.2	7.5	8.0	10.0	5.0	6.0
Never	66.7	56.3	79.1	69.1	70.0	60.0	80.0	70.0
Total	100.0	100.0	100.0	100.0	100.0	100.0	100.0	100.0

Source: Field Survey.

The respondents were asked whether their relatives and friends visit them. About two-third respondents reported that their relatives and friends never visit them. This was found more pronouncing in Varanasi as compared to Vrindavan. About one-fourth respondents reported that sometimes their relatives and friends visit them while only 9 per cent respondents said that their relatives and friends visit them often (Table 6.84).

Table 6.84

Do Your Relatives and Friends Visit You

	Varanasi	%	*Vrindavan*	%	*Total*	%
Never	150	66.7	329	64.8	479	65.44
Sometimes	55	24.4	132	26.1	187	25.55
Often	20	8.9	46	9.1	66	9.02
Total	225	100.0	507	100.0	732	100.0

Source: Field Survey.

The respondents were further asked that whether their relatives and friends invite them on festivals. About 69 per cent respondents admitted that their relatives and friends never invite them on festivals. This was found more pronouncing in Vrindavan. About 27 per cent respondents reported that their relatives and friends sometime invite them on festivals. This was found more pronouncing in Varanasi. About 4 per cent respondents further reported that their relatives and friends invite them often on festivals. It is to be noted that for the first time, with the initiative of Sulabh International Social Service Organisation, New Delhi, widows from Vrindavan and Vrindavan visited their native place in West Bengal during the festival of Durga Puja in 2013 (Table 6.85).

Table 6.85

Do Your Relatives and Friends Invite You on Festivals

	Varanasi	%	*Vrindavan*	%	*Total*	%
Never	151	67.1	354	69.1	505	68.99
Sometimes	59	26.2	141	28.8	200	27.32
Often	15	6.7	12	2.1	27	3.68
Total	225	100.0	507	100.0	732	100.0

Source: Field Survey.

Emotional Conditions

About 58 per cent respondents reported that they feel sometime unhappy. This was found more pronouncing in Varanasi (61.8%) as compared to Vrindavan (56.3%). About 11 per cent respondents further reported that they feel often unhappy. This was reported significantly high in Varanasi (22.2%). About 38 per cent respondents in Vrindavan said that they never feel unhappy. This is to be noted that widows are living in isolation. They are cut off from society and do not frequently participate in socio-cultural gatherings. Thus, their emotions are being affected. This causes unhappiness among them (Table 6.86).

Table 6.86
Do You Feel Unhappy

	Varanasi	%	Vrindavan	%	Total	%
Never	36	16.0	195	38.4	231	31.56
Sometimes	139	61.8	285	56.3	424	57.92
Often	50	22.2	27	5.3	77	10.52
Total	225	100.0	507	100.0	732	100.0

Source: Field Survey.

The respondents were asked whether they get angry. About 54 per cent respondents reported that sometimes they get angry. This was found more pronouncing in Vrindavan (66.6%) as compared to Varanasi (24.8%). About 36 per cent respondents reported that they never get angry. This was found more pronouncing in Varanasi (58.2%). About 11 per cent respondents said they often get angry. This was found more pronouncing in Varanasi (16.9%) (Table 6.87).

Table 6.87
Do You Get Angry

	Varanasi	%	Vrindavan	%	Total	%
Never	131	58.2	131	25.9	262	25.79
Sometimes	56	24.8	337	66.6	393	53.69
Often	38	16.9	39	7.7	77	10.51
Total	225	100.0	507	100.0	732	100.0

Source: Field Survey.

The respondents were further asked whether they feel sleeplessness. About 18 per cent respondents said that they never feel sleeplessness. This was found more pronouncing in Vrindavan (22.1%). About 58 per cent respondents reported that they sometimes feel sleeplessness while about one-fourth respondents often feel sleeplessness. This was found more pronouncing in Varanasi (Table 6.88).

Table 6.88
Do You Feel Sleeplessness

	Varanasi	%	Vrindavan	%	Total	%
Never	20	8.9	112	22.1	132	18.03
Sometimes	127	56.4	295	58.2	422	57.65
Often	78	34.7	100	19.7	178	24.32
Total	225	100.0	507	100.0	732	100.0

Source: Field Survey.

Reasons for emotional feelings are shown in Table 6.89. Fear of future (55.33%), socio-economic conditions (28.83%), bad health (9.02%) and sense of insecurity (6.83%) are some of the main reasons for emotional feelings. The reasons for emotional feelings vary across the selected districts.

Table 6.89

Reasons for Your Emotional Feelings

Reasons	*Varanasi*	*%*	*Vrindavan*	*%*	*Total*	*%*
Sense of Insecurity	22	9.8	28	5.5	50	6.83
Socio-Economic Condition	126	56.0	85	16.7	211	28.83
Fear of Future	77	34.2	328	64.7	405	55.33
Bad Health	0	0	66	13.1	66	9.02
Increase of Problems Due to Old Age	0	0	0	0	0	0
Others	0	0	0	0	0	0
Total	225	100.0	507	100.0	732	100.0

Source: Field Survey.

Cultural and religious ties (35.11%), listening to taunts from neighbours and relatives (25.96%), circumstances (23.63%) and staying in touch with family (4.37%) are some of the main reasons that support the logic that widows should not live alone (Table 6.90).

Table 6.90

Why Widows Should Not Live Alone

Reasons	*Varanasi*	*%*	*Vrindavan*	*%*	*Total*	*%*
They Stay in Touch With Their Family	14	6.2	18	3.3	32	4.37
Cultural and Religious Ties	114	50.8	143	28.2	257	35.11
Due to Circumstances	75	33.3	98	19.3	173	23.63
Do Not Want to Die	5	2.2	36	7.1	41	0.14
Do Not Want to Listen Taunts from Neighbours and Relatives	14	6.2	176	34.1	190	25.96
Others	3	1.3	36	7.1	39	5.33
Total	225	100.0	507	100.0	732	100.0

Source: Field Survey.

Table 6.91

To Whom You Like to Talk

	Varanasi	*%*	*Vrindavan*	*%*	*Total*	*%*
Nobody	35	15.6	55	10.9	90	12.30
Friends and Neighbours	25	11.1	213	42.0	238	32.51
Relatives	75	33.3	44	8.7	119	16.26
Family Members	10	4.4	68	13.4	78	10.66
Others	80	35.6	127	25.0	207	28.28
Total	225	100.0	507	100.0	732	100.0

Source: Field Survey.

The respondents were asked that to whom they like to talk. About one-third respondents reported that they like to talk with their friends and neighbours. This was found more pronouncing in Vrindavan (42%). More than one-fourth respondents reported that they want to talk with their relatives and family members. This was found more pronouncing in Varanasi as compared to Vrindavan. About 12 per cent respondents were not found interested to talk anybody (Table 6.91).

The respondents were asked that in which circumstances they remember their deceased husbands. Slightly less than one-third respondents reported that they remember their deceased husbands at the time of family problem. This was found more pronouncing in Varanasi (49.8%). About 21 per cent respondents reported that they remember their deceased husbands during family functions. About 20 per cent respondents reported that they remember their deceased husbands on seeing someone similar looking. Similarly, about 16 per cent respondents said that they remember their deceased husbands on seeing things he used to use. About 11 per cent respondents remember their deceased husbands on their birth day (Table 6.92).

Table 6.92

In Which Circumstances Do You Remember Your Deceased Husband

	Varanasi	*%*	*Vrindavan*	*%*	*Total*	*%*
Family Functions	45	20.0	108	21.3	153	20.90
Birth Day	22	9.8	58	11.4	80	10.93
On Seeing Someone Similar Looking	35	15.6	111	22.0	146	19.95
On Seeing Things He Used to Use	11	4.8	110	21.7	121	16.53
At the Time of Family Problem	112	49.8	120	23.6	232	31.69
Total	225	100.0	507	100.0	732	100.0

Source: Field Survey.

Health Conditions

Majority of the respondents revealed that they are unhealthy (63.66%). This was found more pronouncing in Vrindavan (54.1%). Thus, about 36 per cent respondents were found healthy. This was found more pronouncing in Varanasi (37.3%). It is to be noted that the health conditions of widows is being affected by their living conditions. Most of the widows are living in unhygienic, narrowed space and lack proper clothing, bedding, furniture, etc. In the absence of proper bed, they are forced to sleep on floor while they do not get nutritious and healthy food on regular basis besides they are not able to afford their proper treatment and health care. In absence of health care and medical treatment, the health of widows further deteriorates (Table 6.93).

Table 6.93
How is Your Health

	Varanasi	*%*	*Vrindavan*	*%*	*Total*	*%*
Healthy	84	37.3	182	35.9	266	36.34
Unhealthy	141	62.7	325	64.1	466	63.66
Total	225	100.0	507	100.0	732	100.0

Source: Field Survey.

About one-fourth respondents reported that they treat their diseases from widow home. This was found more pronouncing in Varanasi (66.8%). About 21 per cent respondents reported that they treat their diseases from their pension. This was found more pronouncing in Vrindavan (38.8%). Thus, about 17 per cent respondents reported that they treat their diseases in hospitals. This was found more pronouncing in Vrindavan (32.3%) (Table 6.94).

Table 6.94
How Do You Treat Your Diseases

	Varanasi	*%*	*Vrindavan*	*%*	*Total*	*%*
From Widow Home	94	66.8	94	28.9	188	25.68
Hospital	22	15.4	105	32.3	127	17.32
Pension	25	17.8	126	38.8	151	20.63
Others	0	0	0	0	0	0
Total	141	100.0	325	100.0	466	100.0

Source: Field Survey.

Cultural Conditions

The respondents were asked that for what reasons they celebrate religious festivals. About 61 per cent respondents said that they believe in religious festivals and thus, they do celebrate them. This was found more pronouncing in Vrindavan (81.2%). About 29 per cent respondents are celebrating religious festivals for purity of soul. This was found more pronouncing in Varanasi (76%). About 10 per cent respondents are celebrating religious festivals for their self satisfaction (Table 6.95).

Table 6.95
For What Reasons Do You Celebrate Religious Festivals

Reasons	*Varanasi*	*%*	*Vrindavan*	*%*	*Total*	*%*
Do Not Believe in Them	0	0	0	0	0	0
Believe in Them	31	13.8	412	81.2	443	60.52
For Purity of Soul	171	76.0	43	8.5	214	29.23
For Self Satisfaction	23	10.2	52	10.3	75	10.25
Total	225	100.0	507	100.0	732	100.0

Source: Field Survey.

The respondents were further asked that whether they visit temples. Most of the respondents revealed that they visit temples. This was found more pronouncing in Varanasi (95.6%). Those who do not visit temples reported that they do not believe in temples and lack time (Table 6.96).

Table 6.96
Do You Visit Temple

	Varanasi	*%*	*Vrindavan*	*%*	*Total*	*%*
Yes	215	95.6	456	89.9	671	91.67
No	10	4.4	51	10.1	61	8.33
Total	225	100.0	507	100.0	732	100.0
If No, reasons						
Do Not Believe in Temples	8	53.3	30	58.8	38	57.58
Lack of Time	7	46.7	21	41.2	28	42.42
No Interest	0	0	0	0	0	0
Total	15	100.0	51	100.0	66	100.0

Source: Field Survey.

Majority of the respondents admitted that they participate in Satsang (68.85%). This was found more pronouncing in Vrindavan (88.7%). Less than one-third respondents do not participate in Satsang due to lack of time. This was found more pronouncing in Varanasi (76%) (Table 6.97).

Table 6.97
Do You Participate in Satsang

	Varanasi	*%*	*Vrindavan*	*%*	*Total*	*%*
Do Participate	54	24.0	450	88.7	504	68.85
Not Interested	0	0	0	0	0	0
Lack of Time	171	76.0	57	11.3	228	31.15
Others	0	0	0	0	0	0
Total	225	100.0	507	100.0	732	100.0

Source: Field Survey.

Table 6.98
Do You Visit Religious Centres

	Varanasi	*%*	*Vrindavan*	*%*	*Total*	*%*
Yes	221	98.2	451	88.9	672	91.88
No	4	1.8	56	11.1	60	8.20
Total	225	100.0	507	100.0	732	100.0
If No, Reasons						
Do Not Believe	4	100.0	36	64.3	40	66.67
Financial Problem	0	0	0	0	0	0
Old Age	0	0	20	35 7	20	33.33
Total	4	100.0	56	100.0	60	100.0

Source: Field Survey.

The respondents were further asked whether they visit religious centres. Most of the respondents admitted that they are visiting religious centres (91.88%). About 8 per cent respondents do not visit religious centres. This was found more pronouncing in Vrindavan (11.1%). Those who do not visit religious centres reported that they do not believe in them. More than one-third respondents are not visiting religious centres in Vrindavan due to old age (Table 6.98)

About 27 per cent respondents never participated in religious festivals and functions. This was found more pronouncing in Varanasi (72.4%). However, slightly less than three-fourth respondents admitted that they sometimes participate in religious festivals and functions. It was recorded as high as 93.2 per cent in Vrindavan (Table 6.99).

Table 6.99

Do You Participate in Religious Festivals and Functions

	Varanasi	*%*	*Vrindavan*	*%*	*Total*	*%*
Never	163	72.4	34	6.8	197	26.91
Sometimes	62	27.6	473	93.2	535	73.09
Often	0	0	0	0	0	0
Total	225	100.0	507	100.0	732	100.0

Source: Field Survey.

Reasons for non-participation in religious festivals and functions are shown in Table 6.100. Those who are not participating in religious festivals and functions said that they are not being invited (21.83%) while most of the respondents in Varanasi reported that due to economic reasons they are not participating in religious festivals and functions.

Table 6.100

Reasons for Non-Participation in Religious Festivals and Functions

Reasons	*Varanasi*	*%*	*Vrindavan*	*%*	*Total*	*%*
Not Invited	9	5.5	34	100.0	43	21.83
Social Distance	0	0	0	0	0	0
Forbidden	0	0	0	0	0	0
Due to Economic Reasons	154	94.5	0	0	154	21.04
Total	163	100.00	34	100.0	197	100.0

Source: Field Survey.

The respondents were asked whether they keep fast during religious functions. Slightly less than half of the respondents reported that they keep fast during religious functions. This was found more pronouncing in Vrindavan (58.9%) as compared to Varanasi (44.4%). Those who do not keep fast during religious functions reported that they believe but do not keep fast while a large segment of respondents do not keep fast due to bad health/old age (Table 6.101).

Table 6.101
Do You Keep Fast during Religious Functions

Reasons	*Varanasi*	*%*	*Vrindavan*	*%*	*Total*	*%*
Yes	100	44.4	248	48.9	348	47.54
No	125	55.6	259	51.1	384	52.46
Total	225	100.0	507	100.0	732	100.0
If No, Give Reasons						
Do Not Believe	13	10.4	23	8.6	36	9.38
Believe but Does Not Keep Fast	32	25.6	132	52.5	164	42.71
Hindrance in Work	14	11.2	24	8.9	38	9.90
Bad Health/Old Age	66	52.8	80	30.0	146	38.02
Total	125	100.0	259	100.0	384	100.0

Source: Field Survey.

Change in life after being widowed is shown in Table 6.102. There has been significant change in life of widows. Most of the respondents reported that they do not put sindoor, wear *mangalsutra*, bangles and dark colour clothes after becoming a widow. Thus, the major change after being widowed is change in attire.

Table 6.102
Change in Life After Being Widowed

	Varanasi	*%*	*Vrindavan*	*%*	*Total*	*%*
Change in Attire	21	9.3	11	2.1	32	4.37
Do Not Put Sindoor	—	—	—	—	—	—
Do Not Wear *Mangalsutra*	—	—	—	—	—	—
Do Not Wear Bangles	—	—	—	—	—	—
Wear White and Light Colour Cloth	—	—	—	—	—	—
All Changes	204	90.7	496	97.9	700	95.63
Total	225	100.0	507	100.0	732	100.0

Source: Field Survey.

The respondents were asked how they break or alter the traditional lifestyle of widows. About half of the respondents said that they wear all types of clothes. This was found more pronouncing in Varanasi (68%). About 23 per cent respondents reported that they eat all types of food. This was found more pronouncing in Vrindavan (27.4%). About 13 per cent respondents further reported that they make their presence in religious and marriage *mandap* and also cook *prasad*. Thus, about 16 per cent respondents revealed that they still believe in traditional lifestyle of widows. This was found more pronouncing in Vrindavan (17.6%) (Table 6.103).

Table 6.103

How You Have Broken the Traditional Lifestyle of Widow

	Varanasi	*%*	*Vrindavan*	*%*	*Total*	*%*
Wear All Types of Clothes	153	68.0	206	40.6	359	49.04
Eat All Types of Food	27	12.0	139	27.4	166	22.68
Present in Religious and Marriage *Mandap* and Cook *Prasad*	19	8.4	73	14.4	92	12.57
Wear Jewellery	0	0	0	0	0	0
None	26	11.6	89	17.6	115	15.71
Total	225	100.0	507	100.0	732	100.0

Source: Field Survey.

Caste-wise breaking the traditional lifestyle of widows is shown in Table 6.104. Widows from lower communities are found more liberal towards the lifestyle of widows while widows from General Caste are more rigid towards the practice of traditional lifestyle of widows.

Table 6.104

Caste-wise Breaking the Traditional Lifestyle of Widows

	Varanasi				*Vrindavan*			
	General	*SC*	*ST*	*OBC*	*General*	*SC*	*ST*	*OBC*
Wearing of All Type of Clothes	75.5	83.3	87.5	73.1	80.5	80.3	90.5	75.1
Taking All Types of Foods	17.9	9.5	8.3	11.5	14.9	9.5	5.3	10.5
Presence in Worship, Marriage *Mandap* and Cooking *Prasad*	6.6	7.2	4.2	15.4	4.6	10.2	4.2	14.2
Use of Jewellery	0.0	0.0	0.0	0.0	0.0	0.0	0.0	0.0
Total	100.0	100.0	100.0	100.0	100.0	100.0	100.0	100.0

Source: Field Survey.

Table 6.105

Age-wise Breaking the Traditional Lifestyle of Widows

	Varanasi				*Vrindavan*			
	26–35 Years	*36–45 Years*	*46–55 Years*	*56 Years and Above*	*26–35 Years*	*36–45 Years*	*46–55 Years*	*56 Years and Above*
Wearing of All Types of Clothes	58.3	62.5	75.0	65.3	62.3	64.5	75.0	65.3
Taking All Types of Foods	16.7	18.8	15.5	14.7	15.7	15.8	15.5	14.7
Presence in Worship, Marriage *Mandap* and Cooking *Prasad*	8.3	12.5	8.3	8.2	9.3	10.5	8.3	8.2
Use of Jewellery	16.7	6.2	1.2	11.8	12.7	9.2	1.2	11.8
Total	100.0	100.0	100.0	100.0	100.0	100.0	100.0	100.0

Source: Field Survey.

Age-wise breaking the traditional lifestyle of widows is shown in Table 6.105. A higher proportion of respondents from higher age group was found against the traditional lifestyle of widows while significant proportion of respondents from lower age group was found in favour of the practice of traditional lifestyle of widows.

Education-wise breaking the traditional lifestyle of widows is shown in Table 6.106. Educated widows are more liberal towards the practice of lifestyle of widows while low educated women still follow the traditional lifestyle of widows.

Table 6.106

Education-wise Breaking the Traditional Lifestyle of Widows

	Varanasi				*Vrindavan*			
	Illiterate	*Primary*	*Middle*	*Higher Studies*	*Illiterate*	*Primary*	*Middle*	*Higher Studies*
Wearing of All Types of Clothes	58.3	62.5	75.0	65.3	60.0	65.0	75.0	65.0
Taking All Types of Foods	20.7	18.8	15.7	14.1	20.0	18.0	15.0	15.0
Presence in Worship, Marriage *Mandap* and Cooking *Prasad*	12.7	12.5	8.3	8.2	12.0	10.0	10.0	8.0
Use of Jewellery	8.3	6.2	0.0	12.4	0.0	0.0	0.0	0.0
None	0.0	0.0	0.0	0.0	8.0	7.0	0.0	12.0
Total	100.0	100.0	100.0	100.0	100.0	100.0	100.0	100.0

Source: Field Survey.

Majority of the respondents reported that they wear plain and white coloured clothes. This was found more pronouncing in Vrindavan (77.5%). The significant proportion of respondents further reported that they do not wear bangles, do not go to kitchen and do not wear *bindi* after being widowed (Table 6.107).

Table 6.107

What You Do After Being Widowed

	Varanasi	*%*	*Vrindavan*	*%*	*Total*	*%*
Wear Plain and White Coloured Cloth	113	50.3	393	77.5	506	69.13
Do Not Go to Kitchen	1	0.4	45	8.9	45	6.28
Do Not Go to Marriage *Mandap*	10	4.4	11	2.2	21	2.87
Eating One Time Only	4	1.8	11	2.2	15	2.05
Do Not Wear Bangles	87	38.7	16	3.2	103	14.07
Do Not Wear *Bindi*	10	4,4	31	6.0	41	5.60
Cutting of Hair	0	0	0	0	0	0
Others	0	0	0	0	0	0
Total	225	100.0	507	100.0	732	100.0

Source: Field Survey.

About two-fifth respondents reported that they were supported by their neighbours and friends. This was found more pronouncing in Varanasi (69.8%). About 30 per cent respondents reported that their siblings/children supported them. This was found more pronouncing in Vrindavan (35.9%). Slightly less than one-third respondents in Vrindavan reported that their parents/in-laws supported them (Table 6.108).

Table 6.108
Who Have Supported You

	Varanasi	*%*	*Vrindavan*	*%*	*Total*	*%*
Parents/In-Laws	34	15.1	156	30.8	190	25.96
Siblings/Children	34	15.1	182	35.9	216	29.51
Neighbours/Friends	157	69.8	169	33.3	326	44.54
Others	0	0	0	0	0	0
Total	225	100.0	507	100.0	732	100.0

Source: Field Survey.

Kind of support is shown in Table 6.109. Majority of the respondents reported that the support was in terms of basic amenities. This was found more pronouncing in Vrindavan (65.3%). Financial support, job and education were other kind of support, while 18 per cent respondents reported that support was in terms of agriculture land. This was found more pronouncing in Varanasi (28.8%).

Table 6.109
Kind of Support

	Varanasi	*%*	*Vrindavan*	*%*	*Total*	*%*
Basic Amenities	125	55.6	331	65.3	456	62.30
Money, Job, Education	35	15.6	112	21.1	147	20.08
Agriculture Land	65	28.8	64	12.6	129	17.62
Others	0	0	0	0	0	0
Total	225	100.0	507	100.0	732	100.0

Source: Field Survey.

Table 6.110
Who Have Contacted You for Help

	Varanasi	*%*	*Vrindavan*	*%*	*Total*	*%*
Relatives of Husband	36	16.0	128	25.3	164	22.40
Relatives of Parents	53	23.6	163	32.1	216	29.51
State/Central Government	38	16.8	100	19.7	138	18.85
NGOs	98	43.6	116	22.9	214	29.23
Others	0	0	0	0	0	0
Total	225	100.0	507	100.0	732	100.0

Source: Field Survey.

The respondents were asked that who have contacted them for help. More than half of the respondents reported that their relatives, including parents, approach them for help. This was found more pronouncing in Vrindavan as compared to Varanasi. About 29 per cent respondents said that NGOs contacted them for help. This was found more pronouncing in Varanasi (43.6%). About 19 per cent respondents admitted that state/central government officials contacted them for help (Table 6.110)

About one-third respondents reported that they contacted their friends/neighbours during the time of crisis. This was found more pronouncing in Vrindavan as compared to Varanasi. Less than one-fourth respondents admitted that they contacted widow home during the time of crisis. This was found more pronouncing in Varanasi (48.9%). About two-fifth respondents said that they contacted their relatives during the time of crisis. This was found more pronouncing in Vrindavan (Table 6.111).

Table 6.111

To Whom You Contact During the Time of Crisis

	Varanasi	*%*	*Vrindavan*	*%*	*Total*	*%*
Parents/In-Laws	35	15.6	123	24.2	158	21.58
Siblings/Children	15	6.6	136	26.9	151	20.63
Friends/Neighbours	65	28.9	187	36.9	252	34.43
Widow Home	110	48.9	61	12.0	171	23.36
Total	225	100.0	507	100.0	732	100.0

Source: Field Survey.

Caste-wise contact of respondents in problems is shown in Table 6.112. About one-fourth respondents from OBC communities in Varanasi reported that they contact to their parents and in-laws during problems as against only 3.9 per cent respondents from General Caste who contact their parents and in-laws during problems. Similarly, about 11 per cent respondents from Scheduled Tribes in Vrindavan reported that they contact their parents and in-laws during problems as against only 3.9 per cent respondents from General Caste who contact their parents and in-laws during problems. Thus, most of the respondents are depending on widow homes even during their problems.

Table 6.112

Caste-wise Contact of Respondents in Problems

Relations	*Varanasi*				*Vrindavan*			
	General	*SC*	*ST*	*OBC*	*General*	*SC*	*ST*	*OBC*
Parents/In-laws	3.9	7.3	9.2	23.1	3.9	10.3	11.2	11.1
Siblings/Children	8.5	4.7	8.2	11.5	5.5	3.7	11.2	11.5
Friends/Neighbours	11.3	14.2	7.6	11.5	10.3	10.2	7.6	12.5
Widow Homes	76.3	73.8	75.0	53.9	80.3	75.8	70.0	65.9
Total	100.0	100.0	100.0	100.0	100.0	100.0	100.0	100.0

Source: Field Survey.

Age-wise contact of respondents in problems is shown in Table 6.113. A higher proportion of respondents from lower age group reported that they contact their parents and in-laws during their problems while about three-fourth respondents from the age group of 46–55 years reported that they contact widow homes during their problems.

Table 6.113

Age-wise Contact of Respondents in Problems

Relations	*Varanasi*				*Vrindavan*			
	26–35 Years	*36–45 Years*	*46–55 Years*	*56 Years and Above*	*26–35 Years*	*36–45 Years*	*46–55 Years*	*56 Years and Above*
Parents/In-laws	8.5	7.3	6.1	5.8	4.5	7.3	6.1	5.8
Siblings/Children	8.5	7.5	8.2	18.4	8.5	7.5	8.2	10.4
Friends/Neighbours	16.3	6.5	10.4	21.8	16.3	6.5	10.4	13.8
Others	66.7	68.7	75.3	54.0	70.7	68.8	75.3	70.0
Total	100.0	100.0	100.0	100.0	100.0	100.0	100.0	100.0

Source: Field Survey.

Education-wise contact of respondents in problems is shown in Table 6.114. There is no correlation between education and contact with family members and relatives during problems. About three-fourth respondents from middle level education in Varanasi and Vrindavan reported that they contact widow homes in their problems. However, about 11 per cent illiterate respondents reported that they contact their parents and in-laws during their problems.

Table 6.114

Education-wise Contact of Respondents in Problems

Relations	*Varanasi*				*Vrindavan*			
	Illiterate	*Primary*	*Middle*	*Higher Studies*	*Illiterate*	*Primary*	*Middle*	*Higher Studies*
Parents/In-laws	11.0	6.5	4.2	11.3	10.0	6.0	5.0	10.0
Siblings/Children	10.5	6.4	4.2	11.3	10.0	6.0	5.0	10.0
Friends/Neighbours	10.2	18.4	16.6	22.7	10.0	18.0	15.0	20.0
Others	68.3	68.7	75.0	54.7	70.0	70.0	75.0	60.0
Total	100.0	100.0	100.0	100.0	100.0	100.0	100.0	100.0

Source: Field Survey.

The respondents were asked who held them responsible for death of their spouse. About 57 per cent respondents said that nobody held them responsible for death of their spouse. This was found more pronouncing in Varanasi (63.1%). However, 30 per cent respondents reported that they are themselves responsible for death of their spouse. This is because of the fact that these women believe in *karma*. A significant proportion of respondents said that their relatives held them responsible for death of their spouse (Table 6.115).

Table 6.115
Who Held You Responsible for Death of Your Husband

	Varanasi	%	Vrindavan	%	Total	%
Family of Husband	14	6.2	18	3.5	32	4.37
Parents	9	4.0	29	5.7	38	5.19
Neighbours	9	4.0	12	2.3	21	2.87
Self	51	22.7	170	33.5	221	30.19
Nobody	142	63.1	278	55.0	420	57.38
Total	225	100.0	507	100.0	732	100.0

Source: Field Survey.

Majority of the respondents reported that they felt big shock when they were told about the death of their spouse. This was found more pronouncing in Vrindavan (70.2%). About 16 per cent respondents reported that they became numb when they were told about the death of their spouse. Similarly, about 10 per cent respondents reported that they fainted when they were told about the death of their spouse (Table 6.116).

Table 6.116
What Did You Feel When You Were Told About the Death of Husband

	Varanasi	%	Vrindavan	%	Total	%
Senseless	45	20.0	75	14.8	120	16.39
Nothing	34	15.2	38	7.5	72	9.84
Faint	37	16.4	38	7.5	75	10.25
Big Shock	109	48.4	356	70.2	465	63.52
Total	225	100.0	507	100.0	732	100.0

Source: Field Survey.

About two-fifth respondents reported that they took about 3 years time to recover from this condition while about one-third respondents reported that more than 3 years were taken by them for recovery from this condition. Thus, only 13 per cent respondents could recover from the condition within a year (Table 6.117).

Table 6.117
Time Taken in Recovery of This Condition

	Varanasi	%	Vrindavan	%	Total	%
Less Than One Year	25	11.1	71	14.0	96	13.11
One to Three Years	93	41.3	194	38.3	287	39.21
Three Years and Above	107	47.6	242	47.7	349	34.02
Total	225	100.0	507	100.0	732	100.0

Source: Field Survey.

About 36 per cent respondents admitted that their *karma* has been responsible for being widowed while about one-third respondents held circumstances responsible for being widow. Less than one-third respondents held God responsible for being widow (Table 6.118).

Table 6.118

What Do You Held Responsible for Being Widowed

	Varanasi	*%*	*Vrindavan*	*%*	*Total*	*%*
Circumstances	57	25.3	184	36.3	241	32.92
Karma	73	32.0	187	36.9	260	35.52
God	95	42.9	136	26.8	231	31.56
Others	0	0	0	0	0	0
Total	225	100.0	507	100.0	732	100.0

Source: Field Survey.

Table 6.119

Who Is Responsible for Your Current Condition

	Varanasi	*%*	*Vrindavan*	*%*	*Total*	*%*
Religious Believe	69	30.7	112	22.1	181	24.73
Social and Caste Induced Condition	24	10.7	47	9.3	71	9.70
Lack of Education Among Women	69	30.7	230	45.4	299	40.85
Unemployment	17	7.5	47	9.3	64	8.74
Dependency	46	20.4	71	13.9	117	15.98
Total	225	100.0	507	100.0	732	100.0

Source: Field Survey.

The respondents were further asked who is responsible for their current condition. About two-fifth respondents reported that lack of education is the main cause of their current condition. About one-fourth respondents reported that religious belief is responsible for their current condition. Dependency of women, unemployment and social and caste-induced conditions are also responsible for their current condition (Table 6.119).

Table 6.120

What Should be Done to Improve the Condition of Widows

	Varanasi	*%*	*Vrindavan*	*%*	*Total*	*%*
Women Education	63	28.0	62	12.2	125	17.08
Employment for Women	33	14.7	37	7.3	70	9.56
Law for Property	15	6.7	64	12.6	79	10.79
Social Reforms	60	26.7	80	15.8	140	19.13
Awareness Among Women	54	24.0	264	52.1	318	43.44
Others	0	0	0	0	0	0
Total	225	100.0	507	100.0	732	100.0

Source: Field Survey.

Awareness about welfare schemes, education, social reforms, law for property, employment for women are some of the important suggestions to improve the condition of widows. However, suggestions vary across the selected districts (Table 6.120).

Attitude of youth towards widows is shown in Table 6.121. About 60 per cent respondents reported that the outlook of youth towards their problems is respectful. This was found more pronouncing in Varanasi (65.3%). About 29 per cent respondents reported that the outlook of youth towards their problems is neutral. This was found more pronouncing in Vrindavan (81.8%). Thus, only 11 per cent respondents revealed that the outlook of youth towards them is disrespectful.

Table 6.121

What is the Outlook of Youth towards Your Problems

	Varanasi	%	*Vrindavan*	%	*Total*	%
Disrespectful	25	11.1	55	10.9	80	10.93
Neutral	53	23.6	161	31.8	214	29.23
Respectful	147	65.3	291	57.3	438	59.83
Others	0	0	0	0	0	0
Total	225	100.0	507	100.0	732	100.0

Source: Field Survey.

In order to save the plight of women who suffered on account of the death of their husbands, Brahmo Samaj launched a campaign advocating widow remarriage. Despite the campaign that led to the legislation of widow remarriage (1856) in India, Hindu society had many reservations on this issue. The Brahmo Samaj campaigned against such prejudices. To reinforce their commitment to this, many young men of the Brahmo Samaj movement made a positive point of marrying widows. Besides championing the cause of widows the Brahmo Samaj also came to the aid of unmarried women as well. It was not just the lower castes who suffered in the caste system. Despite their caste status, the girls from the upper caste families suffered because of their position. If a suitable bridegroom could not be found for such a girl in their caste, their options were limited, as marriage to lower caste men was not permitted. These girls often found themselves being married off to very old men who were already married several times over. Or worse still, sometimes these girls would be poisoned to death. Again the Brahmos campaigned against such unjust practices and saved the lives of many such girls. Widow re-marriage was not permitted among Hindus, except in certain tribal communities. Widow re-marriage is considered a taboo in India. Widow re-marriage among the Hindus is not common. People marrying widows are considered to be of inferior status. Despite best efforts made by the Arya Samaj in the field, there has been no perceptible progress. Among the Scheduled Castes widow remarriage is performed not according to custom but as an economic necessity. Amongst the Sikh Jats widows are remarried to their *dewar* or *jeth*. Naamdharis also preach widow remarriage. Widow re-marriage among Jains is also not popular. Christians and Muslims, however, remarry widows. There has never been a total ban on widow remarriage in India as often assumed. Anthropological studies have given ample evidence that in all non-Brahmins, i.e. lower caste groups, widow remarriages are quite prevalent. It is said that young virgin widows and child widows are allowed to remarry provided it is within their caste groups. Widows of all communities carried the stigma of inauspiciousness and were not permitted to participate in religious or auspicious social functions like marriages or other celebrations. A widow was not even allowed to perform the ritual ceremony to welcome her own daughter-in-law. Reformers like Raja Ram Mohun Roy, Iswar Chandra Vidyasagar and other fought for doing away with the evil of *sati* and tried to encourage the practice of widow remarriage.

About half of the respondents were found in favour of remarriage. This was found more pronouncing in Varanasi (75.1%). Thus, about 60 per cent respondents in Vrindavan were against remarriage. Those who are against remarriage said that remarriage is not allowed in Hindu religion. About 21 per cent respondents said that they do not get respect while about 20 per cent respondents fear from society and children. Those who are in favour of widow marriage reported that widow should remarry till the age of 30 years. The respondents further reported that young widows and childless widows should remarry (Table 6.122).

Table 6.122

Do You Favour Widow Remarriage

	Varanasi	*%*	*Vrindavan*	*%*	*Total*	*%*
Yes	169	75.1	202	39.9	371	50,68
No	56	24.9	305	60.1	361	49.32
Total	225	100.0	507	100.0	732	100.0
If No, Give Reasons						
Remarriage is not allowed in Hindu Religion	20	35.0	192	62.9	212	58.73
Fear of Society and Children	20	35.0	53	17.4	73	20.22
Do Not Get Respect/Old Age	16	30.0	60	19.7	76	21.05
Total	56	100.0	305	100.0	361	100.0

Source: Field Survey.

Above analysis simply demonstrates that the conditions of widows at religious places are no better than widows in general in India. The widows shifted to the religious places to worship and pray gods and goddesses and, thus, live in peaceful and dignified life; however, their living conditions have become worse due to lack of social security measures, negligence by their relatives and their exploitation. Most of the widows at religious places are from poor families mainly from Scheduled Caste, OBCs and Scheduled Tribes Communities. They are living in the city from a long time. They have strong belief in socio-cultural traditions. Most of the widows do not have regular contact with their relatives and, thus, live in isolation at religious places. Some of the old and young widows have attempted to break the traditional lifestyle of widows.

7

Social Security and Rehabilitation

The poorest of poor are sometimes referred to as destitute. Destitute is a kind of deprivation in the space of income or monetary poverty. It involves the absence of any control over assets and the loss of access to income from one's own labour. Destitute is being conceived as an individual phenomenon because by the time a person is destitute they are usually an individuated remnant of a collapsed household. But the process also requires the loss of insurance mechanism to protect themselves from the shocks of uncertain events. The social aspects of destitution are related with social structure and relations. As social constructs, belonging to Scheduled Caste, Scheduled Tribe, minority, old age, disabled and widow may create multiple disadvantages for destitution. The departure or death of those whose duty is to support, or their failure to support through dispute, physical inability and incapacity, or their neglect or abuse of the obligation to support, may be other triggers. The loss of access to public goods and services also creates destitution among the people. Destitute people have also lost the social relations by means of which potential capability is converted to actual functioning. Survival in life requires income, food, clothing, medicine and other necessities of life. Thus, rehabilitation, though mainly refers to the process of helping a person to readapt to society or to restore someone to a former position or rank, requires access to public goods and services besides creating conducive environment. Social security and rehabilitation process is imperative for the majority of the widows who are lacking their family support for their survival and fulfilling their individual needs.

Soon after the attainment of freedom, the popular government introduced several security measures. Several provisions were incorporated in the Constitution of India guaranteeing people protection against underserved want. Article 38 says that 'the State shall strive to promote the welfare of the people by securing and protecting as effectively as it may a social order in which justice, social, economic and political shall inform all the institutions of the national life'.

The Constitution guarantees social security in the following words:

> The State shall within the limits of its economic capacity and development make effective provision for securing public assistance in case of unemployment, old age, sickness, disablement and other cases of undeserved want.

There is no denying that social security today embraces a wider field than ever before. In addition to labour welfare and economic protection of workers, it covers also socio-economic progress and development of the weaker sections and the welfare of children, the aged and the handicapped. The following pages contain an analysis of the responses to the questionnaires received from 44 organizations. We have given suggestions for the introduction of social security measures for widows and their children. We have devised some important welfare schemes for the widows and recommended their implementation.

A questionnaire was mailed to 70 government departments, private concerns, autonomous bodies and undertakings. The purpose was to collect data on the existing social security coverage of workers. The information was sought on the following:

1. Family pension scheme as applicable to the various categories of employees.
2. Preference, if any, given to the employees' widows and/or children in the matter of appointment to different categories of jobs on compassionate grounds.
3. Ex-gratia assistance, if any, given to the widows and/or dependents of those employees who die as a result of an accident on duty in addition to what they are eligible under the Workmen's Compensation Act 1923 or who die a natural death prematurely.
4. Insurance scheme and coverage of different categories of employees, if any.
5. Any other social security programme which the organization has for the benefit of widows and dependents of the employees.

We received responses from 44 out of 70 organizations. The distribution of these organizations on the basis of their management viz.; government, government undertaking, autonomous and private is given below:

Preference in Employment

We were interested in knowing preference, if any, given to the employees' widows and/or their children in the matter of appointment to suitable jobs on compassionate grounds. About 75 per cent organizations gave preference to widows or one of their children in appointment to various jobs falling in class III and IV categories. For this purpose, the widow or her child, as the case may be, were given certain concessions like relaxation in age; out of turn employment with relaxation of minimum qualifications and age; preference in employment given to qualified and eligible widows provided vacancies exist; and providing employment to one of the children of the deceased employees. All the six government departments who responded give relaxation in age, etc. to the employees' widows or one of their children for the purpose of employment. In government undertakings also preference in employment with liberal concessions was given to the widows or their children. However, there were 10 such undertakings who strictly followed the laid down minimum qualifications and eligibility conditions as per government rules. In contrast to government departments, there was no uniformity in government Undertakings in the provision of various concessions to the widows or their children. Lack of uniformity also existed in autonomous and private organizations. There were three government undertakings and seven private organizations who did not give any concessions to the widows or their children in the matter of employment. About 41 per cent private concerns follow the same rules as that of the government in the matter of age relaxation, etc.

Do the deceased employees' widows or their dependents get any ex-gratia assistance in case of an employee's death due to accident or natural death pre-maturely? Fifty per cent organizations did not provide any ex-gratia assistance. These included three government departments, nine government undertakings and private concerns each and one autonomous organization. There were three government departments and one private concern which provided ex-gratia assistance of an unspecified amount. In case of five private concerns, two government undertakings and one autonomous organization, grant of ex-gratia assistance depended on the discretion of the managing committee which considered each case on its merits. The amount of ex-gratia assistance varied on the basis of rank, years of service, etc. in case of four government undertakings and two private concerns and one autonomous organization. One government undertaking had kept the amount of assistance fixed at ₹ 1,000 per month up to 5 years.

Insurance Schemes

From the distribution of organizations according to the operation of insurance scheme(s) for different categories of employees, it is evident that a large majority (77.27%) of organizations did not have any insurance coverage for their employees. The 10 organizations which had provided insurance schemes included six private concerns, and two government departments and government undertakings each. The employees of five out of six private concerns which provide insurance were covered under the Employees State Insurance Act. In case of three organizations, one government, government undertaking and private concern each group insurance had been provided for employees engaged in hazardous occupations. One government undertaking provided Term Assurance for class III and IV employees and Group Insurance for class I and II employees. There was one government department in which all the employees were covered under Group Insurance Scheme. We find that the insurance schemes had been implemented by only few organizations where the job was hazardous and the risk of life involved.

Other Provisions

As many as 30 out of 44 organizations had no special social security-provisions for their employees. These organizations were three government departments, 13 government undertakings, two autonomous and 12 private concerns. Out of the rest 14 organizations, six had only one provision whereas eight organizations had more than one provision. There were two government undertakings and one government department which bore the funeral expenses of their employees. Three autonomous organizations and one government department, government undertaking and private concern each gave financial assistance to widows from the Employees' Welfare Fund. One government department and government undertaking each provided financial assistance for the school-going children. Four private concerns and one government department and government undertaking each had established welfare societies for the grant of financial assistance to their employees. In case of two private concerns, financial assistance was granted at the discretion of the managing committee.

We find that the social security programmes are highly inadequate. Baring some concessions in the matter of employment to widows or their children and ex-gratia and financial assistance by some organizations, there were no schemes for the welfare of widows and their children. There were only two organizations assisting widows in the matter of education of their children. No doubt the untimely death of the breadwinner brings in its fold a number of problems for the widows, but it adversely affects the young children when they are still at school. In many cases, it is the children's education which suffers. Therefore, all the organizations should introduce provisions for the financial assistance to widows for children's education. As reported elsewhere in the contents of this book, many children had to dropout of school or college soon after the death of their father. There were some organizations who insisted that a widow or her child should have prescribed minimum qualifications, age, etc. in order to become eligible for a job. Such restrictions should be waived off. The authorities should take all the necessary steps for the economic rehabilitation of the widows. It was reported that many dead husbands did not leave behind any savings. In some cases, the widows had no money even to incur expenditure on the funeral of their husbands. Many widows borrowed money for performing religious ceremonies during the mourning period immediately following the death of their husbands. Still there were others who had no savings, and nothing to eat after the stoppage of husbands' income. Therefore, it will be a great relief to the widows and their families if ex-gratia financial assistance is granted to them within a period of one or two weeks from the date of the death of their husbands. The data showed that many organizations do not provide insurance coverage to their employees. Most of those covered were engaged in hazardous occupations. It cannot be disputed that those employees are exposed to risks but employees in other organizations have also chances of meeting death due to unforeseen circumstances. Therefore, all the employees without any exception should be provided with insurance coverage by the organizations. Detailed recommendations on the socio-economic rehabilitation of the widows and their children are given in the Appendix.

Widows' Expectations

What were the expectations of widows? What kind of assistance did they expect for their socio-economic rehabilitation? In response to these questions, the widows said that they expected help from the government in respect of the following:

Employment: Help in getting a job; help in starting some profitable work for purpose of self-employment; reservation of some percentage of jobs for widows and their children in government jobs.

Education: Organizing condensed courses for the widows; provision of free ships, text-books, uniforms, etc. for school-going children. Free hostel facilities for children.

Financial Assistance: Grant of children's educational allowance; grant of pension to widows; lump-sum grants for daughters' marriage; supply of sewing machines.

Accommodation: Safe-guarding tenancy rights of widows; allotment of Government flats to widows on priority basis. Allotment of shops/business premises to widows/children on preferential basis.

Counselling and Guidance Services: Guidance to widows for their socio-economic rehabilitation. *Counselling* services for resolving their emotional problems.

Medical Facilities: Free medical facilities to widows and their children at government dispensaries and hospitals.

Allotment of Land and Farming Equipment: Allotment of land for cultivation to rural widows; supply of farming equipment on concessional rates.

The analysis of the data reveals that 14.80 per cent widows wanted help in getting some employment including help for self-employment. Help in getting children employed was desired by 5.40 per cent widows; and 7.80 per cent wanted financial assistance for daughters' marriage; 4 per cent wanted help in children's education and 2.20 per cent were in need of suitable accommodation. The rest (40%) desired assistance for more than one of the above mentioned purposes. Religion-wise break-up of widows living in metropolitan areas revealed that a large number of Muslim widows (86.12%) expected some kind of assistance in comparison to Hindu (73.33%) and Christian (55.88%) widows.

Government Role

The widows were asked about the role which, in their opinion, the government should play for the welfare of widows and their children. A majority (85%) of widows desired that the government should play an active role in their socio-economic rehabilitation. In all 33 areas were cited by the widows for Government intervention. These areas range from education, training, employment, etc. to financial help for daughters' marriage, allotment of shops, etc. The responses of the widows on the role of government for the welfare of widows were compressed into the following categories: (1) Education – organizing condensed courses for widows, children's; (2) Training – organizing training courses in suitable vocations for widows intending to get rehabilitated through self-employment; (3) Employment – helping to widows/children in getting suitable jobs in the deceased husbands' organization; (4) Financial – *Lumpsum* grants to widows for their daughters' marriage; (5) Reservations in services and posts and educational institutions for widows and their children; (6) Establishment of a Society for the Welfare of Widows; allotment of accommodation on easy terms; (7) Free medical facilities at government dispensaries and hospitals; (9) Counselling and guidance services for widows and their children; (10) Devising and implementation of

Social Security Programmes; (11) Pension for widows without any economic support; (12) Prevention of unnatural deaths on account of accidents, crime, suicides, occupational diseases, etc.; (13) Day care centres for the children of working widows on nominal charges; (14) Help to young widows desirous of remarriage; (15) Provision of recreational facilities for widows and their children; (16) Supply of farming equipment, on concessional rates, to rural widows.

Since majority of the widows are from higher age group which has been treated as senior citizens, therefore, it is imperative to treat widows also in the category of senior citizens besides treating them as destitute and poor women. If we consider widows as senior citizen, they will be entitled for the development benefits under the government and non-government programmes and schemes meant for senior citizens. Thus, the canvas of social and welfare services will be widened for widows living in religious places. A majority (36.20%) of widows emphasized need for active government role in providing suitable employment avenues for the widows to enable them to support their dependents. The next largest group desired that the government should provide financial assistance to the widows to meet expenditure on their children's education, daughters' marriage, etc. A number of widows (11%) said that the government should provide suitable jobs to the children of widows on preferential basis. They also desired that their children should be given free education. In case, the government was not in a position to provide free education, these children should at least be provided scholarships, text-books, uniforms, etc. they emphasized; 40.18 per cent rural widows stressed the need for setting up of rural vocational training centres for widows; 5.80 per cent wanted that the widows without any economic support should be granted pension. The possibility of government making a provision for the pensionary benefits for all widows irrespective of the employment status of their deceased husbands did not perhaps catch the imagination of the respondents. This, perhaps, explains why very few widows had suggested pension scheme for the widows. Also, 4 per cent widows stressed the need for free medical facilities for the widows and their children. One of the important suggestions made, although by a lone widow, was regarding the prevention of unnatural deaths due to accidents, suicides, and alcoholism. She also stressed the need for the prevention, control and treatment of occupational diseases. Some of the widows wanted the government to mobilize public opinion in favour of remarriage of Widows.

Rehabilitation

Socio-economic rehabilitation of widows includes various services in the areas of education, training, employment, counselling and remarriage. Financial assistance for education of children and for meeting expenses of marriage of their daughters assumes greater significance in the rehabilitation of widows. Rehabilitation of widowed women needs concerted efforts of all the concerned, i.e. central and state governments; voluntary agencies and the community at large. The Department of Women and Child Development, Ministry of Human Resource Development, Government of India, has the responsibility of providing opportunities for widows. Widows need a varied kind of services depending upon their age, health status, family background, educational level, occupational status and dependent children. Widows can be rehabilitated through remarriage, education, vocational training, employment and welfare programmes for dependent children. In particular they will need help in the following areas: (1) Remarriage, (2) Education for self and children, (3) Vocational training, (4) Employment, (5) Welfare services for children, e.g. foster care and sponsorship, (6) Marriage of daughters, (7) Free legal aid in securing inheritance of property and other matters, (8) Hostels for working widows, (9) Day care facilities for children, (10) Financial assistance for destitute widows, (11) Residential institutions for old, infirm and helpless widows, (12) Counselling and guidance, (13) Short stay homes for widows in distress, (14) Protection of young widows from exploitation and victimization, (15) Community education to bring about changes in the social attitudes towards widows.

From General to Specific: Few Case Studies

In this chapter, we will analyse cases drawn from our respondents to substantiate the arguments presented in chapters 1 to 6, as mentioned in the previous chapter. The analysis will pertain to the nature and type of the main theme of the present study, namely the deprivation, renunciation and formation of social-self among the Bengali widows living in Varanasi city. The case-studies of respondents living within the city, selected from all age-groups, socio-personal backgrounds and of different life conditions, are given below. To maintain confidentiality of the socio-personal information provided by them, their names have been changed. These case-studies are followed with a brief analysis primarily along the main themes or issues covered in the present study.

Bharati Roy (70 years old), a Kayastha by caste, hailed from the family of a cultivator in the erstwhile East Bengal (now Bangladesh). After the death of her mother, her father arranged her marriage at a very early age with an agriculturist. She was not happy with her marital life, in spite of having the company of her husband for a long time. She also did not have any issue. Soon after the death of her husband, she started working in a house in her neighbourhood. At the time of Partition of the country when the members of the family in which she was working migrated permanently to Varanasi city, she also accompanied them. She stayed with that family for some time, but later started working as a cook in the house of some Guruji – an old Bengali gentleman from whom she also took the *diksha* (initiation for becoming a renounce). In the beginning, she stayed in the house of the Guruji, but later she rented a room at ₹ 100 per month in a separate *mohalla* (locality). Her Gurubhai (the son of her Guruji) arranged to pay 50 per cent of the room rent, but later he stopped doing so for reasons not known to her. As far as her sustenance in the city was concerned, she was getting a pension of ₹ 60 per month from the state government under its Old Age Pension Scheme. But for the last two-three years or so, instead of that she was getting a pension of ₹ 100 per month from the Ramakrishna Mission Ashrama. Besides, she was also begging at the Kedarghat.

Although she could not tell us as how much exactly was she getting daily by begging, but she used to get more money (coins) on every Monday, as it was regarded the day of Lord Shiva. She also used to get a *sari* in the *dona* occasionally. She was somehow managing her livelihood in the city. With regard to her daily routine, she used to take the Ganga bath regularly in the morning and eat a one-time vegetarian meal but was unable to perform *puja* (prayer) twice – in the morning and evening. In fact, unlike the usual Bengali women, she used to perform *puja* only once in the morning and not in the evening. She did not have any relative in Varanasi, except her Gurubhai and his son. Hence, she considered herself a very unfortunate woman and was not at all happy with her widowhood. Not only that, but she often used to remember her deceased husband (not out of any love or affection but due to her own miseries) and wanted to reach to him (die) as early as possible.

Subarna Chakravarty (75 years old), a Brahmin by caste, came from the erstwhile East Bengal (now Bangladesh) with her husband and children. Her husband and four sons died, but her two daughters remained alive. They got married in Varanasi city but they also became widows, though they were still young. After the death of her husband and sons as well as her daughters' marriage, she started working as a cook in a neighbouring family and living separately in a rented room. She worked as a cook for quite some time, but she left the job because of her old-age and also because of her becoming an asthama patient. Her neighbour was good enough to arrange for her the state government pension. Earlier, she used to supplement her livelihood through regular begging, but due to her ill health, now she begged only on Mondays as she got more coins on that day. Though her daughters used to visit her to know about her well-being, but since they themselves were economically poor they could not extend any financial support to her. Hence, she was largely dependent on the government pension (the net amount; after the cut of the commission of the postman and the *dakil)* for her sustenance or survival in the city.

Rebabala Saha (70 years old), belonging to a Scheduled Caste family from West Bengal, got married at the age of 15 years. Her husband, who was not employed in any work, remained alive only for six years after their marriage, i.e. she became widow after six years of their marriage. She had given birth to a few children by that time. After they grew older, the children started managing the land owned by her husband, but they did not take good care of her. Hence, after 7 years of becoming a widow, she left home and went first to Vrindavan and then to Kashi or Varanasi, the abode of Lord Vishwanath or Shiva. In Varanasi, she worked and stayed most of the time in a holiday home. She was not getting any pension either from the state government or from the Ramakrishna Mission Home. Instead, she was sustaining with the help of whatever she used to get from the holiday home and with the *prasada,* in the forms of sweets, cooked food, etc. in small quantities, from the temples. One of her sons, staying in the Gangadaul area in West Bengal, wanted to take her back home, although his economic condition was not good. But she herself refused to go back home because of the poor economic condition of her son, and also because she wanted to live independently and die peacefully in the city of Lord Shiva.

Protima Sirkar (50 years old), a Kayastha by caste, came from Calcutta (now Kolkata) to Varanasi city nearly 25 years ago. She was not a widow in the real sense of the term, as the death of husband was not confirmed. Actually, her husband left home to become a *sanyasi* (renouncer) and never returned home to take up his role of the husband. Hence, according to the *Shastric* prescription that percolated down to the folk-tradition, if a married man did not come back home after a minimum period of 7 years of his being away, he was treated as a dead person and his wife as a widow. In such a situation, Protima came alone to Varanasi and rented a room on the first floor in a house in a *mohalla* located near the Ganga ghat. She neither had any relative in the city nor was she getting pension of the state government or of the Ramakrishna Mission Ashrama. Although she was an asthmatic patient, she did not have any option for sustaining herself except begging regularly at the Ganga ghat. She used to take tea in the morning, since she apprehended that she would suffer from severe headache without it. Since she had rented a room in a house without any tap water facility at the first floor, it was very difficult for her to carry water from the ground floor. That is why she used to eat the dried or parched rice as she was unable to cook her food. She used to get cooked food once in a week from the Kumareshwara Matha. Usually, she did not spend much of her time inside the room but wandered about in the streets since she used to feel restless due to her ailment. She was also quite indifferent about the religious way of life as practised by the widows in general and the majority of our respondents in particular in the religious city of Varanasi.

Ratna Chattopadhyay (77 years old) was born in the erstwhile East Bengal (Bangladesh). Her father was employed in the railways and so were a few other members in the family. After completing her education up to matriculation, she got married in a Zamindar family. Her husband had also bought his maternal uncle's house who was a Jagirdar. Although she was married in a rich family, she did not like to stay at her husband's house. Consequently, her father got the permission *of* her husband and took her back to his own house after some time. Although her father was employed in a transferable job in the railways, her mother never accompanied him when he was transferred from one place to the other. Instead, it was Ratna who always accompanied her father. In fact, she was much closer to her father than to her husband. She was also issueless. After the death of her husband, she took training in some craft, and got employment in Orissa and stayed with her father where he was posted. Her mother died at the age of 69 years and her father at 72 years. After the death of her father, she moved to Vrindavan in Uttar Pradesh and took up the job of a store-keeper in the Anandmai Ma Ashrama there. After sometime, Anandmai ma, the spiritual Mother, shifted to Varanasi and set up her Ashrama there. She also brought Ratna with her. The Mother became so affectionate to Ratna and the latter became so devoted to the Ma that she used to cook *bhoga* (the pious food) for the Mother. So long as the Mother was alive, she used to accept her *bhoga* only from the hands of Ratna. During her old-age, her vision became blurred. In fact, her both the eyes were operated upon. She was unable to read and write. Not only that but one of her legs was injured. As a result, she could walk only with the help of some inmate of the Ashrama. She used to get a little milk from the Ashrama, prepare tea for herself and drink the rest of the milk. She did not have any contact with either the natal or the affinal members of her families.

Aparna Banerjee (80 years old), a descent of the Vedic or Bhattacharya Brahmins, was born in Varanasi city itself. Her father was a professional reciter of the Vedic *mantras (slokas* or hymns) in a temple in the city. She got educated at home and was married at the age of 14 years. Her husband was a professor in Delhi but died immaturely at the age of 42 years due to typhoid. She was only 30 years of age at that time. By then, she had borne five sons and three daughters from him. After the death of her husband, she returned along with her children to her parents' house in Varanasi city. Her father's *Jajmans* (clients) helped in getting her and her children rehabilitated in the city. Her brother, a renowned person of the city, did not have any child of his own; hence, he got her sister's (Aparna's) sons educated up to matriculation level. After that, they completed their graduation and got settled in their lives. Her daughters also got married and settled in their lives. After she became a widow, Aparna used to come to the Ashrama of Anandmai Ma. In fact, soon after becoming a widow, she wanted to come and stay permanently in the Ashrama but the Mother advised her first to complete her household responsibilities like getting her sons and daughters settled in their life. After a lot of difficulty, she got her youngest daughter married and finally came to the Ashrama to stay there permanently. While staying in the Anandmai Ma Ashrama, she used to get some financial support from her sons. She also got ₹ 200 per month, besides foods and clothes from the Ashrama. Within six months of her stay in the Ashrama, she became quite devoted to the Mother. Till the Mother was alive, she used to prepare (cook) *bhoga* for her. But after the death of the Mother, she was unable to prepare the *bhoga* due to her old age. Even then, she liked to stay in the Ashrama. Her daily-routine in the Ashrama was that she used to get up at 4 o'clock in the morning, take bath and worship Lord Shiva. Then, she used to get involved in the worldly-affairs such as cutting vegetables to be cooked for the inmates of the Kanyapeeth – the residential girls school run by the Ashrama, and for the central kitchen, serve breakfast and dinner to the inmates, and then herself take the *bhoga* from the Ashrama. She never cooked separately for herself in the Ashrama. As long as she could work, she wanted to stay in the Ashrama. Aparna had good relations with her sons. Whenever she fell ill, they took her back to their house. They had also arranged for her a cassette *of bhajans* (religious songs) from the Ramakrishna Mission Ashrama. They did not allow her to do any household chores, but she did not like to sit idle and become a burden on others. That is why, she wanted to stay in the Ashrama. But her stay there was possible only till she was able to do some work there. Finally, she had to go home to her sons to live with them.

Ratna Mukherjee (71 years old) was born in a zamindar family in West Bengal. She got married in a zamindar family at the age of 9 years and became widow at the age of 11 year, just after two years of her marriage. Her husband was the only son of his parents who were alive at the time of his death. But after few days of his death, the mother-in-law also died. Then, she lived with her father-in-law so long as he remained alive. Since she was the only daughter-in-law, he loved her very much. She was aware of the fact that the widows did not traditionally have any right either to the family property or even to that of their deceased husbands, except to have food and shelter as long as they were alive. As her father-in-law was also aware of the customary law, he sold a portion of his landed property and gave the money to her. After the death of her father-in-law, she accompanied a neighbour to Puri in Orissa and stayed there for five years. After returning from Puri, she went to her brothers' house and stayed there for some time. Although her brothers liked her to stay in their house, but she herself did not like it. Consequently, she contacted someone in the Ramakrishna Mission Ashrama and came to its branch office in Varanasi. Since she hailed from a zamindar's family and was also married into a zamindar family, she had not only led a cultured life but also enjoyed the services of a host of servants in both her affinal and natal houses. After coming to the Ramakrishna Mission Ashrama in Varanasi, she took the charge of the store of the Ashrama. She also got adjusted soon with the regulated life of the Ashrama as she used to get up early in the morning, take bath, and perform the *puja* (prayer) and meditation. Then, she used to open the door of the *mandir* (temple) and the store. She used to even cook her own food and take one-time meal at around 11 A.M. She had got a separate room in the Ashrama. She was satisfied with her present life and was not willing to remember her previous life.

Deprivation and Renunciation

Although we have already made generalizations about the deprivation, renunciation and formation of social-self of our data collected from 235 Bengali widow-respondents living in different *mohallas* or localities in Varanasi city, yet we shall analyse briefly the data collected from the seven specific respondents through the case-studies method, as mentioned at the outset. The analysis is being done merely to substantiate the arguments given on the basis of responses collected from the relatively larger number of respondents. However, not only is there more possibility of extracting minute details of the life condition of each respondent from a small sample size, but there is also less possibility of making broad generalizations on the basis of detailed information. In any case, our intention here is not to enter into the theoretic-methodological issue(s) pertaining to the analysis of a social phenomenon. Instead, we are simply concerned with a brief analysis of the details of the socio-personal information collected from seven respondents through the case-study method, simply to substantiate our arguments given through various chapters in the present study. Looking at the case-studies, what we find is that the majority of our respondents was deprived materially as well as non-materially or emotionally at both their natal and affiliate families. Their deprivation was well-reflected from their not getting educated to the extent they wanted, not getting proper food and nourishment, and affection and care from their parents during their childhood, getting married at an immature age and consequently bearing more number of children at the cost of their ill-health, experiencing lack of adequate care, and affection from their husbands, and, over and above, being deprived of inheriting property, both ancestral and the one owned by their husbands. The height of their material and non-material or emotional deprivation was when they were disowned and discarded by their own children and/or by their kith and kins in those cases where they were issueless. Thus, in the absence of reciprocity or reciprocal relationship between them and their children or between them and their kith and kins – both in their affiliate and natal families, they were totally left at the mercy of others including philanthropic organizations, state machinery and individual householders. Both their material and non-material or emotional deprivation, after their becoming widows and coming to Varanasi city in the name of doing *Kashivas,* could not be overcome while they were residing in the city. This was so as in most of the cases, they had come to Varanasi city for the first time and the city was totally foreign to them, especially with its unique type of population composition, its cultural tradition of both the *yoga* and the *bhoga,* and, over and above, with the different ethnic traits, especially language spoken by the people, except in a few Bengali *mohallas.* Also, in most of the cases they did not know anybody in the city. In such a situation, they had to struggle hard to locate a place to stay and to find some source of their daily sustenance. After becoming widows, they were also supposed to observe strictly the norms prescribed in the Hindu *Dharmashastras* for a Hindu widow. Since such *Shasitk* prescription has already percolated down to the masses at the practice level, the needs of the Bengali widows in general and of our respondents, including those covered under the case-studies in particular, happened to be bare minimum. For instance, they had to wear a single white *sari,* take a simple vegetarian meal in a small quantity once in a day, live in a small room and sleep on the ground without much comfort, spend their entire time in performing religious activities such as taking Ganga bath, visiting temples and worshipping the gods installed there, remembering gods and goddesses by chanting their names, reciting *katha-kirtan,* etc.

When we look at the cases of our respondents, we find a large majority of them being deprived in one way or the other. For instance, they could not afford to have a proper hygienic accommodation. In fact, quite a sizeable number of our respondents did not have any accommodation as such and they used to reside in the premises of temples, *ashramas,* etc. A large majority of them did not have any permanent source of their sustenance or livelihood but were dependent on begging, reciting *katha-kirtan* in exchange of a few coins, *prasadas* (food in the small quantity), occasionally a *sari* and so forth. All this, however, was based on the religiosity and generosity of the householders and the pilgrims. With regard to their social security, the state government under its Old Age Pension Scheme, the Ramakrishna Mission Ashrama and Sulabh

International Social Service Organisation have prolonged them monthly pension. Some of the *ashramas, bhavanas* and *sanghas* such as Ramakrishan Mission Ashrama, Anandmai ma-ka Ashrama, Ganga ma-ka Ashram etc., and the Mumuksha Bhavana and the Marwari Seva Sangha provided them accommodation, food, medical facilities, etc. The provisions provided to them by these religious and philanthropic institutions served as a means of their social security, on the one hand, but also helped them in pursuing their renunciation or even asceticism. As has already been pointed out, both the forced and voluntary forms of renunciation or asceticism in the case of our respondents were to be understood entirely in the non-conventional sense where it was almost analogous to their observing strictly the prescribed norms of widowhood, including celibacy. Their renunciation was also supplemented by their worshipping gods like Lord Shiva and goddesses such as Durga, Kali, Saraswati or even Anandmai ma, etc. Their renunciation was also different from asceticism in the sense of their living collectively in a *math* or monastery, although in few cases two-three widows were living in a community of their own wherein they were offering prayers or performing *puja* together, and sharing each other's sorrows and helping at the time of sickness, etc.

Life Ahead of Oblivion

In the verandah of Chaitanya Vihar, Phase-I, in Vrindavan stood Jyotika Ghosh helplessly and perhaps remorsefully eager to conceal her identity pushing the broken wheelchair of her handicapped 35-year-old daughter. She did this because she had recorded her husband's name incorrectly in the register of the Ashram, wherein his name was mentioned as Dhirendra Ghosh. I had a long chat with 65-year-old widow, Jyotika Ghosh, about her glorious past in marked contrast to her present life. At one stage she showed me with pride and nostalgia a photo of her late husband posing with a legendary national leader. Isn't he the well known photo journalist?', I asked her. 'Yes, he was a well known photo journalist, she said. 'What was the name of your husband?' I asked again. She said, 'Subhash'. This name is imaginary because Jyotika did not want to mention his real name. She was completely taken aback by my revelation and burst into tears and wondered how after long years it came to her tongue. Senior photo journalist Subhash Ghosh had earned a reputation of being an excellent freelance photographer. 'He used to earn sufficient money to meet the medical expenses of my ailing daughter Meeta Ghosh. She was almost recovering when my husband Ghosh died suddenly in 1990. Since then we have had no source of income. Circumstances compelled me even to sell out his costly cameras to make both ends meet,' Jyotika said mournfully. Her husband had good collection of costly cameras. Jyotika had no alternative but to sell them one by one to run the household. She got her son Gautam Ghosh admitted at St. Thomas School, Kolkata, by selling a camera. She even sold her house for ₹ 3 lakh for meeting the expenses of her son's study (Diploma in Engineering) in the US, with high hopes that good days would come again. Thereafter both the mother and daughter started living in a rented house. After returning from the US, Gautam joined a private firm. The company was paying him ₹ 50,000 per month. But it was not a smooth-sailing for the family. One day Jyotika came to know that Gautam has embraced Christianity and married a Christian girl. For Jyotika, deserting one's own religion is like death. She tried to pacify her son but all in vain. He declined all the good advices showered upon him. 'You are as good as dead to me,' she said in anger and banished him from her house. Twelve years have passed, she has not seen him even once, she said, maybe, he has gone to America, uttered Jyotika in anguish. Jyoyika was a staunch believer in her own religion. She never asked for any help from anybody. But her ailing daughter was her main worry. The economic condition gradually went shattering. Once Christian society volunteered to take the responsibility of looking after the daughter, but her self-respect stood in the way. 'They will hang the cross around her and would make her stand in a church. It is like selling my daughter. No, I won't allow this to happen. It is all my self-respect that forced me to go through all these gruesome situations. Had I not banished my son from the house everything would have been normal. All my relatives, both from the paternal and maternal sides, are well-placed. My elder brother-in-law was a judge. My brother also retired from a high post. But what am I here! Now virtually I am a beggar. It is true that I never beg on road or in temple. Come to the Ashram, you will see me also standing in the queue. Where is my self-respect?' she quibbled.

Anger of Manu Mother

At 9 in the morning when I reached Meera Sahabhagini Mahila Ashram in Vrindavan, I found all the occupants busy in their respective jobs. There I located an old woman named Manu Ghosh. I went to see her and expressed my wish to know something about her. She asked me to wait for some time. She said she would go and come back in 10 to 15 minutes after attending to Lord Krishna along with the daily ritual of 'Vog'. Meanwhile, I met some other occupants of the Ashram. By then it was 1 P.M. and Manu Ghosh had not yet returned. I approached the caretaker of the Ashram and disclosed the purpose of meting her. I was told that she was busy frantically searching her lost ration and Sarvodya cards. After sometime, I again spotted her and dashed to her. Her mood was off. She could not find her missing articles. In terse language she said, 'tell me, what you want to know.' I patiently asked her to relax, and said I am not in a hurry. I told her I only wanted to know all the major events of her life. Manu Ghosh said 'Would you listen to my life story? It is a full book. Your whole copy would be covered. What to know about the past. Let them go. I am 80 years old and I belong to Kolkata. You all collect information about us and do your own job. But who cares for Manu Ghosh and other old ladies of the Ashram. Come along with me, I shall show you how the rooms of the Ashram are decaying. Due to irregular supply of electricity occupants fall in toilets in darkness. They often get injured. We live here with just ₹ 10 per day. We have been telling to enhance kerosene oil quota from 3 ltrs. to 5 ltrs. a month but to no avail. No one listens to us. No one listens to us. We are pulling on here with a single sari for three to four years. This is the reality'. Manu went on to say: 'Once a doctor came here. He examined our eyes and recommended spectacles. But they were found to be useless. It was a big joke with us. Here we need no doctors. We need body-massagers because we run four kilometres in the morning to attend *bhajans* and *kirtan* in the temple. *Bhajans* are our meals, both spiritual and physical. Those mothers who are unable even to move lie down always on bed. In fact they are in need of massagers. We are here to seek salvation. Everyone comes here with that hope. You ought to know, when you go back, another person like you would come and will ask similar questions. But nothing tangible would be done and we shall lead our dejected life as usual. Our ultimate solace is Lord Krishna. He can only protect us.'

Lord Krishna is Everything for Her

The entire room was shining with the radiant look of an elderly lady of 80 years from 24 Parganas, West Bengal. This glory was due to her utter devotion to Lord Krishna in the Ashram of Vrindavan. This new age Radha utters: 'Lord Krishna is everything for me; he is my father, my husband and even my son. My daily routine starts with the early rising, followed by daily chores which include chanting of the Lord's name 108 times.' I met Subhadhra Maa for the first time at Tarash Mandir of Akhil Bhartiya Mahila Parishad. I have always noticed her chanting on her bed, while other ladies take rest after breakfast. It is only the radiant appearance of Maa Subhadhra Devi which attracted me towards her. Chanting Radha-Radha, I went close to her and asked her permission to sit near her. Those who are 70 years and above are residing here; some of them are too ill or aged and they need help for even their simple routine activities, but Subhadhra Maa is quite healthy and does her work herself. She got married at an early age. Her husband Vanmali was jobless, and they owned some land and did farming on it. Recalling her past she said: 'Due to my beauty and dedication towards my work and family, I was loved by one and all at my in-laws' house. All were highly impressed by my culinary skills. Fish curry made by me used to be their favourite dish. I lived in such a healthy atmosphere that I could still remember those joyful days when I used to spend my time watching movies and singing hymns in praise of the lord with my mother-in-law. After two years of marriage, I was blessed with a baby boy. Unfortunately, he could not live for long. After this mishap, I got shattered. My mother-in-law stood with me in all my hardships. But those happy days did not exist for long. My mother-in-law also passed away after a few years. I was lefy all alone mourning the loss as I loved my mother-in-law so much. The misfortune did not stop there and soon my husband also passed away. I was completely left alone. I decided to go on a pilgrimage. When I reached Vrindavan, I felt that this was the best place to spend the rest of my life. I have almost spent 35 years of my life in Vrindavan. I was young when I came here. I came to this ashram only three months ago. I pass my time in prayers in Madan Mohan Temple. I cook myself there, but when I feel exhausted I come here. Here the food is cooked by Samli Bishvas, and she looks after us'. To my question how she could read without spectacles, she replied smiling that her sight is so perfect that she can see Lord Krishna. Suddenly, I noticed a key tied to the corner of her saree. She said, it was the key of the box kept under her bed. To my question, 'Is there anything valuable kept in the box?' she smilingly answered, 'a little bit. But all this will be donated to this Ashram.' I sat beside her for a long time. Samli Bishvas was preparing food for all. I observed that Subhadhra Maa's food was also being served.

Different Faces of Malti Maa

Malti Adhikari seems very different from all those who are staying at Swadhar Ashram. Her commanding voice and smile makes her different from all those staying at Swadhar ashram. She was the one who was instructing others and gathering them. I was amazed to find her so active at the age of 77. I went to her and told her that I wanted to know her story. She laughed and said, 'Wait, I will be back soon'. This is her story: Malti Maa belongs to Kolkata. She got married at the age of 12 years, she studied up to the fifth standard. She became a mother of five children at the age of twenty 22. Her husband Kartik Adhikari ran a flower shop. When her sons grew up, they also joined their father's business. After getting all her children married, Malti Maa was leading a tension free life when suddenly Kartik Adhikari fell ill and passed away. Malti Maa's life was shattered but still she continued to hide her sorrows thinking that she has her sons and daughters-in-law with her. Soon Malti Maa's life started getting miserable day-by-day. Both the sons use to fight on small issues and when Malti Maa interrupted they fought with her also. Her pains added up when she saw that her younger daughter was tortured by her husband. Malti Maa could not take it anymore and decided to leave the house. She went and started living in a nearby temple. She could not find peace there and so without informing anyone she left for Vrindavan. After 18 years, suddenly her younger daughter Archana Das came to Vrindavan looking for her. Seeing her mother after 18 years, Archana cried at lot. She told Malti Maa that her husband had left her. She went back to Kolkata with her daughter and made arrangements for her living. She also arranged for a job for Archana's sons. As Malti Maa was coming back to Vrindavan, her daughter also expressed her desire to accompany her. Malti Maa brought her daughter along with her. Last year, Archana fell ill and passed away. Whenever Malti Maa is asked about her family, she starts crying. She does not want to talk about Kolkata. She is happy here at Vrindavan.

Don't Know Where He Is

Like so many widows, Krishna has been living in Vrindavan. But she is not a widow. She has sought refuge in the temple town because she was fed up of living with her husband. He was not a bad guy when he married her at the age of 12. He was member of a group earning their living by singing *bhajans* and doing *kirtans* in temple and private homes. But Krishna never knew how her husband was earning livelihood. She never asked for money nor was she ever given anything by her in-laws. She gave birth to two sons and a daughter. But always she was living from hand to mouth. Time passed. Her two sons grew up and were married. Whatever dowry she got she used that for the marriage of her daughter. But she was shocked to learn that her husband had started gambling. Whatever little money he used to give her also became rare. 'One day when my elder son came home I asked him to take away his wife and leave me alone as I was unable to look after their needs. I said I want to go on pilgrimage and this is how I came to Vrindavan. My son and others asked me to stay along with them because if I did not stay with them, this would cast a poor reflection on the family. But I was unwilling to stay with him. Later, I came to know that my husband Lokman was in bad company and never visited home. He was least bothered about his family. I don't know whether he is dead or alive. I felt that when husband is not there to look after me, why I should wait and thus spend my life in agony. I was deserted and depressed and finally one day I left my home by putting one or two saris in a bag and alone I came to Vrindavan. Now I am happy, here people are good and alive together. I get food and water. It is nearly one year now. My elder brother lives in Vrindavan. He is willing to keep me but I am happy here and you can better understand why I don't want to be with my brother and bhabhi. Hope you can understand me.' 'I don't feel like knowing about my son or daughter-in-law, because it's of no use, it will trouble me. I want to live along with these ladies in Vrindavan and I am happy. After knowing others I feel comfortable being here.'

Life in Terror

One day at Tarash Temple while talking to Krishna Maa, my attention stuck to a small figure who continuously was trying to squeeze her. Some women were sleeping after breakfast that morning, some comforting themselves with hand-fans as there was a power failure. It was too humid and unbearable. Even in the horrible heat, the lady whom I saw in the morning was lying shivering with a bed-sheet on. 'Is that lady not well'? I asked Krishna. 'No, sometimes she behaves like that'. I was not able to control myself. Feeling bad for her, I wanted to check whether she is having fever or not. I went near her and was about to pull up the sheet covering her, she started screaming loudly; she was breathing heavily and pulled the sheet out more tightly. All the ladies in that room started saying 'please leave her alone, do not disturb her, otherwise she will create nuisance.' Now I became more curious to know about her. Other ladies sitting there began to talk something about her past. According to the register of Akhil Bhartiya Mahila Parishad, she came from Chaurinat Village of Bankura Distt., West Bengal. Her name is 'Hari Dasi' and she is now 85 years old. For the last 50 years, she has been living in Vrindavan. This was the only information about her and no one knows anything about her husband or other family members. How did she come here? People wonder whether 'Hari Dasi' herself remembers anything about her past life and family members. Yes, there is a strong recollection; whenever she remembers that she goes in a fit. She is so scared that she tries to hide herself from every one. This type of attack often takes place twice a week and during which she starts screaming and shouting. In this condition, she runs and closes all doors and windows. She also shouts loudly and says: 'the mob is coming and they will kill everyone. Run quickly and close the door'. Saying this she hides her under the bed and puts a finger on her lips so that others keep quiet. At times Hari Dasi is just normal and behaves like any other women chanting, praying and singing *bhajans*. She also manages all work on her own. She doesn't have appetite and takes very little food. Here in Vrindavan, we met many ladies and heard their stories. The story of 'Hari Dasi' is the first story narrated by other ladies. Back home from Vrindavan, I kept on remembering 'Hari Dasi'. It was a matter of grave concern to me. There might be many others like Hari Dasi who are going through the same predicament of not even remembering their own children. That night I went to bed with fond memories of my mother and tears welled into my eyes.

Widowhood at the Age of Fifteen

In India a child attains adulthood legally only 18 years of age and then only becomes eligible for marriage. Marriage at a younger age is an offence, according to law, but this was not followed in the past when child marriages were common in every part of the country. Gyanuda Viswas was married at the age of 12. What is more, sorrows came one by one in her life. She lost her husband when she was only 15. She got her head shaved and she was asked to wear a white saree. Recalling her past life, Gyanuda Viswas said: 'I was totally unaware of what was happening around me. Without understanding even the meaning of marriage or widowhood, I went on doing what was told to me by my in-laws. I could not understand why the people around me were crying and blaming me for all that had happened. I had not killed my husband, but strangely I was held responsible for his death. I don't even remember my husband's face but only remember that his name was Satish Vishwas, who was a farmer and used to spend the whole day out. I was very ill treated by my in-laws. But I never protested and always kept quiet. I only cried when I was alone, remembering my parents.' 'One day my father came to my in-laws and had heated arguments with my mother-in-law. He then decided to take me along with him. I came back to my parents' house. I was very happy coming back to my village. Since childhood I was very religious and so I started spending most of my time at temples offering prayers and performing religious rituals. After some time I realized that all this had became a part of my life. My family was non-vegetarian and very fond of fish but whenever it was cooked, I could not bear the smell and felt like vomiting. One day I came to know that some of my friends were going to Vrindavan. I also expressed my desire to go there but was not permitted to do so by my 'Baba' (father). With the help of my cousin I somehow convinced my father and he gave me the permission to go along with my cousin. I came to Vrindavan with him. At that time I was 25. My cousin left me at Govind Ashram here in Vrindavan. Since then I have been staying here. Now I am 50 years old. I am staying at Swadhar Ashram for the last five years. Earlier, I also stayed in Pagalbaba Ashram. I cook my own food when I don't get it in *bhandara*.'

Long Life to Live

About 90-years-old Rampyari lives with her divorced daughter Kiran Bala, aged 50, in Room No.-12 of Sector-1 in Chaitanya Vihar. Before coming to this

Ashram, their life was full of struggles. Rampyari was the only bread-earner as her husband was jobless. She was determined to give her proper education and finally get her happily married. She left no stone unturned towards achieving this goal. She belonged to Kathol village of Haryana where women do not enjoy any status worth the name. Rampyari left her home in search of employment. She took embroidery work in a cottage industry. Sometimes she earned some money by selling tea or groceries. After struggling hard, she however fulfilled all the responsibilities of her family. Yet struggles did not end there. The elder daughter's husband met with a road accident and died when she was pregnant. She gave birth to her son in Kathol and got employed in a school. Rampyari tried to convince her daughter to get married again. By the time she was able to convince her for remarriage, her father passed away. The entire family was once again put into greater hardship. Rampyari, however, succeeded in persuading her daughter to remarry. But her husband refused to accept and recognize her first husband's child. Rampyari assured her daughter that she would bear the responsibility of looking after her child and she could come and meet the child on weekends. After two years of Rampyari's elder daughter's marriage, Kiran Bala, the younger daughter got married. Her husband was working in a private firm. He was an alcoholic and was fond of non-vegetarian food. On her repeated pleas to give up these habits, Kiran Bala was told to leave her husband's house. So she filed a case against her husband in the women police cell. When justice was denied to her, she moved the Patiala House Courts in Delhi. Kiran Bala says that she stayed with her uncle while the case was proceeding and in the process incurred debts. She wanted her husband to leave the bad habits and not a divorce. But her uncle insisted to get separated as court issues do not get sorted easily. Ultimately, she got a divorce and received a sum of ₹ 1,50,000 compensation. This she used for repaying her debts. At that time she was aged 40. Her mother had grown old and could not manage by selling vegetables. So Kiran Bala started helping and managed it. When elder daughter's son grew older, both Rampyari and Kiran Bala decided to spend their rest of their life in Vrindavan and came here in 2005. 'My mother's age is now 90, but I have to face many more challenges in my life,' Kiran Bala says confidently without any sign of defeat. It sounds good.

Wish, I Could Die Here-Haripriya Dasi

Sixty-year-old Harpriya Dasi belongs to Dhausera village of West Bengal. Married to Sukhdev Das at the age of 24, has a son and two daughters. Her husband died when she was 42 years old. Carried out manual work, raised the children and got them married. In West Bengal, old rituals still prevail. Because of it, a widow is compelled to live a life of grief and agony. Their life is limited to its surroundings and it is difficult to get out of it. After finishing the responsibility, they go to pious places to take a dip and get clean. First, she went to Ganga Sagar then to Navdeep, the birth place of Chaitanya Mahaprabhu. Then she came to Prayag and Kashi and ultimately she reached Vrindavan. When asked as to why she came to Vrindavan, she said 'I want to spend the remaining life in meditation, worship and serving the God. Only because of this I have made Vrindavan my place. I want to live the remaining life here. Better if I die here so that I could attain the ultimate *moksha*.'

Bowing to Cruel Traditions

Sadhana Chatterjee, aged 68, is the widow of Jeevan Lal Chatterjee, village Srerasaiya, Post Bethula Dori, district Nadia, West Bengal. Sadhana's life is a story of irony. Could anyone imagine that a man who spends every moment of his life worshipping gods and goddesses would be so unfortunate that he would die early, living behind his widow burdened with four children? Unfortunately, this is what had happened to Sadhana's husband who was a very dedicated temple priest and who passed away when his children were still very young. Sadhana says life without her husband, who died of heart ailment 20 years ago, has been a cycle of suffering and torture. Denied any compensation by the temple authority, she did not know how to raise her children. At last, she had no alternative but to start working as a domestic maid on a paltry salary of ₹ 300 per month. She went on working in this way, bringing up her family with what little she could earn. With the passage of time, her children grew up and she settled them and got them married. The elder son is a contractor in Kolkata, the second son works in a book shop and the third one, who had been a problem all through his life, has remained unemployed. When the cruel treatment meted out to widows in West Bengal started weighing on her mind, she felt that her home – where she was born and got up, where she was married and where she raised her family – was no longer a fit place for her to stay. Travelling by a tourist bus, she reached Vrindavan and to her great relief and comfort found a large number of widows living there without any complaint. After remaining in Vrindavan for some days, she decided this could be her permanent home now. She took shelter in an ashram and has been living there like any other widow but she was surprised to find one day that her belongings had been stolen. She did not know what to do. But that there could be thieves even in hallowed places like Vrindavan was a stunning shock to her. She did not know where to go. However, she resolved to spend the rest of her life only in Vrindavan where Gods may grant her *mukti*.

Battling With Destiny

Arti Sarkar, aged 60, is the widow of Narendra Sarkar and originally resident of Village and Post Jhanda, district Purulia, West Bengal. Arti Sarkar was married at the age of 15 and had two daughters. Her husband was a small farmer, able to earn enough to look after the family. But suddenly he died when he was just 44 years. After his death, Arti herself took to farming. Her husband had a small landholding. She was able to raise her daughters and get them married in good families. She was, thus, quite satisfied, though she continued to face the taunts and digs of people for being a widow. She was often reminded of the happy days she had spent with her husband with tears in her eyes. Although, her daughters were loving and affectionate, they could not spend much time with her due to their own preoccupation. She was haunted by the thoughts that there was nobody to take care of her or even spend some time with her. She decided to leave her home and hearth. After giving all her land to her daughters, she went on pilgrimage to various holy places. First of all, she visited the birth place of Chaitanya Mahaprabhu. Then she went to Ganga Sagar, Ayodhya, Kashi and Prayag and ultimately reached Vrindavan. Being in the lap of Lord Krishna, she felt she was in absolute bliss and thus gave away all her belongings. 'Now I want to pass my days remembering and praying to Lord Krishna day and night. I would be really blessed if I breathed my last in this holy place and attain Nirvana'.

Depths of Despair

Nihar Mandal, wife of late Shanker Mandal and native of Julybari, Post Thakur Claura, district Tiripura, West Bengal, lived with her family. Nihar Mandal got married at the age of 11. Mandal had six daughters. The couple was so busy in grooming up their daughters that they ignored their own health. At the age of 35, Nihar Mandal's husband passed away and Nihar had to shoulder the entire responsibility of looking after the family, but left no stone unturned in discharging her duties sincerely and got her daughters married. Even today, women, especially widows, are considered to be a burden on the society in West Bengal. Nihar Mandal says bright colours have no roles in my life. 'I am stuck with this faded white cotton sari, even on auspicious occasions. I am also deprived of the pleasure of participation in my family ceremonies. Bengal is known for its rice and fish but widows are compelled to stay away from rich diet and coloured dresses. It seems as if we are to be punished for being widows. I reached Vrindavan after getting fed up with life and devoted the rest of my life to praying Lord Krishna, who is my protector and I wish to devote the rest of my life in serving him. I will satisfy my hunger by begging alms at the Gate of Radha Rani in Vrindavan. My ultimate wish is to serve Lord Krishna and liberate myself from this materialistic world'.

Miseries of a Young Widow

Veena Pani Mandal, aged 68, widow of Anath Mandal, resident of village Gedhoha, Post Barakhsa, District Bir Bhum, West Bengal. Veena Pani Mandal was destined to be widowed at the age of 18, nearly four years after her marriage, when she was still in her youth. She had neither any issue nor any support from her in-laws. Left to wander and roam about in the widow-hating society of West Bengal, poor Veena did not know what to do. The cup of her misery was full to the brim when custodian of custom and traditions forced her to shave her head, wear a plain whit sari, eat gruel and pass her days in object poverty and want. The custom and traditions of West Bengal, only sough to throttle widows regardless of their age. 'Faced with social hostility and total indifference of my kith and kin, I did not know what to do,' Veena says mournfully. I sought refuge in the birth place of Chaitanya Mahaprabhu but could not live there long. At last, buffeted by cruel society I moved from place to place in search of some home to hide myself. Wandering here and there, I reached Vrindavan, which I found, was the only place where widows were not looked down upon. They were made to chant slogans for Lord Krishna and Radha

Rani in exchange for food. I pray every moment O Lord Krishna, liberate me from the cycle of birth and death and never make anyone a widow.

पढ़े लिखे होते तो भुगतते काहे

बनारस में रहने वाली आविदा की उम्र आज पैंसठ वर्ष है, कभी बडे आराम से जीवन व्यतीत कर रही थी माँ–बाप का साया बचपन में ही उठ गया था। पति स्वर्गीय रूजन बुनकर थे और बनारसी साड़ी का नक्शा बनाते थे। आविदा जी के तीन बेटे और तीन बेटियां हैं, लेकिन जब बत्तीस साल की उम्र में पति की मृत्यु टी.बी. से हुई और एक बेटा भी अचानक चल बसा तो इनके जीवन में बड़ा परिवर्तन आया। पढ़ाई–लिखाई तो पहले ही नहीं हुई थी और पति की बीमारी ने जो भी जमीन थी उसको बेचकर दवा दारू में लगा दिया था। पहले तो परिवार और आस–पड़ोस का व्यवहार ठीक रहा लेकिन पति की मृत्यु के पश्चात् सभी रिश्ते–नाते खराब होने लगे, आविदा अपनी बड़ी लड़की के पास रहने लगी, लेकिन बढ़ती उम्र में जब नातिनों ने भी परेशान करना शुरू किया – तो मजबूरी में बनारस में छावनी परिषद् में स्थित वृद्धा आश्रम का सहारा लेना पड़ा। यहा – तो मजबूरी में बनारस में छावनी परिषद् में स्थित वृद्धा आश्रम का सहारा लेना पड़ा। यहाँ आने के बाद अपने जैसी और महिलाओं से मिलने का मौका मिला तो जैसा लगा मैं ही दुखयारी नहीं हूं सभी की समस्या एक है। जीवन में आने वाली समस्याओं से लड़ने का हौसला यहीं से मिला। यहाँ खाना–पीना, दवा की व्यवस्था के साथ–साथ सम्मान भी मिल जाता है, यहां आने वाले लोग माई करके बात करते हैं तो अच्छा लगता है, कभी–कभी लगता है कि पढ़–लिख लिये होते तो यह दिन देखना न पड़ता। अब तो बस मिलने वाली पेंशन का ही सहारा है। अब यही आश्रम मेरा परिवार है।

पति प्रोविजन भगवान ओरिजनल

कभी उच्च शिक्षा के लिए जाने–जाने वाले बिहार स्थित नालन्दा में 4 नवम्बर, 1942 में जन्मी शान्ति देवी का बचपन घर पर ही बीता, लेकिन दुर्भाग्य रहा कि माता–पिता का देहान्त जल्दी ही हो गया था। उन्हें उनके दादा–दादी ने पाला। शान्ति देवी की शादी 9 वर्ष की उम्र में ही हो गई थी। उनके पति परमेश्वर ब्रह्मदेव मिडिल तक पढ़े थे, और किसानी करते थे। शान्ति देवी का जीवन पति के रहने तक तो बहुत अच्छा चला रहा था। लेकिन जब उन्हें दमे की बीमारी ने जकड़ा तो खेत–खलिहान बेचकर भी हम उनकी जान नहीं बचा सके। 'परिवार में एक बेटा और एक बेटी भगवान ने हमको प्रदान किये थे, 1999 में जब पति की मृत्यु हुई तो भी मैं जीवन से लड़ने का हौसला रखती थी, लेकिन दो हजार तीन में जब डकैती पड़ी और उस डकैती में नौकरी से छुट्टी पर आये मेरे बेटे की हत्या डकैतों ने कर दी, तब शान्ति देवी का हौसला डगमगाया। ऐसी स्थिति में भतीजे ने सहारा दिया, लेकिन वह भी कब तक मुझे पालता और अन्त में उसने मुझे महादेव की नगरी काशी ले जाकर राजघाट पर छोड़, दिया, फिर मुझे याद नहीं कि कब मैं इस राजकीय वृद्धा आश्रम, दुर्गा कुन्ड में आ गई। शान्ति देवी मानती हैं कि पति तो देव होता है, उसको अपनाना चाहिए। जैसा पूर्व जन्म में व्यक्ति कर्म करता है, वैसा ही वर्तमान में भोगता है। इसलिए परमात्मा में लीन हो जाना चाहिए। अब तो यह आश्रम ही मेरा घर है। यहीं पर रहकर भगवान की पूजा करना और उन्हें याद करना मेरा मुख्य काम है। दैनिक जरूरतें यहां आने वाले दानियों से सुलभ से पूरी हो जाता है। इस बूढ़ी चमड़ी के लिए इतना पर्याप्त है। मैं एक सन्देश देना चाहूंगी कि यदि महिला के पति की मृत्यु हो जाती है, तो उसे भगवान को ही अपना लेना चाहिए।

कर भला तो हो भला

शारदा देवी का जन्म बिहार की नगरी सासाराम में हुआ, लेकिन जब बारह वर्ष की उम्र में ही श्री लक्ष्मण चौधरी से विवाह हुआ, तो वह बनारस आ गईं। चूंकि पति यहां नौकरी करते थे। प्रारम्भ में समय बहुत अच्छा बीता सब तरफ खुशहाली बरस रही थी। परिवार भी साथ देता था। समय बीतता रहा और वह दो लड़कों और दो लड़कियों की माता बन गईं। घर का खर्चा पति द्वारा कमाये गये पैसों से ही चलता था, अचानक जब पति की मृत्यु फालिस के अटैक पड़ने से हुई तो सब अस्त–व्यस्त हो गया ऐसा लगा कि भाग्य ने हीं मुंह मोड़ लिया सास–ससुर, देवर–देवरानी सभी ने मुंह मोड़ा लिया है, संघर्ष के दिनों में मैं काम करने लगी और बच्चों को पालने लगी। समय बीतने के साथ–साथ लड़कों की शादी हो गई और जब उनका परिवार बढ़ा तो मेरी देख–रेख कम हो गई। चूंकि मेरा बेटा प्राइवेट नौकर है तो मैं उसकी परेशानी न देख पाई और मैंने वृद्धा आश्रम में आने का फैसला किया। भगवान का शुक्र है कि यहां आने के बाद मुझे ढेर सारा प्यार और सम्मान मिला। मुझे ऐसा लगता है कि सभी महिलाओं को जागरूक होना चाहिए, पढ़ना चाहिए ताकि वह अपने अधिकारों को जानें और उन्हें पाने का प्रयास करें। शारदा देवी का कहना है कि कम उम्र में महिला अगर विधवा हो तो उसकी शादी कर देनी चाहिए जिससे सामाजिक विषमताओं से बचा जा सके।

हर इंसान को सहारा मिल जाता है

बाबा विश्वनाथ की पवित्र नगरी में कदम–कदम पर घाट हैं, और घाटों पर बने हुए मन्दिर। बनारस नगरी के निकट जिला जौनपुर के एक जमींदार परिवार में ब्याही गई दुर्गा सिंह का जीवन परियों की गाथा जैसा प्रतीत होता है। दुर्गा सिंह का जन्म कोलकाता में हुआ, पति बनारसी सिंह आठवीं पास थे और खेती करके जीवन यापन करते थे। भरे–पूरे परिवार में आई दुर्गा का स्वागत सभी ने किया। कालान्तर में दुर्गा जी के सात बच्चे हुए। सभी कुछ ठीक–ठाक ही चल रहा था। मैं और मेरे पति बाइस एकड़ की जमींदारी का लाभ ले रहे थे, पता नहीं कब पति को दमा की बीमारी ने घेर लिया और बहुत प्रयास करने के बाद भी उनकी मृत्यु हो गई। फिर तो जैसे लगा कि दुर्गा के परिवार को किसी की नजर लग गई और शीघ्र ही चार बेटों में से दो की मृत्यु चेचक की वजह से हो गई। पति के न रहने से पट्टीदारों ने प्रताड़ित करना प्रारम्भ कर दिया और पारिवारिक सम्पत्ति में घाल–मेल करना शुरू कर दिया। बढ़ती उम्र के साथ वह अपने को असहाय महसूस करने लगी, कि तभी एक और बज्रपात हुआ, दुर्गा के दो बड़े बेटे जिनकी उम्र बीस और बाईस वर्ष थी, एक सड़क दुर्घटना में मारे गये। यह बताते–बताते दुर्गा जी की आंखों में कई बार आंस आये और गये आगे की जिन्दगी काटने के लिए बड़ी बेटी के संसुराल का सहारा लिया, लेकिन कब तक एक मां अपनी बेटी के ससुराल में रोटी तोड़ सकती थी। अचानक एक दिन दुर्गा जी ने निर्णय किया और महादेव की नगरी वाराणसी आ गई। जमींदारनी अब एक भिच्छुक की स्थिति में आ चुकी थी। यहां भगवान का सहारा मिला और पिछले पांच वर्ष से राजकीय वृद्धा आश्रम वाराणसी में रह रही हैं। अब इनका मन यहीं रमता है, और यहां से जाने को नहीं करता। अब तो जीना–मरना काशी में ही है, क्योंकि यहां हर किसी को सहारा मिल जाता है।

समय बड़ा बलवान

वृद्धा आश्रम उम्र का एक पड़ाव होता है, जहां पहुंचकर मनुष्य को किसी न किसी सहारे की आवश्यकता अवश्य होती है, यह बात जिला सीवान, बिहार में जन्मी इन्दरासना देवी पर लागू होती है। इन्दरासना देवी पढ़ी–लिखी तो नहीं हैं, लेकिन चिट्ठी और किताब पढ़ लेती हैं। इन्दरासना जी की शादी नौ वर्ष में ही बदरी जी के साथ हुई थी, लेकिन जल्द ही एक घटना में पति की हत्या हो गई। ससुराल में खेती का प्रचलन था, और उसी से जीवन यापन चल रहा था। पति की मृत्यु के बाद भी इन्दरासना ससुराल में ही रहीं। चूंकि उनके कोई सन्तान नहीं थी फिर भी सास–ससुर से प्यार मिलता रहा। इन्दरासना जब पचपन वर्ष की हुईं, तब तक सास–ससुर की मृत्यु हो चुकी थी और ससुराल में भतीजों का व्यवहार अब रास नहीं आ रहा था, अचानक उन्होंने काशी आने का निर्णय ले लिया और लोगों की सहायता से दुर्गा कुन्ड स्थित आश्रम में आ गईं। यहां रहते हुए इन्दरासना जी को अपने परिवार से बिछड़ने का गम नहीं होता। यहां आने वाले व्यक्तियों से सम्पूर्ण रूप से प्यार मिलता है। इन्दरासना अब खुश होती हैं और कहती हैं कि अब समय बदल गया है। अब कम उम्र की विधवा लड़कियों को शादी होने में बहुत समस्या नहीं आती हैं, वह चाहती हैं तो उन्हें सहारा मिल जाता है। अब तो मैं भगवान के पूजन–अर्चन में ही अपना समस्त जीवन अर्पित कर रहीं हूँ। यहां रहकर सब ठीक लगता है।

Women seeking care and protection in the shelter homes come from various challenging situations. Women need food, shelter and clothing. The role of care giver does not stop by providing only the basic needs. There are various other needs that women in shelter homes require. These are related with food, education, vocational skill, entertainment, sports, music, dance, drama, singing, clothing, counselling, medical help, legal aid and advice, celebration of festivals, shelter, love, affection, kindness, reunion with family and social network, etc. Understanding the psychological need of women in shelter homes is crucial to address the comprehensive psychological care for destitute women. The psychological care for women in shelter homes is restricted not only to providing care and support to the women but it encompasses the arena of interventions at individual, family and community level. There is a need to understand that there are many aspects of psychological care. The destitute women cannot be helped in isolation. While working with the women one need to focus not only upon psychological support of helping her in relieving her distress associated with the difficult situation but also in helping her to move beyond the trauma to rebuild her life. Widows living in ashrams at religious places need a comprehensive package of social security and rehabilitation including shelter, food, clothing, health care, education, vocational training, entertaining and amusement, counselling and psychological care along with love and affection, participation in the celebration of festivals, religious functions and reunion with family during important social gatherings such as marriage, birth, death, etc.

8

Conclusion and Recommendations

The status of ageing in India reflects that the issues pertaining to socio-economic and demographic profiles, living arrangements, problems of and services to the elderly, interpersonal relationships especially of the urban elderly are highlighted to a great extent. No doubt, concerted efforts made by researchers have so far led to a better understanding of ageing issues. However, the diversity that has emerged in the ageing process necessitates our research efforts to focus on different ageing issues in society. This, in turn, is expected to promote development of effective age-related policies and programmes. In India, the family is most important institution that has survived through ages. The Indian family is considered to be strong, well knit, resilient and enduring. There are regional and cultural variations in family structure and functioning. The norms and values related to family life vary according to religion, caste, social class and residential patterns. A joint or a multi-generational household includes kinsmen, and generally embraces three to four living generations. It is a group composed of a number of family units living in separate rooms in the same house. These members eat and food is cooked on one hearth, they share a common income and common property and are related to one another through kinship ties. In traditional Indian society older people lived within the multi-generational family. They enjoyed honour and legitimate authority over the family functions and relationships. However, with a demographic transition and impact of western culture, Indian society is witnessing a decline in traditional or joint family system and thus, proper care and legitimate authority of the older persons in the family is gradually shrinking. This has caused the negligence, exploitation, abuse and isolation of the older people. The problems of older people have also increased manifolds with the change of time and degradation of socio-cultural value system. A large segment of the older people requires rehabilitation services and proper care, protection and support for their survival and well-being. A large number of ashrams, well-age homes, aged homes and day care centres have been set up by government, private and non-government organizations including corporate houses for providing rehabilitation services to the aged. The present study purports to examine the performance of scheme of Integrated Programme for Older Persons in selected states of India.

Widowhood is a universal phenomenon. The rate of widowhood varies from country to country and within countries from time to time. In addition to natural factors relating to general mortality, man-made factors like wars and terrorism also can increase the incidence of widowhood in a population. According to 2001 Census, India had 34 million widows, 8 million more than in the 1991 Census; whereas, according to 2011 Census, there are around 43 million, about 8 per cent of the entire Indian female population. As per 2011 Census, widows, divorcees and separated women (20 and above years) constituted 8.2 per cent. This was reported high in Tamil Nadu followed by Kerala, Karnataka and Andhra Pradesh. In the state of Uttar Pradesh, widows, divorcees and separated women from the age group of 20 and above years accounted for 5.7 per cent. As per Sample Registration Survey, persons below 10 years of age are being treated as unmarried. Widows, divorcees and separated women constituted more than 10 per cent of the population. This was found more pronouncing in Tamil Nadu, Karnataka, Kerala, Andhra Pradesh and West Bengal. In the State of Uttar Pradesh, it was recorded 7.1 per cent. The socio-cultural profile of Varanasi and Vrindavan presents interesting scenario. Varanasi has been abode of Lord Shiva and thus, it is the place of Shaiv sect while Vrindavan and Vrindavan being the place of Lord Krishna is known for Vaishnav sect. A large number of widows from neighbouring states like West Bengal, Madhya Pradesh, Rajasthan, Odisha, Gujarat, Maharashtra and other places migrated to these two religious places to settle their life as both the places are known for *moksha* – the liberation from cycle of birth and death. Vrindavan has comparatively larger concentration of widows and destitute women; however, their life in the city is worse.

Main Findings

- Most of the respondents were found from the higher age group, mainly from General and OBC communities. Majority of the respondents were illiterate and educationally backward.
- Most of the respondents in Vrindavan were found living in widow homes while more than two-fifth respondents in Varanasi were found living independently. About two-fifth respondents reported that they are living in the city from more than 10 years while more than one-fourth respondents were found living in the city from five years. Majority of the respondents revealed that they are depending on charity and menial work for fulfillment of financial needs.
- More than half of the respondents were from nuclear families. The main occupation of their deceased husbands was labour, petty business and private job. Thus, their income was reported low i.e. less than ₹ 5,000. Majority of the respondents were from lower class. The main occupation of the head of the family was reported to be labour, agriculture, private job and petty business.
- About half of the respondents reported that their relations with head of the family are normal. Only 14 per cent respondents revealed that their relations with head of the family are strained. About half of the respondents reported that they do not have any dependent members.

- Majority of the respondents were found satisfied with their family conditions. A significant number of respondents revealed that the nature of behaviour of parents and other family members towards them has been normal and harmonious. However, about 21 per cent respondents reported that the behaviour of their parents and family members towards them is strained.
- Majority of the respondents reported that they never received support from their family. Thus, majority of the respondents revealed that they do not get financial support from their family. Most of the respondents further reported that their deceased husbands did not leave any property for them.
- Majority of the respondents revealed that they have children. Their children are mainly engaged in labour, agriculture, small business and trade. More than half of the respondents reported that their children never consulted them.
- About two-third respondents reported that they believe in traditional social values. Most of the respondents further reported that they get respect from society. The behaviour of their colleagues and relatives towards them has been reported to be harmonious and normal. Thus, majority of the respondents were found satisfied with their conditions. They also do not feel insecure and alone.
- About three-fourth respondents reported that they were less than 15 years at the time of their marriage while the age of their deceased husbands was less than 25 years. Most of the respondents were satisfied with their marital life. Majority of the respondents reported that they became widows at the age of 45 years and above. The main cause of the death of their deceased husbands was prolonged decease, heart decease and cholera. They further reported that treatment was provided to their deceased husband for their diseases/ailments.
- Majority of the respondents reported that they knew about widow homes from their relatives, neighbours and NGOs. Most of the respondents reported that people perceive widows with sympathy. Majority of the respondents further reported that they themselves came to widow homes, while a large number of respondents came to widow homes due to family members and pressure of neighbours and society.
- The environment in a widow home has been found normal and harmonious. Most of the respondents further reported that they have proper facilities for accommodation, drinking water, bathroom and toilet, cleanliness, entertainment and security and mess.
- Only one-third respondents were found aware about the government welfare programmes and thus, about one-third respondents revealed that they are getting government support. About half of the respondents reported that they are getting widow pension.
- About three-fourth respondents reported that they faced financial problems after death of their deceased husbands. In order to resolve economic problems, they initiated work and took borrowings.
- A large proportion of respondents reported that their family members hade not been treating them fair after they became widows. Their

relations with family members are stressful and family members do not bother for them. Thus, about 45 per cent respondents reported that they never visited their family. About two-third respondents further reported that their relatives and friends never visited them. Moreover, about 69 per cent respondents revealed that their relatives and friends do not invite them on festivals.

- A significant proportion of respondents reported that they remember their deceased husbands at the time of family problem, family functions, on seeing someone similar looking and on seeing things he used to use.
- Majority of the respondents were found unhealthy. They are receiving treatment for their diseases from widow homes, and in hospital.
- Most of the respondents are celebrating religious festivals as they believe in them and also for purity of soul. Most of the respondents further reported that they are visiting temples and participating in *satsang*. Most of the respondents further revealed that they are visiting religious centres. However, about three-fourth respondents are participating in religious festivals and functions sometime only. About half of the respondents are also keeping fast during religious functions.
- There has been significant change in the lifestyle of respondents after being widowed. However, young and old-aged widows are breaking the traditional lifestyle of widows.
- Lack of education, religious belief, dependency, social and caste induced conditions and unemployment among women are some of the important factors responsible for poor condition of widows. Thus, awareness regarding welfare programmes, social reforms, women education, enforcement of laws and employment among women may improve the conditions of widows.
- About half of the respondents were found in favour of remarriage. They further reported that widows below the age of 30 years should remarry while childless young widows should be married.

Policy Recommendations

- The benefits of government sponsored social security schemes are yet to trickle to widows due to technical difficulties. At present pension can only be sanctioned to widows living in their native places. Thus the existing pension schemes need to be re-drafted to include a clause keeping in mind the demography and the mobility of these widows.
- There is a need to provide alternative housing to the widows who live in makeshift shanties, streets, verandahs, etc. Initiation of Swadhar project will help in providing accommodation, improvement in skill training, providing health care measures and connecting them into the various activities of the temple like making garlands, incense sticks etc. This will be an effort to bring them into the mainstream of the society. Alternatively, shelter homes could be organized and basic weekly ration should be provided as widows go out in the morning to the temples/mazars/ashrams and have their lunch there.

- Financial inclusion including opening of bank account, and life and health insurance should be ensured. Zero balance bank accounts should be opened for the widows so that they could properly save from their meagre earnings which could simultaneously act as their pension account.
- Short stay homes for younger widows and the abandoned women should be established where proper vocational training needs to be imparted as per local market demands.
- Sensitization of the Panchayats and local governments about the provisions of Maintenance and Welfare of Parents and Senior Citizens Act, 2007, especially the obligations of the siblings towards their parents/grandparents as well as the right of a senior citizen to claim maintenance for her near ones is the need of the hour.
- Information dissemination on availability of widow's pension, amount of pension and how to access it should be intensified through innovative IEC campaigns by the Panchayats and local governments through involving civil societies.
- Social conditioning plays a great role in the deprivation of the widows. This conditioning is so strong that the widows see themselves as inauspicious. They internalize their victimized status which results in very low self-esteem. A properly integrated counselling facility is needed in these shelter homes, keeping in mind their geriatric issues as well as psycho-social disorders to rebuild their self esteem.
- There is a need to link the aged and widows with appropriate governmental/non-governmental organizations/national programmes such as literacy, social awareness, family planning, motivation, environment and sanitation, etc. as per their will so that the experience, expertise and competencies of the aged may be utilized for the betterment of the society.
- Proper mechanism needs to be placed to ensure the comprehensive protection, promotion and security of the aged widows. All the available government programmes should have Older People Component (OPC) and programmes designed exclusively for older people need to be implemented.
- It is suggested that government should include awareness generation component in all their schemes initiated for the welfare and development of older people and funds should be released directly to local governments for generating awareness among the older people. In this regard, NGOs should also be supported with financial assistance to become pro active to generate awareness among the older people and widows.
- It is recommended that under the existing scheme of the Ministry of Social Justice and Empowerment, priority should be given to those NGOs who are ready to construct widow homes. NGOs' involvement is good alternative for the welfare and development of the widows. They need support of the government in order to provide them social security and dignity.
- Guidance and counselling services to the families for proper care and protection of aged and widows are required for rehabilitation of the aged

and widows and their mainstreaming in the family and society as inter-generational ideological differences may destroy the relationships.

- The management of widow homes/day care centres should ensure the provision of basic amenities, services and infrastructure for their inmates. This may be created and provided on sustainable basis through imposing of nominal user charges and convergence of programmes and schemes.
- There is a need to ensure convergence of government programmes, schemes and projects with the existing widow homes/day care centres run by corporate, private and religious trusts in order to deliver the health care, rehabilitation and care and protection services to the aged inmates.
- Resource mobilization by the management of these widow homes/day care centres may be ensured through launching a social campaign in the schools, colleges, government and private offices and pooled resources may be utilized to create infrastructure facilities and delivery of rehabilitation services to the aged.
- Health care system for widows needs to take into account their health problems and should be accessible without cumbersome formalities. Appointment of trained social workers to be considered for placement at hospitals and institutions of women.
- There is imperative need of large widow ashrams, accommodating thousands of widows, for providing shelter to widows at religious places. In these Ashrams, all types of facilities and amenities, including food, clothing, health and medical care and physiotherapy, library, etc. should be created for widows. These ashrams may be established through mobilizing resources from corporate and private sectors as well as temples, mosques, and churches as people liberally donate in the religious places. A large mess with modern equipment and facilities may be started with the support of religious trusts and associations for widows. Widows living in widow ashrams may also be involved in supervision, cooking and serving food to inmates.
- All widows living in religious places should be provided social security schemes such as Indira Gandhi National Widow Pension, Indira Gandhi National Old Age Pension, Indira Gandhi National Disability Pension, Rashtriya Swasthya Bima Yojana, Annapoorna Scheme, Pradhan Mantri Jan Dhan Yojana, and Aam Admi Bima Yojana so that widows may get the benefits. The procedures for availing benefits under these schemes should be made easy.
- It is the need of the hour that single widow system of services should be initiated by different departments. For the purpose, registration of all widows needs to be ensured besides they should be provided photo identity cards so that they may get the benefits under social welfare programmes of government.
- Social reform movements are to be encouraged so that young and childless widows may get married while there should be effective enforcement of Hindu Succession Act 1956, Hindu Widow Remarriage Act 1856, Child Marriage Restraint Act and other legal provisions for protection of widows.

- It is necessary to build social awareness and to change the mindset of people towards widows. It is necessary to educate girls encouraging them to be independent and fight for their own rights. Education will give them a sense of independence and will help them become self reliant. This will change the attitude of people towards widows and they will not be treated as parasites in the society.
- The social mindset has also to be changed in the sense that widowers should marry widows rather than marrying unmarried girls or only childless widows. None of the reforms contemplated by various legislations enacted for the benefit of widows can achieve success unless and until the mindset of the society is changed and they become more receptive to reduce the suffering of widows.
- Social festivals should be organized by NGOs and other civil society organizations from time to time to encourage widows living in ashrams for participation effectively on the occasion of Dussehra, Deepawali, Chhat, Holi, Christmas, Id, so that they may feel good and become energized.
- Training-cum-production centres should be established for widows making them independent and develop the confidence to live with dignity and honour.
- Any strategy to rehabilitate the widows in religious centres has two-pronged aim. One is to improve their conditions within that particular place as most of the widows have shown reluctance in moving out from Vrindavan. Secondly, awareness should be created among widows that they do not leave their homes and move miles away just for survival. This will involve intensive social intervention by government, civil society organizations, NGOs, welfare organizations and also involvement of religious leaders. More focus would be required in those areas where migration results in the pathetic conditions of the widows who move to religious centres and to convince them to stay back with their families.
- There is a need to encourage the NGOs and civil society organizations and charitable trusts to provide boarding and lodging facilities for widows and abandoned women, particularly living in religious centres. Government agencies should enforce existing laws and guidelines regarding social security of widows. All widows and destitute women living in religious centres should be provided social security benefits under government run schemes.
- District Probation Officer should be made accountable for maintaining statistics related with widows and destitute women living in religious centres. The officer should be made responsible for preparing action plan for rehabilitation of widows and destitute women in consultation with district level officials, civil societies, NGOs, and charitable trusts.
- Government should also open Women Help Line in association with civil society organizations, NGOs and charitable trusts so that women in need may get access to social security and other government and non-government services for their rehabilitation.

Bibliography

Aaronson, W.E., Zinn, J.S. and Rosko, M.D. (1994) Do For-Profit and Not-For-Profit Nursing Homes Behave Differently?, *The Gerontologist*, Vol. 34, No. 6.

Abrahams, Ruby (1972) Mutual Help for the Widowed, *Social Work*, Vol. 17, No. 5, pp. 54–61.

Agarwal, A.G. (Ed.) (1978) *Poverty, Deprivation and Intelligence*, New Delhi: Criterion Publications.

Agarwala, A.K. (1974) Intelligence Differences and Affectional Deprivation, *Indian Psychological Review*, Vol. 28, No. 3, pp. 39–44.

Agarwala, S.N. (1962) Remarriage Rates in Some Delhi Villages, *Medical Digest*, Vol. 30, No. 10, pp. 548–57.

——. (1967) Widow Remarriage in Some Rural Areas of Northern India, *Demography*, Vol. 4, No. 1, pp. 126–34.

Agewell Foundation (2010) *A Study on Isolation in Old Age*, New Delhi: Agewell Research and Advocacy Centre.

Ahmed, J. (2004) Reaching the Body: Future Directions. In H. Thomas and J. Ahmed (Eds), *Cultural Bodies: Ethnography and Theory*, Malden, MA: Blackwell Publishing.

Ahuja, Ram (2001) *Social Surveys and Research Methods*, Jaipur: Rawat Publications.

——. (2007) *Indian Social System*, Jaipur: Rawat Publications.

Akundy, A. (2004) *Anthropology of Ageing: Contexts, Culture and Implications*, New Delhi: Serials Publications.

Alam, Khurshid (1986) Effects of Prolonged Socio-Cultural and Economic Deprivation on Retention: A Comparative Study, *Indian Psychological Review*, Vol. 30, No. 2, pp. 21–24.

——. (1988) Categorical Organization in Free Recall as a Function of Social Deprivation and Observer Presence, *Psychological Studies*, Vol. 3, No. 2, pp. 123–28.

Alam, Moneer (2006) *Ageing in India: Socio-Economic and Health Dimensions*, New Delhi: Academic Foundation.

Alexander, I.E. and Adlerstein, A.M. (1958) Affective Responses of the Concept of Death in Population of Children and Early Adolescents, *Journal of General Psychology*, Vol. 93, No. 2, pp. 167–77.

Alexopoulos (2005) Stress, Social Engagement and Psychological Well-being in Institutional Settings: Evidence Based on the Minimum Data Set 2.0, *Canadian Journal on Ageing*, Vol. 19, No. 2.

Allen, Michael and Mukherjee, S.N. (Eds) (1982) *Women in India and Nepal*, Canberra: ANU Publications.

Altekar, A.S. (1956) *The Position of Women in Hindu Civilization*, Banaras: Motilal Banarsidass.

Anand, U.K. (2001) Dilemmas of Aged in the New Millennium, *Contemporary Social Work*, Vol. XVIII, October.

Anantharaman, R.N. (1979a) Adjustment and its Correlates in Old Age, *Indian Journal of Clinical Psychology*, Vol. 6, No. 2.

Anderson, K.N., Glanze, W.D. and Anderson, L.E. (Eds) (1998) *Mosby's Medical, Nursing and Health Dictionary* (5th Edn), Los Angeles: Times Mirror Company.

Anderson, T.B. (1984) Widowhood as a Life Transition: Its Impact on Kinship Ties, *Journal of Marriage and the Family*, Vol. 46, No. 1.

Andreoletti, C., Veratti, B. and Lachman, M.E. (2006) Age Differences in the Relationship between Anxiety and Recall, *Ageing Mental Health*, Vol. 10.

Andrews, A. (1999) The Seductiveness of Agelessness, *Ageing and Society*, Vol. 19, No. 3.

Andrews, C.R. (2001) Draft Research Agenda on Ageing for the 21st Century, United Nations Department of Social and Economic Affairs, New York.

Anetzberger, G.J. (1997) Elderly Adult Survivors of Family Violence: Implications for Clinical Practice, *Violence Against Women*, Vol. 3, No. 5.

Anshe, R.N. (1949) *The Family: Its Function and Destiny*, New York: Harper and Brothers.

Applegate, M. and Morse, J.M. (1994) Personal Privacy and Interactional Patterns in a Nursing Home, *Journal of Aging Studies*, Vol. 8, No. 4.

Apte, Mahadev L., Lokahitavadi and Chiplunkar, V.K. (1973) Spokesmen of Change in Nineteenth Century Maharashtra, *Modern Asian Studies*, Vol. 7, No. 2.

Apte, Usha M. (1978) *The Sacrament of Marriage in Hindu Society: From Vedic Period to Dharmasastras*, Delhi: Ajanta Publications.

Aradhya, B.M.M. (1987) What it Means to be a Widow, *Social Welfare*, Vol. 34, No. 9, pp. 2–3.

Arber, S. and Ginn, J. (Eds) (1995) *Connecting Gender and Ageing: A Sociological Approach*, Philadelphia, PA: Open University Press.

Arling, Greg T. (1976) The Elderly Widow and Her Family Neighbours and Friends, *Journal of Marriage and the Family*, Vol. 38, No. 4, pp. 757–68.

Athvale, Parvati (1930) *My Story: The Autobiography of a Hindu Widow* (Marathi), translated by Rev. Justin E. Abbott, New York: G.P. Putnam's Sons.

Bailey, F.G. (1960) *Tribe, Caste, Nation*, Manchester: Manchester University Press.

Balagopal, Gayathri (2009) Access to Health Care Among Poor Elderly Women in India: How Far Do Policies Respond to Women's Realities?, *Gender and Development*, Vol. 17, No. 3.

Balasubramanian, C. (1976) *The Status of Women in Tamil Nadu During the Sangam Age*, Madras: University of Madras Press.

Balasubramanyam, V. (1970) A Savior of Widows: A Profile on R.S. Subbalakshmi Ammal, *Social Welfare*, Vol. XVII, No. 3, p. 27.

Bali, A. (Ed.) (1999) *Understanding Greying People of India*, New Delhi: ICSSR and Inter-India Publications.

Banerjee, G. (1984) *Hindu Law of Marriage and Stridhana*, Delhi: Mittal Publications.

Banker, K., Prajapati, B. and Kedia, G. (2011) Study of Health Profile of Residents of Geriatric Home in Ahmedabad District, *National Journal of Community Medicine*, Vol. 2, No. 3.

Bankoff, Elizabeth A. (1983) Social Support and Adaptation to Widowhood, *Journal of Marriage and the Family*, Vol. 45, No. 41, pp. 827–39.

Bansal, Vimla (1979) Widows: Murauna, Ph.D. Thesis, ICSSR Library, New Delhi.

Barbara, Ward (1963) *Women in New Asia*, Paris: UNESCO.

Baron, Omar and Rolf, Ehrenfels (1941) *Mother-Right in India*, Hyderabad: Oxford University Press.

Baum, A.S., Burnes, D.S. and Lamb, H. (1993) *A Nation in Denial: The Truth About Homelessness*, Boulder, CO: Westview Press.

Baxter, E. and Hopper, K. (1981) *Private Lives/Public Spaces: Homeless Adults on the Streets of New York City*, New York: Community Service Society.

——. (1984) Shelter and Housing for the Homeless Mentally Ill. In H.R. Lamb (Ed.), *The Homeless Mentally Ill*, Washington, D.C.: American Psychiatric Association.

Becker, Howard and Hill, Rueben (1948) *Family Marriage and Parenthood*, Boston: D.C. Health Company.

Benson, Leonard (1971) *The Family Bond: Marriage, Love and Sex in America*, New York: Random House Inc.

Berardo, F.M. (1967) Social Adaptation to Widowhood Among a Rural-Urban Aged Population, *Agricultural Experiment Station Bulletin*, Washington: College of Agriculture, Washington State University, p. 4.

——. (1968) Widowhood Status in the United States Perspective on a Neglected Aspect of the Family Life Cycle, *The Family Coordinator*, Vol. 17, No. 3, July.

——. (1970) Survivorship and Social Isolation: The Case of the Aged Widower, *The Family Coordinator*, Vol. 19, No. 1, pp. 11–25.

Bergmann, K. (1971) The Neuroses of Old Age, *British Journal of Psychiatry Special Publication*, Vol. 6.

Bernard, Farber (Ed.) (1966) *Kinship and Family Organization*, New York: John Wiley and Sons Inc.

Berthelot, J.M. (1991) Sociological Discourse and the Body. In M. Featherstone, M. Hepworth and B.S. Turner (Eds), *The Body: Social Process and Cultural Theory*, Newbury Park, CA: Sage.

Beteille, Andre, (1983) *Equality and Inequality: Theory and Practice*, Delhi: Oxford University Press.

Bey, Hamid (1971) Saved from the Funeral Pyre but an Eyesore, *Thought*, May 22, pp. 11–12.

Bhagat, B. Ram and Unisa, Sayeed (2006) Ageing and Dependency in India: A New Measurement, *Asian Population Studies*, Vol. 2, No. 2, July.

Bhaktavatsalam, M. (1964) Women in Changing India, *Women on the March*, Vol. 8, No. 10, pp. 76–77.

Bharat, Shalini (1986) Single Parent Family in India: Issues and Implications, *The Indian Journal of Social Work*, Vol. XLVII, No. 1, pp. 55–65.

Bhate, G.C. (1907) *Permitting Widow Marriages*, Poona: Widow Marriage Association.

Bhatia, H.S. (1983) *Aging and Society: A Sociological Study of Retired Public Servants*, Udaipur: Arya's Book Centre.

Bhattacharya, Amitabha (1977) Molding Man's Attitude for Woman's Progress, *Social Welfare*, Vol. XXII, No. 4, pp. 10–17.

Bhattacharya, K. (1881) *Institute of Parasara*, Calcutta: Asiatic Society of Bengal.

Bhattacharya, Prakash (2005) *Implications of an Ageing Population in India: Challenges and Opportunities*, Hyderabad: Institute of Chartered Financial Analysis of India.

Bhim, Raja (1969) *Marriage of Hindu Widows* (2nd Edn), Bombay: Indu Prakash Press.

Bhingradiya, P. and Kamala, R. (1997) An Intergenerational Study on the Situation of the Elderly in Rural Saurashtra, *Indian Journal of Gerontology*, Vol. 11, Nos 3–4.

Bhuler, G. (Trans.) (1886) *Laws of Manu*, Delhi: Motilal Banarsidass.

Bhushan, Jamila Brij (1973) War Widows, Weekly Round Table, July 1, pp. 26–30.

Bidarakoppa, G.S. (1971) Position and Problems of Hindu Widows, *The Journal of Karnataka University Social Sciences*, Vol. VII.

Biggs, S. (1997) Choosing Not to be Old? Masks, Bodies and Identity Management in Later Life, *Ageing and Society*, Vol. 17, No. 5.

——. (2004) Age, Gender, Narratives, and Masquerades, *Journal of Aging Studies*, Vol. 18, No. 1.

Birke, L. (1999) *Feminism and the Biological Body*, New Brunswick, NY: Rutgers University Press.

Biswas, S.K. (1987) *Aging in Contemporary India*, Calcutta: Indian Anthropological Society.

Blood, Robert O. (1960) *The Marriage*, Glencoe: The Free Press.

Bloom, David E. et al. (2010) Economic Security Arrangements in the Context of Population Ageing in India, *International Social Security Review*, Vol. 63, Nos 3–4.

Blow, Z.S. (1973) *Old Age in a Changing Society*, New York: New Viewpoints, Franklin-Watts.

Blumer, H. (1969) *Symbolic Interactionism: Perspective and Method*, Los Angeles: University of California Press.

Bochner, A.P. (2000) Criteria Against Ourselves, *Qualitative Inquiry*, Vol. 6, No. 2.

——. (2001) Narrative's Virtues, *Qualitative Inquiry*, Vol. 7, No. 2.

Bock, E.W. and Webber, Irving L. (1972) Suicide Among the Elderly: Isolating Widowhood and Mitigating Alternatives, *Journal of Marriage and the Family*, Vol. 34, No. 1, pp. 24–31.

Bold (2001) Health Status of Elderly in India, International Institute of Ageing, United Nations, Malta.

Bombaywale, Usha (1993) *Growing Old in Young India*, Pune: Snehavardhan Publishing House.

Bond, J. (1992) The Medicalization of Dementia, *Journal of Aging Studies*, Vol. 6, No. 4.

Bose, A. and Shankardass, M.K. (2004) *Growing Old in India: Voices Reveal, Statistics Speak*, Delhi: B.R. Publishing Corporation.

Bose, A.B. and Sen, M.L.A. (1966) Some Characteristics of the Widows in Rural Society, *Man in India*, Vol. 46, No. 3.

Bottomore, Tom (1970) Conservative Man, *The New York Review of Books*, Vol. 15, No. 6.

Bougle, C. (1958) Essence in the Reality of the Caste System, *Contributions to Indian Sociology*, Vol. 2, No. 2, p. 30.

Bourdieu, P. (1990) *The Logic of Practice*, Stanford, CA: Stanford University Press.

Bourret, E.M., Bernick, L.G., Cott, C.A. and Kontos, P.A. (2002) The Meaning of Mobility for Residents and Staff in Long-Term Care Facilities, *Journal of Advanced Nursing*, Vol. 37, No. 4.

Bowden, P. (2000) An 'Ethic of Care' in Clinical Settings: Encompassing 'Feminine' and 'Feminist' Perspectives, *Nursing Philosophy*, Vol. 1, No. 1.

Bowman, Henry A. (1960) *Marriage for Moderns*, New York: McGraw Hill.

Boyd, R. and Mcguire, F. (1996) The Efficacy of Humour in Improving Psychological Well-being of Residents of Long-Term Care Facilities, *Journal of Leisurability*, Vol. 23, No. 4.

Bricker, K.S. and Kerstetter, D.L. (2000) Level of Specialization and Place Attachment: An Exploratory Study of Whitewater Recreationists, *Leisure Sciences*, Vol. 22, No. 4.

Brill, P.A., Jensen, R.L., Koltyn, K.F. and Morgan, L.A. (1998) The Feasibility of Conducting a Group-Based Progressive Strength Training Program in Residents of a Multi-Level Care Facility, *Activities, Adaptation and Aging*, Vol. 4.

Brough, J.B. (2001) Temporality and Illness: A Phenomenological Perspective. In S.K. Toombs (Ed.), *Handbook of Phenomenology and Medicine*, Dordrecht, The Netherlands: Kluwer Academic Publishers.

Brown, A. (1998) 'Doing Time': The Extended Present of the Long-Term Prisoner, *Time and Society*, Vol. 7, No. 1.

Brown, B., Perkins, D. and Brown, G. (2003) Place Attachment in a Revitalizing Neighborhood: Individual and Block Levels of Analysis, *Journal of Environmental Psychology*, Vol. 23, No. 3.

Brown, B.B. and Perkins, D.D. (1992) Disruptions in Place Attachment. In I. Altman and S.M. Low (Eds), *Place Attachment*, New York: Plenum Press.

Brubaker, T.H. (1985) *Later Life Families*, London: Sage Publications.

Buettner, L.L. (1995) Therapeutic Recreation as an Intervention for Agitation in Persons with Dementia: A Case Study for Mrs. M, *Therapeutic Recreation Journal*, Vol. 29, No. 1.

Buettner, L.L. and Fitzsimmons, S. (2002) Adventure Program: Therapeutic Biking for the Treatment of Depression in Long-Term Care Residents with Dementia, *American Journal of Alzheimer's Disease and Other Dementias*, Vol. 17, No. 2.

Burgess, E.W. (1960) *Aging in Western Society*, Chicago: The University of Chicago Press.

Burgess, E.W. and Locke, H.J. (1945) *The Family: From Institution to Companionship*, New York: American Book Co.

——. (1963) *The Family*, New York: American Book Co.

Burns, I., Cox, H. and Plant, H. (2000) Leisure or Therapeutics? Snoezelen and the Care of Older Persons with Dementia, *International Journal of Nursing Practice*, Vol. 6, No. 3.

Calasanti, T.M. (2004) Feminist Gerontology and Old Men, *Journal of Gerontology*, Vol. 59b, No. 6.

Caton, A.R. (Ed.) (1930) *The Key Progress: A Survey of the Status and Conditions of Women in India*, London: Oxford University Press.

Census of India (2001) Population Projection for India and States, Office of the Registrar General and Census Commissioner, India.

Centers, Richard (1949) *The Psychology of Social Classes*, Princeton, NJ: Princeton University Press.

Central Statistical Organization (2000) Elderly in India: Profile and Programmes, Ministry of Statistics and Programme Implementation, Government of India, New Delhi.

Chadha, N.K. and Singh, S. (1996) Inter-Generational Gap and Psychological Health. In Vinod Kumar (Ed.), *Ageing: Indian Perspective and Global Scenario*, New Delhi: All India Institute of Medical Sciences.

Chakravarty, Indrani (1997) *Life in Twilight Years*, Calcutta: Kwality Book Company.

Chakravarty, T. (2002) Case Studies. In M.V. Giri (Ed.), *Living Death: Trauma of Widowhood in India*, New Delhi: Gyan Publishing House.

Chambers, R. (1983) *Rural Development: Putting the Last First*, Harlow: Longman.

Chanana, H.B. and Talwar, P.P. (1987) Aging in India: Its Socio-Economic and Health Implications, *Asia Pacific Population Journal*, Vol. 2, No. 3.

Chandra, Sudhir (1985) Widow Remarriage and Later Nineteenth Century Indian Literature (for Private Circulation only).

Charmaz, K. (1983) Loss of Self: A Fundamental Form of Suffering in the Chronically Ill, *Sociology of Health and Illness*, Vol. 5, No. 2.

Chatterjee, Bishwa B. (1980) Effects of Social Deprivation: Some Contradictory Findings, *Social Change*, Vol. 10, Nos 1–2, pp. 9–14.

Chattopadhyaya, Sudhakar (1965) *Social Life in Ancient India*, Calcutta: Academic Publications.

Chen, A.M. (1998) *Widows in India*, New Delhi: Sage Publications.

Cherry, Russell (1981) *The Aging Experience*, Australia: George Allen and Unwin Co.

Cheung, C.K. and Ngai, N.P. (2004) Humanist Approach to Youth Development in the Summer Youth Programme of Hong Kong, *Journal of Social Science Research*, Vol. 31, No. 2, pp. 1–24.

Chevan, Albert and Korson, J. Henry (1972) The Widowed Who Live Alone: An Examination of Social and Demographic Factors, *Social Forces*, Vol. 51, No. 1, pp. 45–53.

Chhabra, Rami (1975–76) Where the Wind of Change Lies Low, *Social Welfare*, Vol. 22, Nos 6–7.

Choubey, N.P., Pandey, L.P. and Patni, Rajani (1986) *Deprivation and Human Personality: Current Theory and Research*, Allahabad: Indian Academy of Social Sciences.

Christensen, Harold T. (1950) *Marriage Analysis: Foundations for Successful Family Life*, New York: The Ronald Press.

Christian, D. (1994) *Two-Way Bilingual Education: Students Learning through Two Languages*, Santa Cruz, CA: National Center for Research on Cultural Diversity and Second Language Learning.

Christian, J. (2003) Homelessness: Integrating International Perspective, *Journal of Community and Applied Social Psychology*, Vol. 13, No. 2.

Clayton, A. Hartjen (1978) *Crime and Criminalization* (2nd Edn), New York: Praeger Publishers.

Clough, P.T. (2000) Comments on Setting Criteria for Experimental Writing, *Qualitative Inquiry*, Vol. 6, No. 2.

Cohen, D. and Eisdorfer, C. (1986) *The Loss of Self: A Family Resource for the Care of Alzheimer's Disease and Related Disorders*, New York: Norton.

Cohen-Mansfield, J., Golander, H. and Arnheim, G. (2000) Self-Identity in Older Persons Suffering from Dementia: Preliminary Results, *Social Science and Medicine*, Vol. 51, No. 3.

Coleman, James C. (1976) *Abnormal Psychology and Modern Life*, Bombay: D.B. Taraporevala and Sons Co.

Collins, P.H. (1991) *Black Feminist Thought: Knowledge, Consciousness, and the Politics of Empowerment*, New York: Routledge.

Colman, A.M. (Ed.) (2001) *A Dictionary of Psychology*, Oxford: Oxford University Press.

Condorelli, Rosalia (2015) An Emergent vs a Linear Approach to Social Change Processes: A Gender Look in Contemporary India between Modernity and Hindu Tradition, *Springer Plus*, Vol. 4, No. 1.

Cooley, C.H. (1902) *Human Nature and the Social Order*, New York: Charles Scribner's Sons.

Cooper, Elizabeth (1983) *The Harem and the Purdah* (2nd Edn), Delhi: Bimala Publishing House.

Cormack, Margaret (1953) *The Hindu Woman*, New York: Bureau of Publications, Teachers College, Columbia University.

Coser, L.A. (2002) *Masters of Sociological Thought*, Jaipur: Rawat Publications.

Cosneck, Bernard J. (1970) Family Patterns of Older Widowed Jewish People, *The Family Coordinator*, Vol. 19, No. 2, pp. 368–73.

Crawford, R. (1980) Healthism and the Medicalization of Everyday Life, *International Journal of Health Services*, Vol. 10, No. 3.

Crossley, N. (1996) Body-Subject/Body-Power: Agency, Inscription, and Control in Foucault and Merleau-Ponty, *Body and Society*, Vol. 2, No. 2.

Csordas, T.J. (1994) Introduction: The Body as Representation and Being-in-the-World. In T.J. Csordas (Ed.), *Embodiment and Experience: The Existential Ground of Culture and Self*, Cambridge: Cambridge University Press.

Cumming, E. and Howry, W.E. (1961) *Growing Old: The Process of Disengagement*, New York: Basic Books.

D'Souza, V.S. (1989) Changing Social Scene and Its Implications for the Aged. In K.G. Desai (Ed.), *Aging in India*, New Delhi: Ashish Publishing House.

Dahrendorf, R. (1959) *Class and Class Conflict in Industrial Society*, Stanford, CA: Stanford University Press.

Dak, T.M. and Sharma, M.L. (1987) Changing Status of the Aged in North Indian Villages. In M.L. Sharma and T.M. Dak (Eds), *Aging in India*, New Delhi: Ajanta Publications.

Dandavate, Pramila, Kumari, Ranjana and Verghese, Jamila (1989) *Widows, Abandoned and Destitute Women in India*, New Delhi: Radiant Publishers.

Dandekar, K. (1993) The Aged, Their Problems and Social Intervention in Maharashtra, *Economic and Political Weekly*, Vol. XXVII, No. 23, June 5.

——. (1996) *The Elderly in India*, New Delhi: Sage Publications.

Dange, Sindhu S. (1980) Yaska on Widow's Share, *Vishveshvaran and Indological Journal*, Vol. XVIII, pp. 385–87.

Dari, Deepa (1985) Department of Information and Broadcasting, Government of Karnataka, Bangalore.

Darshan, S. et al. (1987) Health Needs of Senior Citizens. In M.L. Sharma and T.M. Dak (Eds), *Ageing in India: Challenge for the Society*, Delhi: Ajanta.

Das, J.P. (1973) Cultural Deprivation and Cognitive Competence, *International Review of Research in Mental Retardation*, Vol. 2, pp. 1–53.

Das, J.P. (1973) Cultural Deprivation and Cognitive Competence, *International Review of Research in Mental Retardation*, Vol. 6, No. 2, pp. 1–53.

Das, Mansingh and Badris, Panos D. (Eds) (1978) *Family in Asia*, New Delhi: Vikas Publications.

Das, N.P. and Shah, Urvi (2001) The Social and Health Status of the Elderly in India: Evidence from Recent National Level Data, A Special Report Prepared as a Part of the Research Initiative at the Population Research Centre, Baroda for the MOHFW, New Delhi.

Das, R.M. (1962) *Women in Manu and His Seven Commentators*, Varanasi: Kanchana Publications.

Datta, Jatindra Mohan (1956) Is Enforced Widowhood the Only Cause of the Slower Growth of the Bengalee Hindus, *Man in India*, Vol. 36, No. 4, pp. 272–75.

Datta, K.K. (1972) *Socio-Cultural Background of Modern India*, Meerut: Meenakshi Prakashan.

——. (1975) *A Social History of Modern India*, Delhi: The Macmillan Co. of India Ltd.

Davies, S. and Nolan, M. (2003) Making the Best of Things: Relatives' Experiences of Decisions About Care Home Entry, *Ageing and Society*, Vol. 23, No. 4.

Davis, R.E. (1968) Social Deprivation and Cognitive Function in Low-class Children, Vol. 29, Dissertation, Abstracts International, pp. 1505–07.

De Souza, Alfred (Ed.) (1980) *Women in Contemporary India and South Asia* (2nd Edn), New Delhi: Manohar Publications.

De Souza, A. (1981) *Ageing Among the Urban Poor*, New Delhi: Indian Social Institute.

Denzin, N.K. (2000) Aesthetics and the Practices of Qualitative Inquiry, *Qualitative Inquiry*, Vol. 6, No. 2.

——. (2001) *Interpretive Interactionism* (2nd Edn), Thousand Oaks, CA: Sage Publications.

Derret, J. Ducan (1963) *Introduction to Modern Hindu Law*, Bombay: Oxford University Press.

Desai, A.R. (1985) Women's Movement in India: An Assessment, *Economic and Political Weekly*, Vol. XX, No. 23, p. 3.

Desai, K.G. (1985) Situation of Aged in India, *Journal of Indian Anthropological Society*, Vol. 20, No. 3.

Deuech, M. (1975) Equity, Equality and Need: What Determines Which Value will be Used as the Basis of Distributive Justice?, *Journal of Social Issues*, Vol. 21.

Deutsch, M., Katz, I. and Jensen, A.R. (Eds) (1968) *Social Class, Race and Psychological Development*, New York: Holt, Rinehart and Winston Inc.

Devi, N. et al. (2006) Institutional Care for the Elderly, *Journal of the Indian Academy of Geriatrics*, Vol. 2, No. 1, March.

Dhar, S. and Dhar, M.K. (1986) *Evolution of Hindu Family Law*, Delhi: Deputy Publications.

Dhumatkar, M.G. (1928) Position of Hindu Women with Special Reference to Maharashtra, Ph.D. Thesis, Bombay University, Bombay.

Diamond, T. (1992) *Making Gray Gold: Narratives of Nursing Home Care*, Chicago: The University of Chicago Press.

Diane, Beeson (1975) Women in Studies: A Critique and Suggestion, *Social Problems of Aging*, Vol. 23, No. 1, pp. 52–59.

Dixon, J. and Durrheim, K. (2000) Displacing Place-Identity: A Discursive Approach to Locating Self and Other, *British Journal of Social Psychology*, Vol. 39.

Dobbs, D. (2004) The Adjustment to a New Home, *Journal of Housing for the Elderly*, Vol. 18, No. 1.

Doniger, W. and Smith, B.K. (Eds) (1991) *The Laws of Manu*, London: Penguin.

Donnenwerth, G.V. and Petersen, L.R. (1992) Institutionalization and Well-being Among the Elderly, *Sociological Inquiry*, Vol. 62, No. 4.

Doranne, Jacobson and Wadley, Susan (1986) *Women in India: Two Perspectives*, Delhi: Manohar Publications.

Duberman, Lucile (1977) *Marriage and Other Alternatives* (2nd Edn), New York: Praeger Publishers.

Dubey, A., Bhasin, S., Gupta, N. and Sharma, N. (2011) A Study of Elderly Living in Old Age Home and Within Family Set-Up in Jammu, *Studies on Home and Community Science*, Vol. 5, No. 2.

Dubey, Bhagwant Rao (1965) Widow Remarriage in Madhya Pradesh, *Man in India*, Vol. 45, No. 1, pp. 50–55.

Dubois, Abbe J.A. (1906) *Hindu Manners, Customs and Ceremonies* (3rd Edn), Trans. by Henry K. Beauchamp, London: Oxford University Press.

Dumont, L. (1958) For a Sociology of India, *Contributions to Indian Sociology*, Vol. 1.

——. (1978) Women and Aging: A Report on the Best of Our Lives, Advisory Council on the Status of Women, Ottawa.

Duncan, M.T. and Morgan, D.L. (1994) Sharing the Caring: Family Caregivers' Views of Their Relationships with Nursing Home Staff, *The Gerontologist*, Vol. 34, No. 2.

Dupaquier, J., Helin, E. and Lastett, P. (Eds) (1981) *Marriage and Remarriage in Population of the Past*, New York: Academic Press.

Dupuis, S.L. and Smale, B.J.A. (2003) *In-House and Community Access Recreation Programs in Long-Term Care Facilities in Canada*, Waterloo, Ontario: Murray Alzheimer Research and Education Program, University of Waterloo.

Dupuis, S.L. and Wiersma, E. (2006) Meanings Attached to Responsive Behaviours in Long-Term Care Settings, Paper Presented at the Alzheimer Society of Canada Conference, Toronto, Ontario, Canada.

Dupuis, S.L., Smale, B.J.A. and Wiersma, E. (2005) Creating Open Environments in Long-Term Care Settings: An Examination of Influencing Factors, *Therapeutic Recreation Journal*, Vol. 39, No. 4.

Durkheim, Emile (1951) *Suicide*, New York: The Free Press.

——. (1965) *Elementary Forms of Religious Life*, New York: The Free Press.

Dutt, Nripendra Kumar (1968) *Origin and Growth of Caste in India*, Calcutta: Firma Publications.

Dutt, Romesh C. (1972) *History of Civilization in Ancient India*, Vol. II, Delhi: Vishal Publishers.

Dutt, Ruby (1965) The Property Rights of Women in the Sutra Period, *The Modern Review*, Vol. 118, No. 3, pp. 239–46.

Duval, E.M. (1971) *Family Development*, New York: J.B. Lippincott Co.

Dyck, I., Kontos, P., Angus, J. and Mckeever, P. (2005) The Home as a Site for Long-Term Care: Meanings and Management of Bodies and Spaces, *Health and Place*, Vol. 11.

Dyson, T. and Moore, M. (1983) On Kinship Structure, Female Autonomy and Demographic Behavior in India, *Population and Development Review*, Vol. 9, No. 1, pp. 35–60.

Eichler, Margri (1988) *Families in Canada Today: Recent Changes and Their Policy Consequences*, Toronto: Gage Educational Publishing Co.

Eisdorfer, C. and Cohen, D. (1980) The Issues of Biological and Psychological Defects. In E.F. Borgotta and N.G. Mccluskey (Eds), *Ageing and Society*, London: Sage Publications.

Eisenstadt, S.N. (1973) *Tradition, Change and Modernity*, New York: John Wiley and Sons.

Ejaz, F. (2002) Family Satisfaction with Nursing Home Care for Relatives with Dementia, *Journal of Applied Gerontology*, Vol. 21, No. 3.

Elias, N. (1978) *The Civilizing Process: The History of Manners*, New York: Urizen Books.

——. (1983) *The Court Society*, New York: Pantheon Books.

Eliot, Thomas D. (1922) A Step Towards the Social Psychology of Bereavement, *Journal of Abnormal and Social Psychology*, Vol. 27, No. 3.

——. (1930) The Adjustive Behaviour of Bereaved Families: A New Field for Research, *Social Forces*, Vol. 8, No. 4.

——. (1943) Of the Shadow of Death, *Annals of the American Academy of Political and Social Sciences*, Vol. 229, No. 1.

——. (1948) Bereavement: Inevitable but Not Insurmountable. In Howard Becker and Rueben Hill (Eds), *Family Marriage and Parenthood*, Boston: D.C. Health and Company.

——. (1953) The Bereaved Family. In J.T. Landis and M.G. Landis (Eds), *Readings in Marriage and the Family*, New York: Prentice Hall, pp. 288–94.

Ellis, C. (2004) *The Ethnographic I: A Methodological Novel About Autoethnography*, Walnut Creek, CA: Altamira Press.

Eloise, C. Sgyder (Ed.) (1979) *The Study of Women-Endangering Perspectives of Social Reality*, New York: Harper and Row Publishers.

Embree, A. (1988) *Sources of Indian Tradition*, Vol. 1, New York: Columbia University Press.

English, Horace B. (1961) *Dynamics of Child Development*, New York: Holt, Rinehart and Winston Inc.

Eshleman, J. Ross (1974) *The Family: An Introduction* (2nd Edn), Boston: Allyn and Bacon Inc.

Essex, Marilyn J. and Sunghee, Nam (1987) Marital Status and Loneliness Among Older Women: The Differential Importance of Close Family and Friends, *Journal of Marriage and the Family*, Vol. 49, No. 1, pp. 93–106.

Estes, C.L. (2001) Political Economy of Aging: A Theoretical Framework. In C.L. Estes and Associates (Eds), *Social Policy and Aging: A Critical Perspective*, Thousand Oaks, CA: Sage.

Estes, C.L. and Binney, E.A. (1991) The Biomedicalization of Aging: Dangers and Dilemmas. In M. Minkler and C.L. Estes (Eds), *Critical Perspectives on Aging: The Political and Moral Economy of Growing Old*, Amityville, NY: Baywood.

Estes, C.L., Harrington, C. and Pellow, D.N. (2001) The Medical-Industrial Complex and the Aging Enterprise. In C.L. Estes and Associates (Eds), *Social Policy and Aging: A Critical Perspective*, Thousand Oaks, CA: Sage.

Estes, C.L., Mahakian, J.L. and Weitz, T.A. (2001) A Political Economy Critique of Productive Aging. In C.L. Estes and Associates (Eds), *Social Policy and Aging: A Critical Perspective*, Thousand Oaks, CA: Sage.

Estes, C.L., Wallace, S.P., Linkins, K.W. and Binney, E.A. (2001) The Medicalization and Commodification of Aging and the Privatization and Rationalization of Old Age Policy. In C.L. Estes and Associates (Eds), *Social Policy and Aging: A Critical Perspective*, Thousand Oaks, CA: Sage.

Farmer, Mary (1979) *The Family* (2nd Edn), London: Longman Group Ltd.

Faroqi, M.A., Misra, Girishwar and Tripathi, L.B. (1981) Psychological Consequences of Prolonged Deprivation, *Psychological Studies*, Vol. 26, No. 7.

Farrel, Ronald A. and Lynnswigrert, Victoria (1979) *Social Deviance* (2nd Edn), Philadelphia: J.B. Lippincott Co.

Featherstone, M. (1991) The Body in Consumer Culture. In M. Featherstone, M. Hepworth and B.S. Turner (Eds), *The Body: Social Processes and Cultural Theory*, Newbury Park, CA: Sage.

Featherstone, M. and Hepworth, M. (1991) The Mask of Ageing and the Postmodern Life Course. In M. Featherstone, M. Hepworth and B.S. Turner (Eds), *The Body: Social Process and Cultural Theory*, Newbury Park, CA: Sage.

Fine, M. and Weis, L. (1996) Writing the Wrongs of Fieldwork: Confronting Our Own Research/Writing Dilemmas in Urban Ethnographies, *Qualitative Inquiry*, Vol. 2, No. 3.

Fine, M., Weis, L., Weseen, S. and Wong, L. (2000) For Whom? Qualitative Research, Representations, and Social Responsibilities. In N.K.D.Y.S. Lincoln (Ed.), *Handbook of Qualitative Research* (2nd Edn), Thousand Oaks, CA: Sage Publications.

Fitzsimmons, S. (2001) Easy Rider Wheelchair Biking: A Nursing-Recreation Therapy Clinical Trial for the Treatment of Depression, *Journal of Gerontological Nursing*, Vol. 27, No. 5.

Flynn-Reuss, G., Dupuis, S.L. and Whitfield, K. (2005) Understanding the Experience of Moving a Loved One to a Long-Term Care Facility: Family Members? Perspectives, *Journal of Gerontological Social Work*, Vol. 46, No. 1.

Foner, N. (1995) *The Caregiving Dilemma: Work in an American Nursing Home*, Berkeley: University of California Press.

Foucault, M. (1975) *Discipline and Punish: The Birth of the Prison*, New York: Random House.

Frank, A. (1991) For a Sociology of the Body: An Analytical Review. In M. Featherstone, M. Hepworth and B.S. Turner (Eds), *The Body: Social Process and Cultural Theory*, Newbury Park, CA: Sage.

Freeman, Howard E. and Simmons, Ozzie G. (1961) Feelings of Stigma Among Relatives of Former Mental Patients, *Social Problems*, Vol. 8, No. 4, pp. 313–21.

Fritz, Mary (1929) A Study of Widowhood, *Sociology and Social Research*, Vol. XIV, No. 1, pp. 553–61.

Fuchs, Z., Blumstein, T., Novikov, I., Walter-Ginzburg, A., Lyanders, M., Gindin, J., Habot, B. and Modan, B. (1998) Morbidity, Comorbidity and Their Association with Disability Among Community-Dwelling Oldest-Old in Israel, *The Journal of Gerontology Series A: Biological Sciences and Medical Sciences*, Vol. 53.

Gadow, S. (2004) Body and Self: A Dialect. In the Aberdeen Body Group (A. Blaikie, M. Hepworth, M. Holmes, A. Howson, D. Inglis and S. Sartain) (Eds), *The Body: Critical Concepts in Sociology, Vol. IV: Living and Dying Bodies*, New York: Routledge.

Gajendragadkar, P.B. (1951) The Hindu Code Bill, Two lectures delivered on 12th and 13th April, Karnatak University, Dharwad.

Gandhi, M.K. (1942) *Women and Social Injustice*, Ahmedabad: Navajivan Publishing House.

——. (1964) *The Role of Women*, Bombay: Bharatiya Vidya Bhavan.

Gangrade, K.D. (1999) Emerging Conception of Ageing in India: A Socio-Cultural Perspective. In Arun P. Bali (Ed.), *Understanding Greying People of India*, New Delhi: Inter-India Publications.

Gardner, Jane F. (1986) *Women in Roman Law and Society*, London: Groom Helm.

Gass, T.E. (2004) *Nobody's Home: Candid Reflections of a Nursing Home Aide*, Ithaca, NY: Cornell University Press.

Gathorne-Hardy, Jonathan (1981) *Love, Sex, Marriage and Divorce*, London: Jonathan Cape.

Geiger, C.W. and Miko, P.S. (1995) Meaning of Recreation/Leisure Activities to Elderly Nursing Home Residents: A Qualitative Study, *Therapeutic Recreation Journal*, Vol. 29, No. 2.

Gerald, L.R. (1977) *Marriage in Changing World*, New York: John Wiley and Sons Co.

——. (1979) *The Family in Social Context*, New York: Oxford University Press.

Gerdner, L.A. (2000) Music, Art, and Recreational Therapies in the Treatment of Behavioural and Psychological Symptoms of Dementia, *International Psychogeriatrics*, Vol. 12, No. 1.

Gergen, K.J. (1991) *The Saturated Self: Dilemmas of Identity in Contemporary Life*, New York: Basic Books.

Geschwender, J.A. (1968) Status Inconsistency, Social Isolation and Individual Unrest, *Social Forces*, Vol. 46, No. 4, pp. 477–83.

Gesler, W.M. (1999) Words in Wards: Language, Health, and Place, *Health and Place*, Vol. 5, No. 1.

Gharapure, J.R. (1932) *Yajnavalkya*, Poona: Oriental Book Agency.

——. (1936) *Yajnavakya Smruti*, Bombay: Hindu Law Texts.

Ghosh, Jogesa Chandra (1982) *Hindu Woman of India*, Delhi: Bimala Publishing House.

Ghurye, G.S. (1936) Marriage and Widowhood in India: A Study of a Middle-Class Sample of 3400 Marriages, *Marriage Hygiene*, Vol. II, No. 3, pp. 258–70.

——. (1961) *Caste, Class and Occupation*, Bombay: Popular Prakashan.

——. (1969) *Caste and Race in India*, Bombay: Popular Prakashan.

Gibbons, Don C. and Jones, Joseph F. (1975) *The Study of Deviance: Perspectives and Problems*, New Jersey: Prentice-Hall Inc.

Gibson, D. (1996) Broken Down by Age and Gender: The Problem of Old Women Redefined, *Gender and Society*, Vol. 10, No. 4.

Gibson, D. and Allen, J. (1993) Parasitism and Phallocentrism in Social Provisions for the Aged, *Policy Sciences*, Vol. 26, No. 2.

Giddens, A. (1984) *The Constitution of Society: Outline of the Theory of Structuration*, Berkeley and Los Angeles, CA: University of California Press.

——. (1991) *Modernity and Self-Identity: Self and Society in the Late Modern Age*, Stanford, CA: Stanford University Press.

Gielow, D. and Hobler, R.C. (1986) Sensory Integration Activity in Nursing Home Residents' Cognitions, Affect, Self-Esteem and Behavior, *Perceptual and Motor Skills*, Vol. 62, No. 2.

Gieryn, T.F. (2000) A Space for Place in Sociology, *Annual Review of Sociology*, Vol. 26.

Giri, M.V. (2005) *Emancipation and Empowerment of Women*, New Delhi: Gyan Publishing House.

Giri, Mohini (2002) *Status of Widows of Vrindavan and Varanasi: A Comparative Study*, New Delhi: The Guild Services.

Giuliani, M.V. (1991) Towards an Analysis of Mental Representations of Attachment to the Home, *Journal of Architectural and Planning Research*, Vol. 8, No. 2.

Giuliani, M.V. and Feldman, R. (1993) Place Attachment in a Developmental and Cultural Context, *Journal of Environmental Psychology*, Vol. 13, No. 3.

Gladstone, J. and Wexler, E. (2000) A Family Perspective of Family/Staff Interaction in Long-Term Care Facilities, *Geriatric Nursing*, Vol. 21, No. 1.

Goffman, E. (1959) *The Presentation of Self in Everyday Life*, New York: Doubleday.

——. (1961) *Asylums*, New York: Anchor Books/Doubleday.

——. (1963) *Behavior in Public Places: Notes on the Social Organization of Gatherings*, New York: The Free Press.

——. (1964) *Stigma: Notes on the Management of Spoiled Identity*, New Jersey: Prentice-Hall Inc.

Gokhale, S.D. (2005) Towards a Policy for Ageing in India. In Phoebe S. Liebig and S. Irudaya Rajan (Eds), *An Ageing India: Perspectives, Prospects and Policies*, Jaipur: Rawat Publications.

Golander, H. (1995) Chronically Ill, Old, and Institutionalized: Being a Nursing Home Resident, *Family and Community Health*, Vol. 17, No. 4.

Goodale, T.L. (1990) Perceived Freedom as Leisure's Antithesis, *Journal of Leisure Research*, Vol. 22, No. 4.

Goode, W.J. (1959) The Theoretical Importance of Love, *American Sociological Review*, Vol. 24, No. 1, pp. 38–47.

——. (1963) *World Revolution and Family Patterns*, London: The Free Press.

——. (1965) *The Family*, New Delhi: Prentice-Hall of India (Pvt.) Ltd.

Gopal, Meena (2006) Gender, Ageing and Social Security, *Economic and Political Weekly*, Vol. 41, No. 42, October 21.

Gordon, E.A. (1965) Review of Compensatory Education, *American Journal of Orthopsychiatry*, Vol. 35, pp. 640–51.

Gordon, Michael, Whelan, Brendan and Vaughan, Richard (1981) Old Age and Loss of Household Headship: A National Irish Study, *Journal of Marriage and the Family*, Vol. 43, No. 3, pp. 741–47.

Gore, M.S. (1968) *Urbanization and Family Change*, Bombay: Popular Prakashan.

——. (1990) Social Factors Affecting the Health of the Elderly. In R.L. Kane, J.G. Evans and D. Macfadyen (Eds), *Improving the Health of Older People: A World View*, New York: Oxford University Press.

——. (1996) Studying Problems of Ageing, Unpublished Paper Presented at All-India Sociological Conference, Shivaji University, Kolhapur, November 18.

Gorwaney, Naintara (1977) *Self-image and Social Change*, New Delhi: Sterling Publishers Pvt. Ltd.

Gould, H. (1960) Castes, Outcastes and Sociology of Stratification, *International Journal of Comparative Sociology*, Vol. 1, No. 2, September.

Gour, Horising (1971) *The Hindu Code* (5th Edn), Allahabad: Law Book Publishers.

Government of India (1991) Socio-Economic Profile of the Aged Persons: NSS 42nd Round, July 1986 and June 1987, *Sarvekshana*, Vol. 15, No. 2, Issue No. 49, October – December 1991, National Sample Survey Organization (NSSO), Department of Statistics, Ministry of Planning, New Delhi.

——. (1998) The Aged in India: A Socio-Economic Profile, NSS 52nd Round, July 1995 and June 1996, NSSO, Department of Statistics, Ministry of Planning and Programme Implementation.

——. (1999) National Policy on Older Persons, Ministry of Social Justice and Empowerment, New Delhi.

——. (2000) Elderly in India, Profile and Programmes, Central Statistical Organization, Ministry of Statistics and Programme Implementation, New Delhi.

Gray, Robert F. and Gulliver, P.H. (1964) *The Family State in Africa: Studies in the Role of Property in Family Structure*, London: Routledge and Kegan Paul.

Green, Ernest J. (1977) *Marriage and Family: A Basic Self-Instructional Guide*, New York: McGraw Hill Book Co.

——. (1978) *Personal Relationships*, New York: McGraw Hill Book Co.

Greg, A. (1976) The Elderly Widow and Her Family, Neighbors and Friends, *Journal of Marriage and the Family*, Vol. 38, No. 4.

Groger, L. (1995) A Nursing Home Can be a Home, *Journal of Aging Studies*, Vol. 9, No. 2.

Grosz, E. (1994) *Volatile Bodies: Toward a Corporeal Feminism*, Bloomington, IN: Indiana University Press.

——. (1999) Bodies-Cities. In J. Price and M. Shildrick (Eds), *Feminist Theory and the Body: A Reader*, New York: Routledge.

Gubrium, J.F. and Holstein, J.A. (1993) *Speaking of Life: Horizons of Meaning for Nursing Home Residents*, Hawthorne, NY: Aldine de Gruyter.

——. (1999) The Nursing Home as a Discursive Anchor for the Ageing Body, *Ageing and Society*, Vol. 19.

——. (2000) The Self in a World of Going Concerns, *Symbolic Interaction*, Vol. 23, No. 2.

——. (2001) *Institutional Selves: Troubled Identities in a Postmodern World*, New York: Oxford University Press.

Gubrium, J.F. (1975) *Living and Dying at Murray Manor*, New York: St. Martin's Press.

Gulati, Saroja (1985) *Women and Society: North India in the 11th and 12th Century*, Delhi: Chanakya Publications.

Gupta, Giri Raj (1974) *Marriage, Religion and Society: Pattern of Change in an Indian Village*, Delhi: Vikas Publishing House.

Gupta, Niharika (1999) Two Papers and a Monograph of Field Practicum (Mimeo), TISS, Mumbai.

——. (2004) Successful Ageing and its Determinants, Ph.D. Thesis, Tata Institute of Social Sciences, Mumbai.

Gupta, Sankar Sen (Ed.) (1962) *Indian Folklore: A Short Survey of Their Social Status and Position*, Calcutta: Indian Publications.

Gustavson, L.C. and Cytrynbaum, J.D. (2003) Illuminating Spaces: Relational Spaces, Complicity and Multisited Ethnography, *Field Methods*, Vol. 15, No. 3.

Haggard, L.M. and Williams, D.R. (1992) Identity Affirmation Through Leisure Activities: Leisure Symbols of the Self, *Journal of Leisure Research*, Vol. 24, No. 1.

Hall, B.L. and Bocksnick, J.G. (1995) Therapeutic Recreation for the Institutionalized Elderly: Choice or Abuse, *Journal of Elder Abuse and Neglect*, Vol. 7, No. 4.

Halldorsdottir, S. and Hamrin, E. (1997) Caring and Uncaring Encounters within Nursing and Health Care from the Cancer Patient's Perspective, *Cancer Nursing*, Vol. 20, No. 2.

Hamada, T. et al. (2003) Abnormal Nocturnal Blood Pressure Fall in Senile-Onset Depression with Sub Cotrical Silent Cerebral Infarction, *Neuro Psychology*, Vol. 47, No. 4.

Hamalanien, J. et al. (2005) Major Depression Relationship with Long-Term Unemployment and Frequent Alcohol Intoxication, *Archives of General Psychiatry*, Vol. 62, No. 6, June.

Haraway, D. (1988) Situated Knowledge: The Science Question in Feminism and the Privilege of Partial Perspective, *Feminist Studies*, Vol. 14, No. 3.

Harding, S. (1991) *Whose Science? Whose Knowledge? Thinking from Women's Lives*, Ithaca, NY: Cornell University Press.

Harichandra, C. (1982) Socio-Economic Conditions of Widows, *Yojana*, Vol. XXVI, No. 10, pp. 11–12.

Harrington, C. et al. (2001) Does Investor Ownership of Nursing Homes Compromise the Quality of Care?, *American Journal of Public Health*, Vol. 91, No. 9.

Harris, P.B. and Sterin, G.J. (1999) Insider's Perspective: Defining and Preserving the Self of Dementia, *Journal of Mental Health and Ageing*, Vol. 5, No. 3.

Harvey, Carol D. and Bahr, Howard M. (1974) Widowhood, Morale and Affiliation, *Journal of Marriage and the Family*, Vol. 36, No. 1, pp. 97–106.

Hate, C.A. (1946) The Social Position of Hindu Widows, Ph.D. Thesis, Bombay University, Bombay.

Hate, Chandrakala A. (1948) *Hindu Women and Her Future*, Bombay: New Book Co. Ltd.

Hazan, H. (2002) The Home Over the Hill: Towards a Modern Cosmology of Institutionalization, *Journal of Aging Studies*, Vol. 16, No. 4.

Heidegger, M. (1958) *The Question of Being*, New Haven, CT: College and University Press.

Helves, Helena (2005) Global and Local Perspectives of Youth Research, Paper Presented in VII International Conference on Asian Youth Issues: Opportunities and Challenges of Youth in New Era, Organized by the Education and Youth Affairs Bureau, Macao Special Administrative Region, China, December 5–9.

Hemingway, J.L. (1996) Emancipating Leisure: The Recovery of Freedom in Leisure, *Journal of Leisure Research*, Vol. 28, No. 1.

Henderson, J.N. (1995) The Culture of Care in a Nursing Home: Effects of a Medicalized Model of Long-Term Care. In J.N.H.M.D. Vesperi (Ed.), *The Culture of Long-Term Care: Nursing Home Ethnography*, Westport, CT: Bergin and Garvey.

Hepworth, M. (2003) Ageing Bodies: Aged by Culture. In J. Coupland and R. Gwyn (Eds), *Discourse, the Body and Identity*, New York: Palgrave Macmillan.

Hilary, Standing (Ed.) (1981) *Punjabi Kinship and Marriage*, Delhi: Hindustan Publishing Corporation.

Hillmer, M.P. et al. (2005) Nursing Home Profit Status and Quality of Care: Is There Any Evidence of an Association?, *Medical Care Research and Review*, Vol. 62, No. 2.

Hims, S. Joseph (1964) Some Work-related Cultured Deprivations of Lower-Class Negro Youths, *Journal of Marriage and the Family*, Vol. 25, No. 2, pp. 447–48.

Holman, Robert (Ed.) (1970) *Socially Deprived Families in Britain*, London: The Bedford Square Press.

Holstein, J.A. and Gubrium, J.F. (2000) *The Self We Live By: Narrative Identity in a Postmodern World*, New York: Oxford University Press.

Hormuth, S.E. (1990) *The Ecology of the Self: Relocation and Self-Concept Change*, New York: Cambridge University Press.

Horner, I.B. (1930) *Women Under Primitive Buddhism*, Delhi: Motilal Banarsidass.

Howell, S.C. (1983) The Meaning of Place in Old Age. In G.D. Rowles and R.J. Ohta (Eds), *Aging and Milieu: Environmental Perspectives on Growing Old*, New York: Academic Press.

Howson, A. and Inglis, D. (2001) The Body in Sociology: Tensions Inside and Outside Sociological Thought, *The Sociological Review*, Vol. 49, No. 3.

Hubbard, G., Tester, S. and Downs, M.G. (2003) Meaningful Social Interactions between Older People in Institutional Care Settings, *Ageing and Society*, Vol. 23, No. 1.

Huber, Joan (Ed.) (1973) *Changing Women in a Changing Society*, Chicago: The University of Chicago Press.

Hunt, J.M.C. (1964) The Psychological Basis for Using Pre-school Environment as an Antidote for Cultural Deprivation, *The Merrill- Palmer Quarterly of Behaviour and Development*, Vol. 10, No. 3, pp. 209–43.

Hurlock, Elizabeth B. (1976) *Personality Development*, New Delhi: Tata McGraw Hill Publishing Co. Ltd.

Hurlow, H.F. (1958) The Nature of Love, *American Psychologist*, Vol. 13, No. 4, pp. 673–85.

Hutchison, Ira W. (1975) The Significance of Marital Status for Morale and Life Satisfaction Among Lower-Income Elderly, *Journal of Marriage and the Family*, Vol. 32, No. 2, pp. 287–93.

Hutton, J.H. (1961) *Caste in India: Its Nature, Function and Origin*, Bombay: Oxford University Press.

Hyerah, Miriam and Mitra, Dolly (1988) Synthetic Perception in the Sensorily Deprived, *Psychological Studies*, Vol. 33, No. 2, pp. 110–15.

Hyman, H.H. (1983) *Of Time and Widowhood*, Durham: Duke Press Policy Studies.

Ice, G.H. (2002) Daily Life in a Nursing Home: Has it Changed in 25 Years?, *Journal of Aging Studies*, Vol. 16, No. 4.

ICSSR (1975) *Status of Women in India: A Synopsis of the Report of the National Committee (1971–74)*, New Delhi: Allied Publishers Pvt. Ltd.

Illango, Ponnuswami (2005) Ageing Worldwide Trends and Challenges for Care Giving, *Social Welfare*, Vol. 51, No. 7.

Indira, Mahindra (1980) *The Rebellious Home-makers*, Bombay: S.N.D.T. Women's University Press.

Internal Encyclopaedia of Psychiatry, Psychology Psychoanalysis and Neurology, Vol. 8.

Jacobs, Selby and Ostfeld, Adrian (1977) An Epidemiological Review of the Mortality of Bereavement, *Psychosomatic Medicine*, Vol. 39, No. 5, pp. 344–57.

Jacoby, R. and Bergmann, K. (1986) *The Psychiatry of Old Age in Essentials of Postgraduate Psychiatry*, London: Grume and Stratton.

Jakobsson, U. and Hallberg, I.R. (2006) Quality of Life Among Older Adults with Osteo Arthritis: An Explorative Study, *J Gerontol Nurs*, Vol. 32, No. 8.

Jambagi, Sulochana (1964) Life and Activities of Lingayat Widows, M.A. Dissertation, Karnatak University, Dharwad.

James, K. (2000) You Can Feel Them Looking at You: The Experiences of Adolescent Girls at Swimming Pools, *Journal of Leisure Research*, Vol. 32, No. 2.

Jamuna, D. (2000) Ageing in India: Some Key Issues, *Ageing International*, Vol. 25, No. 4, Spring.

——. (2001) Intergenerational Issues in Elder Care, *The Indian Journal of Gerontology*, Vol. 15, Nos 3–4.

Jayal, Shakambari (1966) *The Status of Women in the Epics*, Delhi: Motilal Banarsidass.

Jersild, A.T. (1963) *The Psychology of Adolescence* (2nd Edn), New York: Macmillan Co.

Jessie, B. and Naik, T. (Eds) (1988) *Indian Womanhood: Then and Now*, Indore: Satyaprakashan Sanchar Kendra.

Jeyalakshmi, S., Chakrabarti, S. and Gupta, N. (2011) Situation Analysis of the Elderly in India, Central Statistics Office, Ministry of Statistics and Programme Implementation, Government of India.

JISC (2009) *The Situational Analysis of Widows in Religious Places of Best Bengal*, Kolkata: Jai Prakash Institute of Social Change.

Jolly, J. (Ed.) (1881) *Vishnu Dharma Sutra*, Calcutta: Motilal Banarsidass.

Jones, M. (1999) *Gentle Care: Changing the Experience of Alzheimer's Disease in a Positive Way*, Vancouver, BC: Hartley and Marks Publishers, Inc.

Jordan, J.A. (Ed.) (1971) *Karl Marx: Economy Class and Social Revolution*, London: Longman.

Joseph, Kirk and Bassett, Marion (1948) *The Family and Democratic Society*, London: Routledge and Kegan Paul Ltd.

Kabir, M. (1992) Effects of Social Change on the Health of Elderly, *Journal of Family Welfare*, Vol. 38, No. 1.

Kaegi, A. (1950) *Life in Ancient India: Studies in Rigvedic India*, Calcutta: Susil Gupta Ltd.

Kahn, D.L. (1999) Making the Best of It: Adapting to the Ambivalence of a Nursing Home Environment, *Qualitative Health Research*, Vol. 9, No. 1.

Kakar, Sudhir (Ed.) (1982) *Identity and Adulthood* (2nd Edn), Delhi: Oxford University Press.

Kamat, A.R. (1963) The Decline in Death Rate and its Effect on the Extent of Widowhood, *Sociological Bulletin*, Vol. XII, No. 7, pp. 18–31.

Kamlani, Ratu (1978) Memories of Widowhood, *Eves Weekly*, August 12–18, pp. 36–37.

Kane, P.V. (1930) *History of Dharmashastra*, Vols II and III, Poona: Bhandarkar Oriental Research Institute.

Kanvi, C.S. (Ed.) (1977) *Women: Her Problems and Her Achievements*, Dharwad: Karnatak University Press.

Kapadia, K.M. (1958) *Marriage and Family in India* (2nd Edn), London: Oxford University Press.

Kapur, Pramila (1973) *Love, Marriage and Sex*, Delhi: Vikas Publishing House.

Kareem, A.S. (1988) *Widowhood in Islam*, Delhi: D.K. Publishers, p. 157.

Karri, Venkat Rango (1889) *Vidhawa Vapana Anachara* (Shaving of Widows Unauthorised), Poona: Oriental Book House.

Karve, Irawati (1953) *Kinship Organization in India*, Bombay: Asia Publishing House.

Karve, Neera (1956) The Lot of a Widow, *Social Welfare*, Vol. IH, No. 4, pp. 30–31.

Katsinas, R.P. (2000) The Use and Implications of a Canine Companion in a Therapeutic Day Program for Nursing Home Residents with Dementia, *Activities, Adaptation and Aging*, Vol. 25, No. 1.

Katti, A.P. and Nagesh, H.V. (1984) A Socio-Economic Study of Widows (in Hubli City and Neighbouring Villages): A Project Report, JSS Institute of Economic Research, Dharwad, pp. 43–44.

Katz, S. (1996) *Disciplining Old Age: The Formation of Gerontological Knowledge*, Charlottesville, VA: University Press of Virginia.

Kaufman, S.R. (1986) *The Ageless Self: Sources of Meaning in Late Life*, Madison, WI: University of Wisconsin Press.

——. (1994) Old Age, Disease and the Discourse on Risk: Geriatric Assessment in U.S. Health Care, *Medical Anthropology Quarterly*, Vol. 8, No. 4.

Kaur, Indrajeet (1983) *Status of Hindu Women in India*, Allahabad: Chugh Publications.

Kaur, Malkit, Grover, R.P. and Aggarwal, Kusum (1987) Socio-Economic Profile of the Rural Aged. In M.L. Sharma and T.M. Dak (Eds), *Aging in India*, New Delhi: Ajanta Publications.

Kaur, Satnam and Kaur, Malkit (1987) Psycho-Social Problems of the Aged. In M.C. Sharma and T.M. Dak (Eds), *Ageing in India: Challenges for the Society*, New Delhi: Ajanta Publications.

Kaur, Sharanjit (1974) Social Adjustment of War Widows, M.A. Dissertation, Punjab University, Chandigarh.

Keith, A.B. (1971) *Rigveda* (2nd Edn), Delhi: Motilal Banarsidass.

Keith, M. and Pile, S. (1993a) Introduction Part I: The Politics of Place. In M. Keith and S. Pile (Eds), *Place and the Politics of Identity*, New York: Routledge.

——. (1993b) Introduction Part II: The Place of Politics. In M. Keith and S. Pile (Eds), *Place and the Politics of Identity*, New York: Routledge.

Kelly, J.R. (1999) Leisure and Society: A Dialectical Analysis. In E.L.J.T.L. Burton (Ed.), *Leisure Studies: Prospects for the Twenty-First Century*, State College, PA: Venture Publishing.

Kelly, M. (1992) Self, Identity and Radical Surgery, *Sociology of Health and Illness*, Vol. 14.

Kelly, M.P. and Field, D. (1996) Medical Sociology, Chronic Illness and the Body, *Sociology of Health and Illness*, Vol. 18, No. 2.

Kenkel, William F. (1977) *The Family in Perspective* (4th Edn), California: Goodyear Publishing Co.

Kephart, William M. (1950) Status After Death, *American Sociological Review*, Vol. 35, No. 5, pp. 635–43.

——. (1981) *The Family, Society and Individuals* (5th Edn), Boston: Houghton Mifflin Co.

Khan, A.M. and Raikwar, Madhu (2010) Relationship between Expectations, Life Satisfaction and Diseases Amongst Elderly from Different Social Groups, *Indian Journal of Gerontology*, Vol. 24, No. 3.

Khan, A.M. (2003) Managing Mindset of Young and Old: Health Aging, *Indian Journal of Gerontology*, Vol. 17, Nos 1–2.

——. (2004) Decay in the Family Dynamics of Interaction, Relation and Communication as Determinants of Growing Vulnerability Amongst Elderly, *Indian Journal of Gerontology*, Vol. 18, No. 2.

Khanna, M. (2002) Widowhood in India: Trauma of Taboos and Tribulations. In M.V. Giri (Ed.), *Living Death: Trauma of Widowhood in India*, New Delhi: Gyan Publishing House, pp. 19–53.

Kimball, Young (1952) *Personality and Problems of Adjustment* (2nd Edn), London: Routledge and Kegan Paul Ltd.

Kincheloe, J.L. and Mclaren, P. (2000) Rethinking Critical Theory and Qualitative Research. In N.K. Denzin and Y.S. Lincoln (Eds), *Handbook of Qualitative Research* (2nd Edn), Thousand Oaks, CA: Sage Publications.

Kishwar, Madhu (1985) Gandhi on Women, *Economic and Political Weekly*, Vol. XX, No. 40, pp. 1691–92.

Kitchlu, T.N. (1979) A Profile of Widows in Delhi, *Social Welfare*, Vol. 25, No. 10, pp. 33–35.

——. (1982) A Study of Socio-Economic Conditions of Widows in Union Territory of Delhi, Report Submitted to Delhi University, p. 5.

Kitwood, T. (1997) *Dementia Reconsidered: The Person Comes First*, Philadelphia, PA: Open University Press.

Kleinman, S., Stenross, B. and McMahon, M. (1994) Privileging Fieldwork Over Interviews: Consequences for Identity and Practice, *Symbolic Interaction*, Vol. 17, No. 1.

Komaromy, C. (2000) The Sight and Sound of Death: The Management of Dead Bodies in Residential and Nursing Homes for Older People, *Mortality*, Vol. 5, No. 3.

Kontos, P.C. (1999) Local Biology: Bodies of Difference in Ageing Studies, *Ageing and Society*, Vol. 19, No. 6.

——. (2003) Embodied Self-Hood: An Ethnography of Alzheimer's Disease, Unpublished Ph.D. Dissertation, University of Toronto.

——. (2004) Ethnographic Reflections on Selfhood, Embodiment and Alzheimer's Disease, *Ageing and Society*, Vol. 24, No. 6.

——. (2005) Embodied Selfhood in Alzheimer's Disease: Rethinking Person-centred Care, *Dementia*, Vol. 4, No. 4.

Koos, E.L. (1953) *Marriage*, Glencoe: The Free Press.

Kumar, Kamal (1987) Deoral: Before and After, *Social Welfare*, Vol. 34, No. 9, p. 7.

Kumar, P., Das, A. and Rautela, U. (2012) Mental and Physical Morbidity in Old Age Homes of Lucknow in India, *Delhi Psychiatry Journal*, Vol. 15, No. 1.

Kumar, Vijaya S. (1991) *Family Life and Socio-Economic Problems of the Elderly*, Delhi: Ashish Publishing House.

——. (1999a) *Quality of Life and Social Security for the Elderly in Rural India*, Hyderabad: Council for Social Development.

——. (1999b) Population Ageing in India: Causes and Consequences, *Research and Development Journal*, Vol. 5, No. 2.

Kumari, Ranjana (1989) *Women-Headed Households in Rural India*, New Delhi: Radiant Publishers.

Kunter, B. et al. (1955) *Five Hundred Over Sixty: A Community Survey on Aging*, New York: Russell Sage Foundation.

Lakshmi, C.S. (1984) *Women in Society: The Face Behind the Mask*, New Delhi: Vikas Publishing House.

Landis, Judson T. and Landis, Marg G. (Eds) (1953) *Readings in Marriage and the Family*, New York: Prentice-Hall Inc.

Landis, P.H. (1954) *Your Marriage and Family Living* (2nd Edn), New York: McGraw Hill Book Co, p. 319.

——. (1955) *Making the Most of Marriage* (2nd Edn), New York: Appleton-Century-Crofts Inc.

Lane, Robert (1959) Fathers and Sons: The Foundation of Political Belief, *American Journal of Sociology*, Vol. 24.

Lantz, H.R. and Synder, E.C. (1966) *Marriage*, Glencoe: The Free Press.

Lasswell, H.D. and Kaplan, A. (1950) *Power and Society*, New Haven: Yale University Press.

Leach, E.R. (1960) *Aspects of Caste in South India, Ceylon, and North-West Pakistan*, Cambridge: Cambridge University Press.

Leacock, E.W. (Ed.) (1971) *Culture of Poverty: A Critique*, New York: Simon and Schuster.

Leading Articles (1961) Broken Hearts, *British Medical Journal*, Vol. 4, No. 1, pp. 2–3.

Leary, M.R. and Tangney, J.P. (2003) The Self as an Organizing Construct in the Behavioral and Social Sciences. In M.R. Leary and J.P. Tangney (Eds), *Handbook of Self and Identity*, New York: Guilford Press.

Leder, D. (1990) *The Absent Body*, Chicago: The University of Chicago Press.

Leonard, Diana and Speakman, Mary Anne (1983) The Changing Experience of Women, The Open University a Second Level Course Unit-9, pp. 53–57; Unit 7–8, pp. 11–12.

Leslie, G.R. (1979) *The Family in Social Context*, New

York: Oxford University Press.

Levitas, R. (1996) The Concept of Social Exclusion and New Durkheimian Hegemony, *Critical Social Policy*, Vol. 16, No. 1.

Lewis, Oscar (1966) *La Vida: A Puerto Rican Family in the Culture of Poverty*, New York: Random House.

Lidz, C.W., Fischer, L. and Arnold, R.M. (1992) *The Erosion of Autonomy in Long-Term Care*, New York: Oxford University Press.

Liebig, Phoebe S. and Rajan, S. Irudaya (2005) *An Ageing India: Perspectives, Prospects and Policies*, Jaipur: Rawat Publications.

Lilley, J. and Jackson, L.T. (1990) The Value of Activities: Establishing a Foundation for Cost-Effectiveness: A Review of the Literature, *Activities, Adaptation and Aging*, Vol. 14, No. 4.

Lincoln, Y.S. (1997) Self, Subject, Audience, Text: Living at the Edge, Writing in the Margins. In W.G. Tierney and Y.S. Lincoln (Eds), *Representation and the Text: Re-Framing the Narrative Voice*, Albany, NY: State University of New York.

Lincoln, Y.S. and Guba, E.G. (2000) Paradigmatic Controversies, Contradictions and Emerging Confluences. In N.K.L. Denzin and Y.S. Lincoln (Eds), *The Handbook of Qualitative Research*, Thousand Oaks, CA: Sage.

Lindemann, Erich (1944) Symptomatology and Management of Acute Grief, *American Journal of Psychiatry*, Vol. 101, No. 2, pp. 141–48.

Lindzey, Gardner and Aronson, Elliot (1975) *The Handbook of Social Psychology* (2nd Edn), New Delhi: Amerind Publishing Co. Pvt. Ltd.

Locke, Harvey J. and Klausner, William J. (1948) Marital Adjustment of Divorced Persons in Subsequent Marriages, *Sociology and Social Research*, Vol. 33, No. 1, pp. 97–101.

Lokare, L., Nekar, M.S. and Mahesh, V. (2011) Quality of Life and Restricted Activity Days Among the Old Aged, *International Journal of Biological and Medical Research*, Vol. 2, No. 4.

London, Perry and Rosenhan, David (Eds) (1968) *Foundations of Abnormal Psychology*, New York: Holt, Rinehart and Winston Co.

Lopata, H.Z. (1969) Loneliness: Forms and Components, *Social Problems*, Vol. 17, No. 2, pp. 248–62.

——. (1970) The Social Involvement of American Widows, *American Behavioural Scientist*, Vol. 14, No. 1, pp. 41–57.

——. (1973) *Widowhood in an American City*, Cambridge: Schenkman Publishing Co.

——. (1978a) Contribution of Extended Families to the Support Systems of Metropolitan Area Widows: Limitations of the Modified Kin Network, *Journal of Marriage and the Family*, Vol. 40, No. 2, pp. 355–64.

——. (1978b) The Absence of Community Resources in Support Systems of Urban Widows, *The Family Coordinator*, Vol. 27, No. 4, pp. 383–94.

——. (1981) Widowhood and Husband Sanctification, *Journal of Marriage and the Family*, Vol. 43, No. 4, pp. 439–50.

Lopez, S.H. (2006a) Emotional Labor and Organized Emotional Care: Conceptualizing Nursing Home Care Work, *Work and Occupation*, Vol. 33, No. 2.

——. (2006b) Culture Change Management in Long-Term Care: A Shop-Floor View, *Politics and Society*, Vol. 34, No. 1.

Low, S.M. and Altman, I. (1992) Place Attachment: A Conceptual Inquiry. In I. Altman and S.M. Low (Eds), *Place Attachment*, New York: Plenum Press.

Lupton, D. (1998) Going with the Flow: Some Central Discourses in Conceptualising and Articulating the Embodiment of Emotional States. In S. Nettleton and J. Watson (Eds), *The Body in Everyday Life*, New York: Routledge.

Lukose, A. (1978) Facing Widowhood, *Eves Weekly*, August 12–18, p. 35.

Macionis, J.J. (1996) *Society: The Basics*, New Jersey: Prentice Hall.

Mackey, Richard A. (1968) Crisis Theory: Its Development and Relevance to Social Case Work Practice, *The Family Coordinator*, Vol. 17, No. 3, pp. 165–73.

Madan, T.N. (1975) Structural Implications of Marriage in North India: Wife-giver and Wife-takers Among the Kashmiri Brahmins, *Contributions to Indian Sociology*, Vol. 9, No. 2, pp. 217–43.

Madden, H.T., Rossiter, L.F. and Klock, D.F. (2003) Study of the Older Prison Population in Virginia and its Budget Implications, The College of William and Mary, Center for Excellence in Aging and Geriatric Health.

Madhawadas, Rugunathdas (1890) *Story of a Widow Remarriage*, Bombay: S.K. Khambata and Co.

Maine, Henry (1934) *Early History of Institutions*, London: John Murray.

Malik, Varun (2013) Problems of Widow Re-marriage in India, *Journal of Business and Social Sciences*, Vol. 2, No. 2.

Mann, R.S. (1979) *Social Structure, Social Change and Future Trends*, Jaipur: Rawat Publications.

Marris, Peter (1958) *Widows and Their Families*, London: Routledge and Kegan Paul Ltd.

Martinson, E. (1970) *Family in Society*, New York: Dodd Mead.

Maurice, Freedom (Ed.) (1970) *Family and Kinship in Chinese Society*, Stanford, CA: Stanford University Press.

Max, Muller F. (1968) *The Dhammapada: Sutta Nipata*, Delhi: SBE.

Mccance, T.V., Mckenna, H.P. and Boore, J.R.P. (1997) Caring: Dealing with a Difficult Concept, *International Journal of Nursing Studies*, Vol. 34, No. 4.

Mccorkel, J.A. (1998) Going to the Crackhouse: Critical Space as a Form of Resistance in Total Institutions and Everyday Life, *Symbolic Interaction*, Vol. 21, No. 3.

Mccormack, B. and Mccance, T.V. (2006) Development of a Framework for Person-centred Nursing, *Journal of Advanced Nursing*, Vol. 56, No. 5.

McCracken, K. and Phillips, D.R. (2005) International Demographic Transitions. In G.J. Andrews and D.R. Phillips (Eds), *Ageing and Place: Perspectives, Policy, Practice*, London: Routledge.

Mcguinn, K.K. and Mosher-Ashley, P.M. (2000) Participation in Recreational Activities and its Effect on Perception of Life Satisfaction in Residential Settings, *Activities, Adaptation and Aging*, Vol. 25, No. 1.

Mchugh, K.E. (2003) Three Faces of Ageism: Society, Image and Place, *Ageing and Society*, Vol. 23, No. 2.

Mead, G.H. (1934) *Mind, Self and Society: From the Standpoint of a Social Behaviourist*, Chicago: The University of Chicago Press.

Meher, Pestonji (1978) Coping with Widowhood: A Challenge, *Eves Weekly*, August 12–18, p. 38.

Mehta, Manubhai N. (1936) Widow Remarriage, *The Indian Social Reform*, Vol. XLVT, No. 58, p. 757.

——. (1961) Widow Marriage and Hindu Society, *The Indian Social Reform*, Vol. XLVI, No. 49, p. 775.

Mehta, Vatsala (1956) The Hindu Widow: With Special Reference to Gujarat, M.A. Dissertation, Bombay University, Bombay.

Menon, Lakshmi N. (1973) Indian Women Since Independence, *Indian and Foreign Review*, Vol. 10, No. 2.

Merleau-Ponty, M. (1962) *Phenomenology of Perception*, New York: Routledge and Kegan Paul.

Merriam-Webster Dictionary (1951) pp. 606–07.

Meyers, R.J., Millor, W.R., Hill, D.E. and Tonigan, J.S. (1999) Engaging Unmotivated Drug Users in Treatment, *Journal of Substance Abuse*, Vol. 10, No. 3.

Milford, Homparey (Ed.) (1978) *The Key Progress: A Survey of the Status and Conditions of Women in India*, London: Oxford University Press.

Miller, Dorothy and Dawson, William H. (1965) Effects of Stigma on Re-employment of Ex-mental Patients, *Mental Hygiene*, Vol. 49, No. 2.

Mishra, S. (1987) *Social Adjustment in Old Age*, Delhi: B.R. Publishing Co.

Misra, G. (1982) Motivational Structure and Prolonged Deprivation, *The Indian Journal of Social Work*, Vol. XLIII, No. 1, pp. 19–25.

Misra, G. and Shashi, B.P. (1977) Prolonged Deprivation and Development of Status Perception, *Journal of Psychological Research*, Vol. 21, No. 2, pp. 185–91.

Misra, G. and Shukla, A. (1979) Experimental Deprivation and Development of Social Memory, *Psychologia*, Vol. 22, No. 2, pp. 115–63.

Misra, G. and Tripathi, L.B. (1978) Prolonged Deprivation and Status Perception, *The Indian Journal of Social Work*, Vol. XXXIX, No. 2, pp. 113–37.

Mitchell, G.J. (1990) Struggling in Change: From the Traditional Approach to Parse's Theory-Based Practice, *Nursing Science Quarterly*, Vol. 3, No. 4.

——. (1991) Human Subjectivity: The Co-creation of Self, *Nursing Science Quarterly*, Vol. 4, No. 4.

Mitter, Dwarikanath (1984) *The Position of Woman in Hindu Law*, Delhi: D.K. Publications.

Moghe, Vrunda Dev (1978) Widowhood Today: A Long Term from the Dark Past, *Eves Weekly*, August 12–18, pp. 33–34.

Mohanty, B. (1980) Effects of Socio-Cultural Deprivation on Some Psychological Characteristics, *Psychological Studies*, Vol. 25, No. 2, pp. 113–17.

Mohanty, S.P. (1989) Demographic and Socio-Cultural Aspects of Ageing in India: Some Emerging Issues. In R.N. Pati and B. Jena (Eds), *Elderly in India: Socio-Demographic Dimensions*, New Delhi: Ashish Publishing House.

Monks, F.J. et al. (1972) *Determinants of Behaviour Development*, New York: Academic Press.

Morell, C.M. (2003) Empowerment and Long-Living Women: Return to the Rejected Body, *Journal of Aging Studies*, Vol. 17, No. 1.

Morgan, L.A. (1981) Economic Change at Midlife Widowhood: A Longitudinal Analysis, *Journal of Marriage and the Family*, Vol. 43, No. 4, p. 899.

——. (1984) Changes in Family Interaction Following Widowhood, *Journal of Marriage and the Family*, Vol. 46, No. 1, pp. 222–32.

Morse, J.M. (1992) Beyond Empathy: Expanding Expressions of Caring, *Journal of Advanced Nursing*, Vol. 17, No. 7.

Morse, J.M. et al. (1990) Concepts of Caring and Caring as a Concept, *Advances in Nursing Science*, Vol. 13, No. 1.

Morton, J.B. (1992) *An Administrative Overview of the Older Inmate*, Washington, D.C.: U.S. Department of Justice, National Institute of Corrections.

Moss, S.E., White, C.L. and Sunderland, T. (2002) Reminiscence Group Activities and Discourse Interaction in Alzheimer's Disease, *Journal of Gerontological Nursing*, Vol. 28, No. 8.

Mukherjee, Ha. (1972) *Social Status of North Indian Women*, Agra: Shivalal Agarwal.

Mukherjee, Prabhatil (1978) *Hindu Women: Normative Models*, New Delhi: Orient Longman Ltd.

Mulla, Dinshah Fardunji (1960) *Principles of Hindu Law* (2nd Edn), Bombay: Tripathi Pvt. Ltd.

Murray, P.C. (1967) Bereavement, *British Medical Journal*, Vol. 3, No. 16.

Mussen, P.H., Conger, J.J. and Kegan, J. (1969) *Child Development and Personality* (3rd Edn), New York: Harper and Row Co.

Mutharayappa, R. and Bhat, T.N. (2008) Is Lifestyle Influencing Morbidity Among Elderly?, *Journal of Health Management*, Vol. 10, No. 2.

Myers, W. (1989) Urban Working Children: A Comparison of Four Surveys from South Africa, *International Labor*, Vol. 128.

Nagesh, H.V. and Katti, A.P. (Eds) (1988) *Widowhood in India*, Dharwad: SDMET and JSS.

Nair, P.T. (1978) *Marriage and Dowry in India*, Calcutta: Minerva Associates.

Nair, Thankappan P. (1970) The First Hindu Widow Remarriage, *Bhavans Journal*, Vol. 17, pp. 39–41.

Nambi, S. (2002) *Psychiatry for Nurses* (1st Edn), New Delhi: Jaypee Brothers Company.

Nandal, D.S. et al. (1987) Ageing Problems in the Structural Context. In M.L. Sharma and T.M. Dak (Eds), *Ageing in India: Challenge for the Society*, New Delhi: Ajanta Publications.

Narain, V.A. (1972) *Social History of Modern India: Nineteenth Century*, Meerut: Meenakshi Prakashan.

Narang, T. (1968) Adjustment of the Aged with Reference to Family Type, M.Sc. Thesis, Punjab University, Chandigarh.

Nasreen, A. (2009) *Urban Elderly Coping Strategies and Societal Responses*, New Delhi: Concept Publishing Company.

Nast, H.J. and Pile, S. (1998) Introduction: Making Places Bodies. In H.J. Nast and S. Pile (Eds), *Places Through the Body*, New York: Routledge.

National Commission for Women (2009) *Study on Widows at Vrindavan*, New Delhi: NCW.

National Sample Survey Organisation (1998) Morbidity and Treatment of Ailments, July 1995 – June 1996, NSS 52nd Round, Report No. 441, Government of India, New Delhi.

Nayar, P.K.B. (2001) Active Ageing, Intergenerational Integration and Related Issues: Theoretical and Empirical Considerations. In A. Chaudhary (Ed.), *Active Ageing in the New Millennium*, New Delhi: Anugraha.

Needam, Rodney (Ed.) (1970) *Classics in Anthropology*, Chicago: The University of Chicago Press.

Nettleton, S. and Watson, J. (1998) The Body in Everyday Life. In S. Nettleton and J. Watson (Eds), *The Body in Everyday Life*, New York: Routledge.

Ngai, N.P. (2007) Youth Research in Asia: Themes and Perspectives, Paper Presented in VIII International Conference on Asian Youths and Childhoods, Lucknow, November 22–24.

Nguyen, H.T. and Zonderman, A.B. (2006) Relationship between Age and Aspects of Depression: Consistency Reliability Across Two Longitudinal Studies, *Psychology and Ageing*, Vol. 21, No. 1.

Nimkoff, M.F. (1934) *The Family*, Boston: Houghton Mifflin Co.

Nuessel, F.H. (1982) The Language of Ageism, *The Gerontologist*, Vol. 22.

Nurcombe, B. (1970) Deprivation: An Essay in Definition with Special Consideration of the Australian Aboriginals, *Medical Journal of Austria*, Vol. 2.

Nussbaum, J. (1993) The Communicative Impact of Institutionalization for the Elderly: The Admissions Process, *Journal of Aging Studies*, Vol. 7, No. 3.

Nye, F. Ivan and Berardo, Felix M. (1973) *The Family: Its Structure and Interaction*, New York: Macmillan Co.

O'Brayant, Shirley L. (1988) Sibling Support and Older Widow's Well-being, *Journal of Marriage and the Family*, Vol. 50, No. 1, pp. 164–84.

Oberoi, K. and Dey, S. (1991) A Study of Physical, Economic, Social and Psychological Problems of Old People, *Indian Psychological Review*, Vol. 36, Nos 1–2.

Oldenberg, H. and Muller, Max (1886) *The Grihyasutras* (Parts 1 and 2), Oxford: The Clarendon Press.

Ostor, Akos, Fruzzetti, Lina and Barret, Steve (Eds) (1983) *Concept of Person, Kinship, Caste and Marriage in India*, Delhi: Oxford University Press.

Packard, V. (1964) *The Statues Seekers*, New York: Penguin Books.

Palmore, E. (1990) *Ageism: Negative and Positive*, New York: Springer.

Pandita, Ramabai (1984) *The High Caste Hindu Women*, Delhi: D.K. Publishers.

Pandya, Samta P. (2010) Ageing and Spirituality: Understanding Some Constructions and Perceived Influences, *Indian Journal of Gerontology*, Vol. 24, No. 3.

Parks, Marray C. (1967) Bereavement, *British Medical Journal*, Vol. 3, Nos 1–6.

Parse, R.R. (1992) Human Becoming: Parse's Theory of Nursing, *Nursing Science Quarterly*, Vol. 5, No. 1.

——. (1998) *The Human Becoming School of Thought*, Thousand Oaks, CA: Sage.

Passow, A. Harry (1963) *Education in Depressed Areas*, New York: Teachers College Press, Columbia University.

Patel, Illa (1998) The Contemporary Women's Movement and Women's Education in India, *International Review of Education*, Vol. 44, No. 2/3.

Patel, Mamta (2010) Crimes Against the Elderly, *Indian Journal of Gerontology*, Vol. 24, No. 3.

Paterniti, D.A. (2000) The Micropolitics of Identity Making in Adverse Circumstance: A Study of Identity Making in a Total Institution, *Journal of Contemporary Ethnography*, Vol. 29, No. 1.

——. (2003) Claiming Identity in a Nursing Home. In J.F.G.J.A. Holstein (Ed.), *Ways of Aging*, Malden, MA: Blackwell Publishing.

Pathak, Bindeswar (2013) *Widows of Vrindavan*, New Delhi: Sulabh International Social Service Organiastion.

Pathak, J.D. (1975) *Inquiry into Disorders of the Old* (Part I), Bombay: Medical Research Centre, Bombay Hospital Trust.

——. (1982) Health Problems of the Elderly in India. In K.G. Desai (Ed.), *Ageing in India*, Bombay: Tata Institute of Social Sciences.

Pathare Reform Association (1869) *Marriage of Hindu Widows*, Bombay: Indu Prakash Press.

Patton, M.Q. (1990) *Qualitative Evaluation and Research Methods* (2nd Edn), Newbury Park, CA: Sage.

Paul, Louis (1966) Crisis Interventions, *Mental Hygiene*, Vol. 50, No. 7, pp. 141–45.

Payton, A. and Porter, V. (1994) Armchair Aerobics for the Cognitively Impaired, *Activities, Adaptation and Aging*, Vol. 18, No. 2.

Peacock, E.W. and Talley, W.M. (1984) Intergenerational Contact: A Way of Counter Ageism, *Educational Gerontology*, Vol. 10, No. 1.

Pedlar, A., Dupuis, S. and Gilbert, A. (1996) Resumption of Role Status Through Leisure in Later Life, *Leisure Sciences*, Vol. 18, No. 3.

Peter, J.S., Judith, R. and Natalie, H. (1977) *The Family: Functions, Conflicts and Symbols*, London: Addison-Wesley Publishing Co.

Peterson, James A. and Briley, Michael (1977) *Widows and Widowhood: A Creative Approach to Being Alone*, Chicago: Association Press.

Phelps, H.A. (1983) *Contemporary Social Problems*, New York: Prentice Hall.

Philiprice, F. (1979) *Marriage and Parenthood*, Boston: Allyn and Bacon Inc.

Phinney, A. (1998) Living with Dementia from the Patient's Perspective, *Journal of Gerontological Nursing*, Vol. 24, No. 6.

Porter, E.J. and Clinton, J.F. (1992) Adjusting to the Nursing Home, *Western Journal of Nursing Research*, Vol. 14, No. 4.

Powell, J.L. and Longino, Jr. C.F. (2001) Towards the Post-Modernization of Aging: The Body and Social Theory, *Journal of Aging and Identity*, Vol. 6, No. 4.

——. (2002) Postmodernism versus Modernism: Rethinking Theoretical Tensions in Social Gerontology, *Journal of Aging and Identity*, Vol. 7, No. 4.

Powers, B.A. (1995) From the Inside Out: The World of the Institutionalized Elderly. In J.N. Henderson and M.D. Vesperi (Eds), *The Culture of Long-Term Care: Nursing Home Ethnography*, Westport, CT: Bergin and Garvey.

——. (1996) Relationships Among Older Women Living in a Nursing Home, *Journal of Women and Aging*, Vol. 8, No. 3/4.

Prakash, I.J. (2001) Role of Intergenerational and Social in Active Ageing. In A. Chaudhary (Ed.), *Active Ageing in the New Millennium*, New Delhi: Anugraha, pp. 32–49.

——. (2004) Widow Pension, *The Economic Studies*, Vol. 4, No. 7, pp. 353–54.

——. (2005) *Ageing in India: Retrospect and Prospect*, Bangalore: Bangalore University Press.

Prakash, Satyendra (2007) *Policies and Programmes on Population Ageing: Indian Perspective*, Bangkok: UNESCO.

Punwani, Jyoti (1978) The Corollaries of Widowhood, *Eves Weekly*, August 12–18, pp. 41–42.

Pushpa, M. (1980) Social Deprivation and Cognitive Development of Primary School Children, *Social Change*, Vol. 10, Nos 1–2, pp. 31–35.

Rabinovich, B.A. and Cohen-Mansfield, J. (1992) The Impact of Participation in Structured Recreational Activities on the Agitated Behavior of Nursing Home Residents: An Observational Study, *Activities, Adaptation and Aging*, Vol. 16, No. 4.

Radhakrishnan, G. (2006) A Study to Assess Depression Among Geriatric Out Patients Attending Selected General Hospitals

at Belgaum, Karnataka, *Nightingale Nursing Times*, Vol. 8, No. 4.

Rajan, Irudaya S. (2000) *Home Away from Home: A Survey of Old Age Homes and Inmates*, Thiruvananthapuram, Kerala: Centre for Development Studies, pp. 11–13.

——. (2001) Social Assistance for Poor Elderly: How Effective?, *Economic and Political Weekly*, Vol. XXVI, No. 8, February 24.

——. (2003) Demography of Indian Ageing, 2001–2051, *Journal of Aging and Social Policy*, Vol. 15, Nos 2–3.

——. (2007) *Population Aging, Health and Social Security in India*, Osaka, Japan: Osaka City University, Centre for Research on Economic Inequality.

Rajan, Irudaya S., Mishra, U.S. and Sarma, P. Sankara (1999) *India's Elderly Burden or Challenge*, New Delhi: Sage Publications.

Rajan, Irudaya S., Risseeuw, Carla and Perera, Myrtle (2008) *Institutional Provisions and Care for the Elderly: Perspectives from Asia and Europe*, New Delhi: Anthem Press.

Ramamurti, P.V. and Jamuna, D. (1984) Psychological Research on the Elderly in India, *Journal of the Anthropological Society of India*, Vol. 19, No. 3.

——. (1992) Markers of Successful Ageing Among Indian Sample, Sandoz Project Report, Switzerland.

——. (1993a) Psychological Dimensions of Ageing in India, *The Indian Journal of Social Science*, Vol. 6, No. 4.

——. (1993b) Some Predictors of Satisfaction with Present Life in an Indian Sample, *Indian Journal of Gerontology*, Vol. 7, Nos 3–4.

——. (1996) Evaluation of Homes and Day Care Centres for the Elderly in Andhra Pradesh, Project Report Submitted to Ministry of Welfare, Government of India, New Delhi.

——. (2002) Ageing in Developing Countries: The Asian Perspective. In S.D. Gokhale and Nirmala Pandit (Eds), *Ageing in Search of its Identity*, Pune: Ameya Prakashan.

——. (2004) *Handbook of Indian Gerontology*, New Delhi: Serials Publications.

Ramamurti, P.V. (1978) *The Sixth Decade and After*, Tirupathi: S.V. University Press.

——. (1991) Correlates of Successful Ageing Among Elderly Men. In Rameshwar Singh and C.S. Singhal (Eds), *Perspectives in Ageing Research*, New Delhi: Today and Tomorrow Printers and Publishers.

——. (1996) Health Behaviour Among the Elderly Men and Women, Project Report Submitted to Indian Council of Medical Research (ICMR), New Delhi.

——. (1997) HRD Training to Meet the Challenges of Old Age. In Indrani Chakravarti (Ed.), *Life in Twilight Years*, Calcutta: Kwality Book Company.

——. (2001) Social Research and Development. In G.R. Andrews, A Research Agenda on Ageing for the 21st Century (Draft Report to U.N.), United Nations Department of Social and Economic Affairs, New York.

——. (2002a) Empowering the Older Persons in India, Paper Presented at International Symposium on Ageing: A Challenge in the New Millennium and X Biennial Meeting of the Association of Gerontology (India), Banaras Hindu University, November 10–12.

——. (2002b) Geropsychology: East-West Scenario, *Journal of Community Guidance and Research*, Vol. 19, No. 2.

——. (2003) Empowering the Older Persons in India, *Research and Development Journal*, Vol. 9, No. 2.

——. (2005) Perspective of Research on Ageing in India. In Phoebe S. Liebig and S. Irudaya Rajan (Eds), *An Ageing India: Perspectives, Prospects and Policies*, Jaipur: Rawat Publications.

Ramchandran, V. and Ramamurthy, B. (1981) Family Structure and Mental Illness in Old Age, *Indian Journal of Psychiatry*, Vol. 2, No. 23.

Ramsey-Klawsnik, H. (2000) Elder-Abuse Offenders: A Typology, *Generations*, Vol. 24, No. 2.

Randhawa, Maninder Singh (1991) *The Rural and Urban Aged*, New Delhi: National Book House.

Rangaswamy, Kalarani and Durairarj (2000) Problems and Remedies of the Aged. In M.A. Sudhir (Ed.), *Ageing in Rural India: Perspectives and Prospects*, New Delhi: Indian Publishers.

Rani, A.M., Palani, G. and Sathiyasekran, B.W.C. (2012) Morbidity Profile of Elders in Old Age Homes in Chennai, *National Journal of Community Medicine*, Vol. 3, No. 3.

Ranjan, Alka (2011) Determinates of Well-being Among Widows, *Economic and Political Weekly*, Vol. 27.

Rao, K.V. (1995) Rural Elderly in Andhra Pradesh: A Study of Their Socio-Demographic Profile (Mimeo), Unpublished Doctoral Dissertation, Andhra University, Visakhapatnam.

Rao, Ramana M.V. (1956a) Hindu Succession Act, *Social Welfare*, Vol. HI, No. 9, pp. 18–20.

——. (1956b) Century of Hindu Widow's Remarriage Act, *Social Welfare*, Vol. III, No. 2, pp. 11–12.

Rao, V.A., Vasudevan, P.M. and Madhavan, T. (1982) Psychosocial Aspects of Geriatric Population. In A. Kiev and A. Venkoba Rao (Eds), *Reading in Transcultural Psychiatry*, Madras: Higginbothams.

Rao, Venkoba (1987) Total Health Care of the Elderly: Kallandir Experience, *Indian Journal of Social Psychiatry*, Vol. 3, No. 4.

Ray, R.E. (1996) A Postmodern Perspective on Feminist Gerontology, *The Gerontologist*, Vol. 36, No. 5.

——. (1999) Researching to Transgress: The Need for Critical Feminism in Gerontology, *Journal of Women and Aging*, Vol. 11, Nos 2–3.

——. (2003) Toward the Croning of Feminist Gerontology, *Journal of Aging Studies*, Vol. 18, No. 1.

Rees, W. Devi and Lutkins, Sylvia G. (1967) Mortality of Bereavement, *British Medical Journal*, Vol. 4, No. 1, pp. 13–16.

Reich, J.A. (2003) Pregnant with Possibility: Reflections on Embodiment, Access, and Inclusion in Field Research, *Qualitative Sociology*, Vol. 26, No. 3.

Relph, E. (1976) *Place and Placelessness*, London: Pion.

Reynolds, R.P. (1991) Leisure Services and Social Control. In T.L.G.P.A. Witt (Ed.), *Recreation and Leisure: Issues in an Era of Change*, State College, PA: Venture Publishing.

Rice, E.P. (1934) *The Mahabharata*, London: Oxford University Press.

Richard, Rubin, Frank, D. and Cyril, M. (Eds) (1969) *Advance in Behavioural Therapy*, New York: The Free Press.

Richardson, L. (1994) Writing: A Method of Inquiry. In N.K. Denzin and Y.S. Lincoln (Eds), *Handbook of Qualitative Research*, Thousand Oaks, CA: Sage.

——. (1997) *Fields of Play: Constructing an Academic Life*, New Brunswick, NY: Rutgers University Press.

Risley, H.H. (1915) *The People of India*, London: W. Thacker and Company.

Robertson, M.J. and Greenblatt, M.E. (1992) *Homelessness: A National Perspective*, New York: Plenum Press.

Rodman, M.C. (1992) Empowering Place: Multilocality and Multivocality, *American Anthropologist*, Vol. 94, No. 3.

Rojek, C. (1993) After Popular Culture: Hyperreality and Leisure, *Leisure Studies*, Vol. 12, No. 4.

——. (1995) *Leisure and Culture*, Thousand Oaks, CA: Sage.

Rose, G. (1999) Women and Everyday Spaces. In J. Price and M. Shildrick (Eds), *Feminist Theory and the Body: A Reader*, New York: Routledge.

Rosenberg, S.W., Ward, D. and Chilton, S. (1988) *Political Reasoning and Cognition: A Piagetian View*, Durham: Duke University Press.

Rosling, L.K. and Kitchen, J. (1992) Music and Drawing with Institutionalized Elderly, *Activities, Adaptation and Aging*, Vol. 17, No. 2.

Rosow, Irwing (1967) *Social Integration of the Aged*, New York: The Free Press.

Ross, Ralph La. (1984) *Family Case Studies: A Sociological Perspective*, New York: The Free Press.

Routasalo, P.E. et al. (2006) Social Contacts and Their Relationship to Loneliness Among Aged People: A Population Based Study, *Gerontology*, Vol. 52, No. 3.

Rowles, G.D. (1987) A Place to Call Home. In L.L. Carstensen and B.A. Edelstein (Eds), *Handbook of Clinical Gerontology*, New York: Pergamon Press.

Rubinstein, R.L. and Parmelee, P.A. (1992) Attachment to Place and the Representation of the Life Course by the Elderly. In I. Altman and S.M. Low (Eds), *Place Attachment*, New York: Plenum Press.

Rudberg, M. (1997) The Researching Body: The Epistemophilic Project. In K. Davis (Ed.), *Embodied Practices: Feminist Perspectives on the Body*, Thousand Oaks, CA: Sage.

Rufus, D. and Sekhar, B. (2011) A Study on Elder Abuse Victims: With Special Reference to the Residents of Old Age Homes in Tirunelveli District of Tamil Nadu, *International Journal of Rural Development and Management Studies*, Vol. 5, No. 2.

Russell, C. (2007) What Do Older Women and Men Want? Gender Differences in the 'Lived Experience' of Ageing, *Current Sociology*, Vol. 55, No. 2.

Sabat, S.R. and Harré, R. (1992) The Construction and Deconstruction of Self in Alzheimer's Disease, *Ageing and Society*, Vol. 12.

Sachchidananda and Sinha, Romesh P. (1984) *Women's Rights: Myth and Reality*, Jaipur: Printwell Publishers.

Sahayam, M. Deva (1988) Aged Females: The Most Deprived Among the Deprived, *Indian Journal of Social Work*, Vol. 49, No. 3.

Sainsbury, P. (1955) *Suicide in London* (Maudsley Monograph No. 1), London: Chapman and Hall.

Saldanha, D. et al. (2010) An Epidemiological Study of Dementia Under the Aegis of Mental Health Program, Maharashtra, Pune Chapter, *Indian Journal of Psychiatry*, Vol. 52, No. 2.

Sanacora, Gerard (2008) Link of Major Depression to Increase Level of Neurons in the Brain, Medicine, *The Journal of Gerontology*, Washington.

Sandhu, P. (1978) A Study of Management Practices and Problems of Rural Aged People in Ropar District, M.Sc. Thesis, Punjab Agricultural University, Ludhiana.

Saraswati, Baidyanath (1983) The Kashivasi Widows, ICSSR Project Report, New Delhi.

——. (1985) The Kashivasi Widows, *Man in India*, Vol. 65, No. 2, pp. 107–20.

Sarkar, S.C. (1928) *Some Aspects of the Early History of India*, London: Humphrey Milford.

Sati, P.N. (1988) *Retired and Ageing People: A Study of Their Problems*, Delhi: Mittal Publications.

Savell, K.S. (1991) Leisure, Perceptions of Control and Well-being: Implications for the Institutionalized Elderly, *Therapeutic Recreation Journal*, Vol. 25, No. 3.

Savishinsky, J. (1991) *The Ends of Time: Life and Work in a Nursing Home*, New York: Bergin and Garvey.

Saxena, D.N. (1988) Senior Citizens: The Problems. In A.B. Bose and K.D. Gangrade (Eds), *The Ageing in India: Problems and Potentials*, New Delhi: Abhinav Publications.

Schneider, David J. (1976) *Social Psychology*, California: Addison-Wesley Publishing Co.

Schoenberg, N.E. and Coward, R.T. (1997) Attitudes About Entering a Nursing Home: Comparisons of Older Rural and Urban African-American Women, *Journal of Aging Studies*, Vol. 11, No. 1.

Sengupta, N. (1965) *Evolution of Hindu Marriage*, Bombay: Popular Prakashan.

Shapiro, S. (1994) Remembering the Body in Critical Pedagogy, *Education and Society*, Vol. 12, No. 1.

Shapiro, S.B. (1999) *Pedagogy and the Politics of the Body: A Critical Praxis*, New York: Garland Publishing.

Sharma, K.L. (Ed.) (2007) *Studies in Gerontology: Inter-Generational Perspectives*, Jaipur: Rawat Publications.

Sharma, K.L. (2009) *Dimensions of Ageing: Indian Studies*, Jaipur: Rawat Publications.

Sharma, R.N. (2005) *Urban Sociology*, New Delhi: Surjeet Publications.

Sharma, S. (1999) Elderly in India: Their Mental Health Problems. In Arun P. Bali (Ed.), *Understanding Greying People of India*, New Delhi: Inter-India Publications.

Sharma, S.P. and Xenos, Peter (1992) Ageing in India: Demographic Background and Analysis Based on Census Materials, Occasional Paper No. 2, Office of the Registrar General and Census Commissioner, Government of India, New Delhi.

Shary, J.M. and Iso-Ahola, S.E. (1989) Effects of a Control-Relevant Intervention on Nursing Home Residents: Perceived Competence and Self-Esteem, *Therapeutic Recreation Journal*, Vol. 23, No. 1.

Shaw, S.M. (2001) Conceptualizing Resistance: Women's Leisure as Political Practice, *Journal of Leisure Research*, Vol. 33, No. 2.

Sherina, M.S. et al. (2006) The Prevalence of Depression Among Elderly Warded in a Tertiary Care Centre in Wilayah Persekutan, *Medical Journal of Malaysia*, Vol. 61, No. 1.

Shilling, C. (2003) *The Body and Social Theory*, Thousand Oaks, CA: Sage.

Shrut, Samuel D. (1958) Attitudes Toward Old Age and Death, *Mental Hygiene*, Vol. 42, No. 2, pp. 259–66.

Shukla, Aradhana and Misra, Girishwar (1988) Deprivation and Development of Colour Competence, *Psychological Studies*, Vol. 33, No. 1, pp. 34–48.

Silver, C.B. (2003) Gendered Identities in Old Age: Toward (De) Gendering, *Journal of Aging Studies*, Vol. 17, No. 4.

Silverman, Phyllis Rolfe (1969) The Widow-to-Widow Programme: An Experiment in Preventive Intervention, *Mental Hygiene*, Vol. 53, No. 3, pp. 333–37.

——. (1979) The Widow as a Care Giver in a Program of Preventive Intervention with Other Widows, *Mental Hygiene*, Vol. 54, No. 4, pp. 540–47.

Singh, Gurmeet et al. (1988) Problems of Widowhood, *The Indian Journal of Social Work*, Vol. XLVII, No. 1.

Singh, Gurmeet M.P. (1988) Restraints to Widow Remarriage, *Social Change*, Vol. 18, No. 3, pp. 59–62.

Singh, Gurmeet M.P. and Gill, Sukhdeep (1986) Problems of Widowhood, *The Indian Journal of Social Work*, Vol. XLVII, No. 1, pp. 67–71.

Singh, Kulwant (1986) *Hindu Women's Right to Property in India*, New Delhi: Deep and Deep Publications.

Singh, Sewa, Kaur, Harjinder and Dube, Renu (1986) Malnutrition and Cognitive Development Among Deprived and Non-Deprived

Children, *Indian Journal of Clinical Psychology*, Vol. 13, No. 1.

Singh, T.R. (1969) Widow Remarriage Among Brahmans: A Sociological Study, *The Eastern Anthropologist*, Vol. 22, No. 1, pp. 75–87.

Singh, Vasta Rajendra (1976) The Remarriage and Rehabilitation of the Hindu Widows in India, 1856–1914, *Journal of Indian History*, Vol. 54, No. 3, pp. 713–30.

Singh, Yogendra (2006) *Modernization of Indian Tradition*, Jaipur: Rawat Publications.

Sinha, B.B. (1982) *Society in Tribal India*, Delhi: B.R. Publishing Corporation.

Sinha, Durgananda, Tirpathi, R.C. and Misra, Girishwar (Eds) (1982) *Deprivation: Its Social Roots and Psychological Consequences*, New Delhi: Concept Publishers.

Siva Raju, S. (1991) Health Care System in India: Need for Comprehensive Evaluation. In C.A.K. Yesudian (Ed.), *Primary Health Care*, Bombay: Tata Institute of Social Sciences.

——. (1997) Medico-Social Study on the Assessment of Health Status of the Urban Elderly (Mimeo), Tata Institute of Social Sciences, Bombay.

——. (2000) Ageing in India: An Overview. In Murli Desai and S. Siva Raju (Eds), *Gerontological Social Work in India*, Delhi: B.R. Publishing Co.

——. (2002a) *Health Status of the Urban Elderly: A Medico-Social Study*, Delhi: B.R. Publishing Co.

——. (2002b) Meeting the Needs of the Poor and Excluded in India, Situation and Voices, The Older Poor and Excluded in South Africa and India, UNFPA, Population and Development Strategies, Vol. 2.

——. (2004a) *Networking of Organisations Working for Care of Older Persons in Mumbai: Issues and Implications*, New Delhi: B.R. Publications.

——. (2004b) Profile of Elderly and Organisations Working for Their Care: A Study in Mumbai (Mimeo), Family Welfare Agency, Mumbai.

——. (2006) *Ageing in India in the 21st Century: A Research Agenda*, Mumbai: Harmony-Celebrate Age.

——. (2008) Report on Situational Analysis of the Elderly Parsis in India, UNESCO-Parzor Foundation, New Delhi.

Slama, C.A. and Bergman-Evans, B. (2000) A Troubling Triangle: An Exploration of Loneliness, Helplessness, and Boredom of Residents of a Veterans Home, *Journal of Psychosocial Nursing*, Vol. 38, No. 12.

Small, J.A., Geldart, K., Gutman, G. and Scott, M.A.C. (1998) The Discourse of Self in Dementia, *Ageing and Society*, Vol. 18.

Smart, M.S. and Smart, L.S. (1976) *Families: Developing Relationships*, New York: Macmillan Publishing Co.

Smith, D.E. (1990) *Conceptual Practices of Power: A Feminist Sociology of Knowledge*, Toronto: University of Toronto Press.

Smith, Ken R. and Zick, Cathleen D. (1986) The Incidence of Poverty Among the Recently Widowed: Mediating Factors in the Life Course, *Journal of Marriage and the Family*, Vol. 48, pp. 619–30.

Smith-Marchese, K. (1994) The Effects of Participatory Music on the Reality Orientation and Sociability of Alzheimer's Residents in a Long-Term Care Setting, *Activities, Adaptation and Aging*, Vol. 18, No. 2.

Soares, G.A.D. (1968) The Active Few: The Student Ideology and Participation in Developing Countries. Cited by Myron Glazer. In Donald K. Emmerson (Ed.), *Students and Politics in Developing Nations*, New York: Praeger Publishers.

Social Security Administration (2007a) *Social Security: A Brief History*, Baltimore, MD: SSA Publications.

——. (2007b) *What Prisoners Should Know About Social Security*, Baltimore, MD: SSA Publications.

Somerville, Rose M. (1971) Death Education as Part of Family Life Education: Using Imaginative Literature for Insights into Family Crisis, *The Family Coordinator*, Vol. 20, No. 3, pp. 209–24.

Spencer, H. (1934) *Sociology*, London: Harrison and Sons Ltd.

——. (1896) *Principles of Sociology*, New York: D. Appleton.

——. (1904) *An Autobiography*, New York: D. Appleton.

Shepherd, M., Cooper, B., Brown, A.C. and Kalton, G.W. (1966) *Psychiatric Illness in General Practice*, Oxford: Oxford University Press.

Spurolock, J. (1970) Social Deprivation in Childhood and Character Formation, *Journal of the American Psychoanalytic Association*, Vol. 18, No. 4, pp. 621–30.

Srinivas, M.N. (1938) Marriage and Family Among the Kannada Castes of the Mysore State, M.A. Dissertation, Bombay University, Bombay.

——. (1942) *Marriage and Family in Mysore*, Bombay: New Book Co.

Srinivas, M.N. (1962) *Caste in Modern India and Other Essays*, Bombay: Media Publishers.

Srinivas, P. (1982) Problems of the Aged in India, *Yojana*, Vol. XXVI, No. 10, pp. 1–15.

Srinivas, S. and Vijayalakshmi, B. (2001) Abuse and Neglect of Elderly in Families, *Indian Journal of Social Work*, Special Issue on Family Violence, Vol. 62, No. 3, July.

Stafford, P.B. (2003) Homebodies: Voices of Place in a North American Community. In P.B. Stafford (Ed.), *Gray Areas: Ethnographic Encounters with Nursing Home Culture*, Sante Fe, NM: School of American Research Press.

Steele, F. (1981) *The Sense of Place*, Boston, MA: CBI Publishing Company.

Stern, M. (1963) *Encyclopedia of Mental Health*, New York: Franklin Watt Inc.

Sterns, Anthony A., Lax, Greta, Sed, Chad, Keohane, Patrick and Sterns, Ronni S. (2008) The Growing Wave of Older Prisoners: A National Survey of Older Prisoner Health, Mental Health and Programming, *Corrections Today*, Vol. 70, No. 4.

Stokowski, P.A. (2002) Languages of Place and Discourses of Power: Constructing New Senses of Place, *Journal of Leisure Research*, Vol. 34, No. 4.

Stroebe, Margaret and Stroebe, Wolfgang (1983) Who Suffers More? Sex Differences in Health Risks of the Widowed, *Psychological Bulletin*, Vol. 93, No. 2, pp. 279–301.

Suen, L.J. and Morris, D.L. (2006) Depression and Gender Differences: Focus on Taiwanese American Older Adults, *J Gerontol Nursing*, Vol. 32, No. 4.

Sullivan, A., Pedlar, A. and Miller, B. (2002) Experiencing Leisure on a Cognitive Support Unit, *Society and Leisure*, Vol. 25, No. 2.

Sweet, James A. (1972) The Living Arrangements of Separated Widowhood and Divorced Mothers, *Demography*, Vol. 9, No. 1, pp. 143–57.

Syamla, M. (1987) Here Widows are Actually Worshipped, *Eves Weekly*, August 8–14.

Sylvester, C. (1991) Recovering a Good Idea for the Sake of Goodness: An Interpretive Critique of the Subjective Debate. In T.L.G.P.A. Witt (Ed.), *Recreation and Leisure: Issues in an Era of Change*, State College, PA: Venture Publishing.

Tabbitts, Clark (Ed.) (1960) *Handbook of Social Gerontology: Social Aspects of Aging*, Chicago: The University of Chicago Press.

Tannenbaum, A.J. (1969) Some Non-intellectual Concomitants of Social Deprivation Israel, *Annals of Psychiatry and Related Discipline*, Vol. 7, No. 1, pp. 9–30.

Tappen, R.M., Williams, C., Fishman, S. and Touhy, T. (1999) Persistence of Self in Advanced Alzheimer's Disease, *Journal of Nursing Scholarship*, Vol. 31, No. 2.

Tatvabhushan, Sitanath (1904) *Social Reform in Bengal*, Calcutta: Papyrus.

Tellis-Nayak, V. and Tellis-Nayak, M. (1989) Quality of Care and the Burden of Two Cultures: When the World of the Nursing Aide Enters the World of the Nursing Home, *Gerontologist*, Vol. 29, No. 3.

The Mahabharata (1962) Poona: Bhandarkar Oriental Research Institute.

Thomas, C. (1993) De-Constructing Concepts of Care, *Sociology*, Vol. 27, No. 4.

Thomas, P. (1939) *Women and Marriage in India*, London: George Allen and Unwin Ltd.

Thomas, W.H. (1996) *Life Worth Living: The Eden Alternative in Action*, Acton, MA: Vanderwyk and Burnham.

Tibbitts, C. (1979) Can We Invalidate Negative Stereotypes of Aging, *The Gerontologist*, Vol. 19, No. 1.

Tinker, A. and McCreadie, C. (1998) Elder Abuse. In R. Tallis, H. Fillit and J.C. Brockelhurst (Eds), *Brockelhurst's Textbook of Geriatric Medicine and Gerontology*, London: Churchill Livingstone.

Tiwari, S.C., Pandey, N.M. and Singh, I. (2012) Mental Health Problems Among Inhabitants of Old Age Homes: A Preliminary Study, *Indian Journal of Psychiatry*, Vol. 54.

Toth, Andre and Toth, Susan (1980) Group Work with Widows, *Social Work*, Vol. 25, No. 1, pp. 63–65.

Travernier, B.J. (1905) *Travernier Travel in India*, Book III, Calcutta: Bangbasi Office.

Traxler, A.J. (1980) Let's Get Gerontologized: Developing a Sensitivity to Ageing, the Multi-purpose Senior Centre Concept, A Training Manual for Practitioners Working with the Ageing, Spring Field, Illness Department of Ageing.

Tripathi, L.B. and Misra, Girishwar (1975) Cognitive Activities as a Function of Prolonged Deprivation, *Psychological Studies*, Vol. 20, No. 2, pp. 54–61.

——. (1976) Some Cognitive Processes as Function of Prolonged Deprivation, *Indian Journal of Psychology*, Vol. 51, No. 2, pp. 129–43.

Troll, Lilliane, Israel, Joan and Israel, Kenneth (1977) *Looking Ahead: A Woman's Guide to the Problems and Joys of Growing Old*, New Jersey: Prentice-Hall Inc.

Truxual, Andrew G. and Merrill, Francis E. (1953) *Marriage and the Family in American Culture*, New York: Prentice-Hall Inc.

Trzinski, A. and Higgins, J. (2001) Therapeutic Play: Building Cohesion and Socialization Among Nursing Home Residents, *Activities, Adaptation and Aging*, Vol. 25, No. 3/4.

Tuan, Y.F. (1977) *Space and Place: The Perspective of Experience*, Minneapolis, MN: University of Minnesota Press.

Turner, B.S. (1995) Aging and Identity: Some Reflections on the Somatization of the Self. In M. Featherstone and A. Wernick (Eds), *Images of Aging: Cultural Representations of Later Life*, New York: Routledge.

Twigg, J. (2000a) *Bathing: The Body and Community Care*, New York: Routledge.

——. (2000b) Carework as Form of Bodywork, *Ageing and Society*, Vol. 20, No. 4.

——. (2004) The Body, Gender and Age: Feminist Insights in Social Gerontology, *Journal of Aging Studies*, Vol. 18.

Twigger-Ross, C.L. and Uzzell, D.L. (1996) Place and Identity Processes, *Journal of Environmental Psychology*, Vol. 16, No. 3.

UNDP (2002) *Human Development Report*, New York: Oxford University Press.

——. (2003) *World Population Prospects*, New York: UNDP.

UNESCAP (1987) *Population Ageing: Review of Emerging Issues*, Asian Population Studies, Series No. 80, Bangkok, Thailand: Economic and Social Commission for Asia and the Pacific.

——. (1992) *Population Ageing: Review of National Policies and Programmes in Asia and Pacific*, Bangkok, Thailand: Economic and Social Commission for Asia and the Pacific.

United Nations (1998) The National Elder Abuse Incidence Study: Final Report, Department of Health and Human Services, National Center on Elder Abuse and Neglect, Washington, D.C.

Upadhyaya, B.S. (1974) *Women in Rigveda*, New Delhi: S. Chand and Co.

Upadhyaya, Usha (1986) Construction and Standardisation of a Tool to Measure Sense of Deprivation, *Indian Psychological Review*, Vol. 30, No. 1, pp. 29–31.

Usita, P.M., Hyman, Jr. I.E. and Herman, K.C. (1998) Narrative Intentions: Listening to Life Stories in Alzheimer's Disease, *Journal of Aging Studies*, Vol. 12, No. 2.

Vaidya, P.L. (1962) *The Valmiki Ramayana*, Poona: Oriental Books Agency.

Vaidya, P.L. (Ed.) (1934) *Dhammapada* (2nd Edn), Poona: Oriental Books Agency.

Valentine, Charles A. (1998) *Culture and Poverty: Critique and Counter Proposals*, Chicago: The University of Chicago Press.

Van Manen, M. (1990) *Researching Lived Experience: Human Science for an Action Sensitive Pedagogy*, London: Althouse Press.

Vasantha Devi, K.P. and Premakumar, S. (2000) Health and Nutritional Problems of the Aged. In M.A. Sudhir (Ed.), *Ageing in Rural India: Perspectives and Prospects*, Delhi: Indian Publishers and Distributors.

Vasta, R.S. (1976) The Remarriage and Rehabilitation of the Hindu Widows in India 1856–1914, *Journal of Indian History*, Vol. 54, p. 719.

Vedvyasa (1931) *The Mahabharata*, Calcutta: Oriental Publishing Co.

Veerasalingam, K. (1970) The First Widow Marriage, *Triveni*, Vol. 39, No. 3, pp. 48–54.

Vidyasagar, I.C. (1976) *Marriage of Hindu Widows*, Calcutta: K.B. Bagchi and Co.

Vidyavati, S.U., Nalini, D. and Masali, K.A. (2012) Morbidity Pattern of Elderly in Rural Field Practice Area at Shivanagi, Karnataka, *International Journal of Current Research and Review*, Vol. 4, No. 10.

Vinick, B.V. (1978) Remarriage in Old Age, *The Family Co-ordinator*, Vol. 27, No. 2, pp. 359–63.

Vinton, L., Mazza, N. and Kin, Y.S. (1998) Intervening in Family-Staff Conflicts in Nursing Homes, *Clinical Gerontologist*, Vol. 19, No. 3.

Visaria, P. (2001) Demographic of Ageing in India, *Economic and Political Weekly*, Vol. 36, No. 22.

Voelkl, J.E., Winkelhake, K., Jeffries, J. and Yoshioka, N. (2003) Examination of a Nursing Home Environment: Are Residents Engaged in Recreation Activities?, *Therapeutic Recreation Journal*, Vol. 37, No. 4.

Vohra, R.N. (1972) Women in Vedic India, *Social Welfare*, Vol. XTX, No. 7.

Waller, Willard (1956) *The Family: A Dynamic Interaction*, New York: The Dryden Press.

Ward, C.R., Kamp, L.L. and Newman, S. (1996) The Effects of Participation in an Intergenerational Program on the Behavior of Residents with Dementia, *Activities, Adaptation and Aging*, Vol. 20, No. 4.

Wason, Neelam and Jain, Karuna (2011) Malnutrition and Risk of Malnutrition Among Elderly, *Indian Journal of Gerontology*, Vol. 25, No. 2.

Watson, J. (2005) *Caring Science as Sacred Science*, Philadelphia, PA: F.A. Davis Company.

Wearing, B. (1998) *Leisure and Feminist Theory*, Thousand Oaks, CA: Sage Publications.

Wendell, S. (1996) *The Rejected Body: Feminist Philosophical Reflections on Disability*, New York: Routledge.

White, J. et al. (2006) Cognitive, Emotional, and Quality of Life Outcomes in Patients with Pulmonary Arterial Hypertension, *Respir Res*, Vol. 7, No. 55.

White, Robert W. and Watt, Norman F. (1973) *The Abnormal Personality* (4th Edn), New York: The Ronald Press Co.

Wiener, C.L. and Kayser-Jones, J. (1990) The Uneasy Fate of Nursing Home Residents: An Organizational-Interaction Perspective, *Sociology of Health and Illness*, Vol. 12, No. 1.

Wiersma, E.C. (2003) Making Meaning: Place and the Experiences of Individuals Living with Dementia, Unpublished Master's Thesis, University of Waterloo, Waterloo, Ontario.

Wight, B.W., Margaret, F.G. and Philip, Keeve (1970) Cultural Deprivation, Operational Deprivation in Terms of Language Development, *American Journal of Orthopsychiatry*, Vol. 40, No. 7, pp. 77–86.

Williams, A. (2002) Changing Geographies of Care: Employing the Concept of Therapeutic Landscapes as a Framework in Examining Home Space, *Social Science and Medicine*, Vol. 55, No. 1.

Williams, D.R. and Vaske, J.J. (2003) The Measurement of Place Attachment: Validity and Generalizability of a Psychometric Approach, *Forest Science*, Vol. 49, No. 6.

Williams, S.J. (2006) Medical Sociology and the Biological Body: Where are We Now and Where Do We Go from Here?, *Health*, Vol. 10, No. 1.

Wilson, K.H. and Reynolds, S.L. (1996) Introducing a Framework for Defining Financial Abuse of the Elderly, *Journal of Elder Abuse and Neglect*, Vol. 8, No. 2.

Wilson, S.A. (1997) The Transition to Nursing Home Life: A Comparison of Planned and Unplanned Admissions, *Journal of Advanced Nursing*, Vol. 25, No. 5.

Winch, Robert F. and Spanier, Graham (Eds) (1974) *Selected Studies in Marriage and Family*, New York: Holt, Rinehart and Winston Inc.

Wolf, R.S. (1996) Understanding Elder Abuse and Neglect, *Aging Magazine*, Vol. 367.

Wolkowitz, C. (2002) The Social Relations of Body Work, *Gender, Employment and Society*, Vol. 16, No. 3.

Womble, Dale (1966) *Foundations for Marriage and Family Relations*, New York: Macmillan.

Wood, D. (1988) *How Children Learn and Think: The Social Context of Cognitive Development*, Oxford: Basil Blackwell.

Wood, S. and Stephens, M. (2003) Vulnerability to Elder Abuse and Neglect in Assisted Living Facilities, *The Gerontologist*, Vol. 43, No. 5.

Woods, P. (1986) *Inside Schools: Ethnology in Educational Research*, London: Routledge and Kegan Paul.

Worsley, P. et al. (1970) *Introducing Sociology*, New York: Penguin Books.

Wyllie, M. (2006) Lived Time and Psychopathology, *Philosophy, Psychiatry and Psychology*, Vol. 12, No. 3.

Yadav, J.P. (2004) *Elderly in India: The Struggle to Survive*, New Delhi: Anmol Publications.

Young, Michael, Benjamin, Bernard and Wallis, Chris (1963) The Mortality of Widowers, *The Lancet*, Vol. II, No. 1, pp. 42–44.

Zarit, Steven H. (Ed.) (1978) *Reading in Aging and Death: Contemporary Perspectives*, New York: Harper and Row Publishers.

Zick, Cathleen D. (1988) Recent Widowhood, Remarriage and Changes in Economic Well-being, *Journal of Marriage and the Family*, Vol. 50, No. 1, pp. 233–44.

Zilboorg, Gregory (1943) Fear of Death, *The Psychoanalytic Quarterly*, Vol. 12, No. 1, pp. 465–75.

Zola, I.K. (1990) Medicine as an Institution of Social Control. In P. Conrad and R. Kern (Eds), *The Sociology of Health and Illness: Critical Perspectives* (3rd Eds), New York: St. Martin's Press.

Index

